Spirit, Mind, & Brain

COLUMBIA SERIES IN SCIENCE AND RELIGION

THE COLUMBIA SERIES IN SCIENCE AND RELIGION

The Columbia Series in Science and Religion is sponsored by the Center for the Study of Science and Religion (CSSR) at Columbia University. It is a forum for the examination of issues that lie at the boundary of these two complementary ways of comprehending the world and our place in it. By examining the intersections between one or more of the sciences and one or more religions, the CSSR hopes to stimulate dialogue and encourage understanding.

Robert Pollack
The Faith of Biology and the Biology of Faith

B. Alan Wallace, ed.
Buddhism and Science: Breaking New Ground

Lisa Sideris
Environmental Ethics, Ecological Theory, and Natural Selection: Suffering and Responsibility

Wayne Proudfoot, ed.
William James and a Science of Religions: Reexperiencing The Varieties of Religious Experience

B. Alan Wallace
Contemplative Science: Where Buddhism and Neuroscience Converge

Spirit, Mind, & Brain

A Psychoanalytic Examination
of Spirituality and Religion

Mortimer Ostow

 Columbia University Press   *New York*

Columbia University Press
Publishers Since 1893
New York   Chichester, West Sussex
Copyright © 2007 Columbia University Press
All rights reserved
Library of Congress Cataloging-in-Publication Data
Ostow, Mortimer.
Spirit, mind, and brain : a psychoanalytic examination of
spirituality and religion / Mortimer Ostow.
—(The Columbia series in science and religion)
Includes bibliographical references and index.
ISBN 0–231–13900–4 (cloth : alk. paper)
— ISBN 0–231–51120–5 (electronic)
1. Psychoanalysis and religion. 2. Psychology and religion.
3. Psychology, Religious. I. Title. II. Series.
BF175.4.R44O088   2006
201'.6150195—dc22   2006004923
∞
Columbia University Press books are printed on permanent and
durable acid-free paper. This book was printed on
paper with recycled content.

Printed in the United States of America
c 10 9 8 7 6 5 4 3 2 1

In memoriam

Miriam Furst Ostow

March 26, 1920–September 14, 2005

The source of my comfort and inspiration for sixty-four years

Thus said the Lord:
I remember with gratitude
The devotion of your youth,
Your love as a bride,
When you trustingly
Followed me into the wilderness,
Into a land unsown.
JEREMIAH 2:2

Contents

Preface

Whereas the religious literature on spirituality, both historic and recent, seems almost boundless, the current psychologic and especially psychoanalytic literature, and also the neuroscientific literature, have but little to say on the subject.

Of course the studies of William James (*The Varieties of Religious Experience*, 1902) and of Rudolf Otto (*The Idea of the Holy*, 1923) are distinguished exceptions to that perhaps overly broad generalization.

Psychoanalysts have historically disdained religion and have not troubled much to distinguish between religion and spirituality. Freud's early statements (*The Future of an Illusion*, and later, *Civilization and Its Discontents* and *Group Psychology and the Analysis of the Ego*) had little to say of religion that was favorable. In his later years, however, beginning with *Moses and Monotheism*, he expressed a more benign view.

The early followers of Freud similarly distanced themselves from even a scholarly interest in the subject. When I was a student at the New York Psychoanalytic Institute soon after World War II, expression of interest in religion, and especially participation in any religious observance, was taken as a sign of either weakmindedness or less than full commitment to the discipline of psychoanalysis.

Neuroscientists have until very recently shown little interest in the subject, probably less because of prejudice against religion than because spirituality seems so difficult to measure and observe experimentally. Even today the field is not as open to affective neuroscience as it might be. Do animals experience affect? Few neuroscientists are willing to allow that they do. Therefore, they believe that affect cannot be studied as an object of scientific endeavor, and certainly not spirituality. In very recent years, I have enjoyed the opportunity to participate in online discussion groups that dealt with the subject of spirituality and included scholars of psychology and sociology. Sociologists have not been quite as allergic to the subject as psychologists and psychoanalysts.

I realize that it may be excessively ambitious for me to undertake this task. I approach it modestly because I am not an expert in spirituality or religion or neuroscience, though I do have a good deal of experience in psychoanalysis and psychiatry. What qualifies me for the task, if it does, is my interest and at least a smattering of ignorance in the first three fields, and expertise in the last two.

My introduction to spirituality arose out of my studies in Jewish mysticism, to which I was introduced by three well-informed and good friends: Gerson D. Cohen and Ismar Schorsch, successive chancellors of the Jewish Theological Seminary, and Rabbi Stanley Schachter. My attempt to apply psychoanalytic understanding to the phenomena of mysticism was published in *Ultimate Intimacy: The Psychodynamics of Jewish Mysticism* (1995), to which I refer often in the pages that follow. That effort was encouraged by the then publisher of Karnac Books, Cesare Sacerdoti.

Although it has not been my field of primary interest, I have taken an active interest in neuroscience and its precursors, neurology and neurophysiology, for the past fifty years, and offered a few published speculations in the field, not all of which turned out to be foolish. My introduction to neuroscience came by way of psychopharmacology, which is, after all, only applied neuroscience. The reader will observe that I make some small use of my expertise in that area in what follows. For my amateur understanding of current neuroscience, I am indebted to my good and wise friend, Jaak Panksepp.

My recent studies of spirituality have been informed by distinguished scholars and good friends who are cooperating with me in an interdisciplinary study of the affective resonance of the Jewish liturgy at the Jewish Theological Seminary: Martin Bergmann, Neil Gillman, Richard Kalmin, Morton Leifman, Menahem Schmelzer, and David Sidorsky.

For encouraging me in all of these endeavors, and keeping me accurate and honest in my application of psychoanalysis to these and other studies over the many years, I owe a profound debt of gratitude to my close friend and colleague Peter B. Neubauer. My good friend Elliot Zupnick has patiently heard me out and encouraged me, and for that I am grateful. Jacob A. Arlow, a serious student of the application of psychoanalysis to Jewish studies, has advised me over the years. Paula J. Hamm, who has taken the lead in encouraging the psychoanalytic study of spirituality and religion, has shared her views with me and offered her significant support. David Pincus came to psychoanalysis and neuroscience via philosophy, and has coached me on matters of epistemology—especially the importance of acknowledging contingencies and emergence in the nature of reality. He has kindly provided some of the important material on which my argument is based.

I am averse to expressing private sentiments in public, but how could I conclude these acknowledgments without expressing my immeasurable debt to my wife, Miriam, who, over sixty years, encouraged and inspired me faithfully and lovingly, even when she had appropriate reservations about my various endeavors?

CHAPTER I

Introduction

"Spirituality" is a word that has no clear-cut meaning, but many resonances. It evokes a strong response from some people and virtually none from others. It is generally recognized as something to be respected or admired. Many people respond to it with enthusiasm, others find it of no interest. Although it has the power to move many people and bore others, it is not easily defined cognitively.

Spirituality and religion are two different domains, but they are usually conflated. Even William James (1902), perhaps the finest student of the psychology of these subjects, does not distinguish them clearly. In fact, he deals with all of spiritual experience under the heading of mysticism.

I shall try in chapter 2 to suggest the dimensions of the spiritual experience and a tripartite classification: awe, Spirituality proper (which I shall spell with a capital S), and mysticism. I shall then, in chapter 3, suggest an explanation for its origin in the psychologic, or more specifically in the psychodynamic processes that emerge sequentially in human development. Briefly, I shall try to demonstrate that pure spiritual experience of whatever kind reproduces the affective component of early contact between mother and infant.

Obviously the interface between spirituality and religion requires examination. Spirituality is not religion and religion is not spirituality, but the spiritual provides the emotional force that underlies interest in and commitment to religion. Chapter 4 is a long discussion of the spiritual basis of religious feeling and practice.

In chapter 5, I shall relate what little information we possess about the brain processes that accompany spiritual experience.

In chapter 6, I shall describe mood regulation, a psychic function that I believe to be a major determining function of our mental life, and how spirituality often contributes importantly to mood regulation. Apocalypse, which is closely related to spirituality, is the subject of chapter 7.

Spirituality and religion do not always enlighten and inspire. On too many occasions, we experience a demonic spirituality and a demonic face of god. It is this type of negative spirituality that gives rise to religious fundamentalism and especially its violent aspects, and much of the terrorism that roils the civilized world today. I approach this subject in chapter 8.

Chapter 9 focuses on the account of a week-long "spiritual quest" by a distinguished psychoanalyst. I apply the conclusions about spirituality that I have developed and compare the report with Psalm 19, a discussion of which runs like a red thread through the whole book. This final chapter serves to knit the many aspects of the argument together.

That some individuals take no interest in spirituality and others disdain it does not mean that it is of limited consequence. Spirituality in its narrow sense inspired the composition of the Bible and other religious scriptures, the construction of the great cathedrals, and the elaborations of the great religions. One could argue that it was the spirituality of the Deists in eighteenth-century England that inspired the founders of the United States in devising the American Constitution. In fact, in at least an indirect way, spirituality could be said to have driven the creation of culture in every civilization of the world. In a more immediate sense, demonic spirituality, as expressed in religious fundamentalism, threatens our culture today, and constructive spirituality drives us to defend it.

Yet science has not dealt with the subject in any serious way. The religious literature abounds with discussions of the spiritual. In the Judeo-Christian tradition, we find it most directly in the autobiographies of the recognized Christian mystics (Underhill 1964). The nineteenth and twentieth centuries saw the growth of a sociology not of spirituality but of religion. Unfortunately the two subjects are usually not properly distinguished, even, as observed, by James, and certainly not by Rudolf Otto, whose contributions to the psychology of religious spirituality stand out (1923). I shall make no effort here to review that copious literature.

What is missing is serious, scholarly study of the psychology of the phenomenon of spirituality itself. Sigmund Freud, who argued against religion, nevertheless had a good deal to say about its supposed prehistory (see Freud 1927, 1913, 1930, 1939). He remarked that he had never experienced anything that would pass as spiritual (1930), and assumed that he had disposed of the matter by explaining the oceanic feeling as a residual memory of the predifferentiated phase of infant development. Although Romain Roland, whose comments on the oceanic feeling he had quoted, argued that that phenomenon is the "source of the religious energy which is seized upon by the various Churches and religious systems" (1930:64), Freud thought that religious needs derive from the infant's helplessness and the longing for the father that it arouses (72). I shall argue in support of Roland's position. Among the psychoanalysts, Ana-Maria Rizzuto has attempted to ascertain, from examining her clinical data, the sources of the images of God (1979). Her theoretical presentation is based upon a system called object relations theory. William W. Meissner, a Jesuit psychoanalyst, also has addressed "The Psychoanalyst and Religious Experience." He quotes Rizzuto's work approvingly and extends it. Note, however, that these deal with religion and not directly with spirituality, speaking of the latter as though it were only an aspect of religious feeling. Pargament (1997) has published an extensive and descriptive study of the usefulness of religious faith, and the "neurotheologists" have tried to establish a "neurophysiology" of spiritual and religious experience.

Some materially minded people, scientists and others, consider a spiritual orientation a sign of mental incapacity. Spirituality does not deal with material, palpable reality. Palpability is our usual criterion for objective, consensual reality. Yet most of these who disparage spirituality do not disparage music or art or poetry or humor or beauty, or for that matter such abstract, nonmaterial disciplines as mathematics and logic, none of which can be touched or felt. Spiritual experience is no less real as a subjective experience than is the appreciation of any of these human encounters. The first four are affective, that is, emotional experiences. Mathematicians and cosmological physicists, impressed by the evident beauty and even awesomeness of the cosmos and the world of mathematical relations, are among the scientists most likely to describe spiritual feeling. Newton divided his time between mathematical and cosmologic physics, and religion. Einstein had many comments about his appreciation of the religious spirituality inherent in science:

> Now, even though the realms of religion and science in themselves are clearly marked off from each other, nevertheless there exist between the two, strong reciprocal relationships and dependencies. Though religion may be that which determines the goal, it has, nevertheless, learned from science, in the broadest sense, what means will contribute to the entertainment of the goals it has set up. But science can only be created by those who are thoroughly imbued with the aspiration toward truth and understanding. This source of feeling, however, springs from the sphere of religion. To this there also belongs the faith in the possibility that the regulations valid for the world of existence are rational, that is, comprehensible to reason. I cannot conceive of a genuine scientist without that profound faith. The situation may be expressed by an image: Science without religion is lame, religion without science is blind. (1956:24)

The resistance to spiritual experience, and to acknowledging it when it exists, may be traced to any of several personal factors, conscious or unconscious. For example, one may feel that spirituality reflects sentimentality, effeteness, or a thoughtless diversion from realism. Perhaps, as I shall suggest below, openness to spiritual experience is a function of perceptual sensitivity in general.

It is important to point out that in fact, reality is not limited to palpable, material substance. We have only limited knowledge of the universe outside our minds. Our senses respond to only a limited range of incident energies—light, sound, heat, pressure—and to a limited number of the chemicals floating in the ambient atmosphere. None of the sensations that these induce is perceived objectively; they acquire distinctive qualities from the instinctual needs and tendencies that greet them with interest. The instincts that are active at any given moment create affects, as do the moods that prevail during most of our lives, waking or dream, and these affects welcome or reject the percepts to which we are exposed, and so color them as we become conscious and aware of them. So if what we discern in the outside world is significantly determined by how we feel, moment to moment, then what is reality? Is life what we think it is early on a spring morning when we are young, or what we think it is on a dark winter night, late in our lives? Is a baby a bundle of vital, happy potential, eliciting our smiles and love, or a noisy nuisance demanding care? Is red the color of love or the color of destructive fire? One could answer that in the end, all we can know of reality is the percepts that impinge upon us, colored by the feelings we attach to them. There is no perception without feeling. If there is an alternate reality that we can extrapolate from our sensations, then we can know it only in a limited way, only inferentially, as a hypothesis. Our feelings and the sensations that they embrace are our immediate reality. (For an extensive discussion of the philosophical and cognitive issues raised by the differences between the unknowable external reality and our internal image of it, see Churchland and Churchland, *Neural Worlds and Real Worlds* [2002].)

Certainly the pleasurable feelings that we enjoy while eating a good meal are real. But so are the feelings evoked by music and art and theatrical performances, even though they are not induced by anything that touches our bodies. And so too are the feelings induced in a patriotic rally. Then what is an illusion? An illusion is a sensation induced by a stimulus that is ordinarily not adequate to induce such a sensation. In the sense that I have been describing, the illusory sensation is real, even though it comes about as a result of a special predisposition of the nervous system to respond to an ordinarily inadequate stimulus. This predisposition leads us to misinterpret the meaning of the percept. A hallucination is a sensation, accompanied by affect (as all sensations are), that comes about in the absence of any external stimulation of any of the organs of perception. Dreams are hallucinations. There may be no external stimulus whatever, but the sensation and the accompanying affect are real. If anyone doubts the reality of dream sensations, his doubts will be overcome when an anxiety dream awakens him.

The thrills that we enjoy while listening to music may be considered illusory if we assume that the sound stimulus is not adequate to cause us to respond that way. And the thrill of participation in a patriotic rally is similarly illusory; the fluttering colored cloth that is the flag would not elicit our enthusiasm if it were not for the patriotic emotion with which we view it. But evidently these nonpalpable stimuli are adequate to elicit the appropriate emotion. So the stimulus is real and the sensory response is real.

What about the sensation of awe, which responds to the perception of scenes of great beauty, enormous structures, extraordinary human qualities, music, and art? The literal qualities of the stimulus do not account for these feelings. I shall argue below that it is not what we see that directly induces in us a sense of awe, but what it reminds us of that we don't see. The sensations themselves and the awe that they inspire must be considered both illusory in that they are not directly given in the stimulating scene, and real in that they embrace us and establish a real mood.

Awe is a spiritual quality, and yet, in the sense in which I have discussed it, real. It is only a small step from externally generated awe to internally generated spiritual experience. The quality of otherworldliness applies to each, and the experience of one is as real as the experience of the other. Even the hallucinations of the mystical experience and the affects that accompany them are no less real than dream hallucinations and reflect the real state of mind and brain.

I am arguing that the events of our minds, no matter how stimulated, are real for us even though it is important to know to what extent they are determined by imposed stimuli and to what extent by the receptive state of our minds.

To summarize these comments about reality and spirituality: some experiences, hallucinations, are determined exclusively by the state of the subject's brain with minimal external input, but all the other subjective experiences are determined by both the qualities and qualia of the impinging stimuli and the affective readiness of the mind-brain. The experience is real no matter what the nature of the impinging stimulus.

That said, we must take note of the difference between spiritual perception and nonspiritual perception. We think of perception as becoming consciously aware of receiving an indication of some change in the outside world within range of our perceptual receptors. For example, when we converse, we hear and take note of what is being said to us, think about it, and reply appropriately. This is a fully attentive conscious experience. But we also perceive things preconsciously. For example, when we drive, we perceive any number of visible and audible signals to which we respond. Our cognitive apparatus cannot process all of these signals in consciousness simultaneously, but we respond to them appropriately even though we may not notice them consciously. We attend to the road, but not to each of the myriad details, many of which guide our responses automatically, that is, without conscious acknowledgment. When asked about a particular detail, we may say that we had not noticed it, as though we had seen it only "out of the corner of my eye." Yet we had probably responded appropriately to it.

Still other percepts are not processed cognitively at all but arouse affective responses. Music, art, attractive people, beautiful landscapes, and offensive scenes as well, for example, may all elicit appropriate emotional responses without the intervention of studied cognition, though we may contemplate them cognitively after processing them. Communication among subhuman animals is probably purely affective in this sense. A lion's roar elicits an affective response among other lions and doubtless, among other animals in the vicinity. I sometimes wonder whether semantic communication may have been differentiated from this affective modality during the evolution of *homo sapiens*.

But spiritual perception is different, a third variety. Here the primary influence is affective, though a cognitive message may accompany it, for example, the revelation that is usually given along with the hallucination. But in perceiving the surrounding world, many of the functions of perceptual consciousness that we ordinarily take for granted are suspended or altered. Time may seem to stand still or to rush by; motion to be arrested or to become frantic; colors to be unusually bright or dull; people and places inappropriately familiar or unfamiliar; objects larger or smaller than we ordinarily see them; sounds louder or softer. God may appear as the thunder and lightning above Mount Sinai or as the still, small voice that Elijah heard in the cave in Horeb. The entire scene may appear unreal or hyperreal. In other words, many or most of the parameters of sensory experience may be altered so that the percept acquires a distinct stamp of the unusual or even unreal.

One could argue that, in a sense, the spiritual experience is real, but one of its parameters, the sense of reality, is altered so that the illusion of unreality is created. *Déjà vu* phenomenon combines a sense of reality with a recognition of unreality. The sense of unfamiliarity or depersonalization, for example, could be triggered by anxiety or other disturbance of mental function or direct abnormalities of brain function. These are individual components of the complex of regulatory parameters that normally keep us in contact with the outside world, so that we can live and function in it effectively.

The spiritual experience, prompted by powerful affective needs, which we shall study below, can apparently derange these regulatory parameters so as to create an alternate sense of reality, in effect, an apparent escape from the world of reality, so as to transport us to a more welcoming world—or, if the effort miscarries, to a more frightening one. It is in this sense that the spiritual experience is unreal. I argue that it only appears to be so; the unreality is an illusion. The phenomenon is essentially a real one in that it is the real mental state that prevails at the time.

The ultimate argument between the religious and the secular is whether the spiritual affect responds to or makes contact with a supernatural external influence, perhaps divine, or is generated only by intrapsychic dynamics. The sensation is real in either case, but it may reflect what it seems to reflect, or may be an illusion.

All of this is, of course, introductory. In what follows I shall deal with the nature of the spiritual experience, its origin, its precipitating causes, its elaboration, its effects, and how it relates to mood and the major orientation of our strivings.

CHAPTER 2

Spirit

This is a letter I received from a close friend, a distinguished scientist, an erudite man, well known as an especially clear thinker.

(REPORT 1)
Here is an account of the unusual experience that I had which I told you about the other evening. It occurred at the beginning of August at a time when Helen was either in the hospital or had just returned home. Now I am not sure exactly which.

I went swimming at our community pool which is located at the edge of the bay. As I regularly do, I looked out over the water before I went into the dressing room to change. Suddenly, everything seemed strangely, fantastically beautiful. The sky was a deep blue, the water seemed motionless and silvery. The clouds in the heavens seemed to be assembled in a very special way; huge and fluffy and very white, yet they were distributed over the heavens in a sparse manner. Over to the side, a White

Heron rested on the water completely motionless. I was aware that this was a scene of transcendent beauty. Nothing moved. Time seemed to stand still. Although I am a complete unbeliever, twice there came into my mind the phrases from the book of Psalms, in Hebrew.

Hashamayim mesaprim Kvod 'El, uma'asey yadayv magid harakia

(The heavens declare the glory of God, and the sky recites the work of His hands)

I looked away and I looked back and the scene remained unchanged. For a moment I had the thought of going to the lifeguard and urging him to come and look, but I knew that there was something very personal about what I was living through.

I had been on that same spot scores, perhaps hundreds of times but never had that sensation before. As I thought about the experience there came to my mind naturally Freud's discussion of the "oceanic feeling" but more than that I thought of two poems; [first was] Wordsworth's "My Heart Leaps up When I Behold a Rainbow in the Sky." Until now I had thought of that as a kind of trite phrase. But after this experience, I can understand what the poet was trying to express, or more accurately, what he was feeling. What really moved me was recalling Keats' sonnet "On First Looking Into Chapman's Homer" in which he described the awesome sensation in terms of "Then felt I like some watcher of the skies when a new planet swims into his ken" and further on, in the same poem, when he imagines what it was to be the first European to stand on a peak and to see the limitless, boundless Pacific Ocean—a mixture of awe and wonder.

Two thoughts may be relevant. First, my mother died at the beginning of August. Second, I recalled when I was a youngster of twelve or thirteen sitting in the front row in the basement synagogue of our Boys' Club on a beautiful Saturday morning looking beyond the neighboring wooden fence and past some decrepit buildings towards a beautiful blue sky. Why I retained that moment in my memory all these years I do not know but it seems to me that it might represent a smaller version of what I experienced on the shores of the bay.

We have here a classic example of a Spiritual experience. It is Spiritual because the observer was suddenly beset by a feeling that he is immersed in a special relation with the surrounding world, different from his usual sense of the world. The surroundings seemed "strangely, fantastically, beautiful." The sky was a deeper blue than usual. The clouds were "assembled in a very special way." The white heron was "completely motionless." A prospect that was very familiar to him now seemed altered in an oddly beautiful way.

His experience is also Spiritual because it was unique, something he had never known before, though there were some childhood reminiscences of similar quality but lesser intensity. It was a feeling with no link to bodily need or social engagement. It had strong aesthetic overtones, but its impact was far more than aesthetic. It seemed to be a reaching out to, a communication or contact with, a natural or religious source of personal fulfillment.

Although my friend considers himself "a complete unbeliever," he nevertheless responded automatically with a verse from Psalm 19 that begins with the acknowledgment of being engaged with God by virtue of his response to the awesome and articulate aspects of the heavens. Profound emotional engagement is automatic; belief is irrelevant.

Let us look more closely at the letter. The man's wife had been seriously ill for several years. They had been married since they were very young and had been unusually close. He had retired from his university position and had stopped seeing faculty, colleagues, and students in order to care for her, and their social life had dwindled to nothing. He was living in virtual solitude. At the pool he seems to have been alone, save for the lifeguard. When he penned this account, he did not recall whether his wife was in the hospital or had recently returned at the time of the occurrence. He was very much alone. It would seem that the experience he described was generated by a sense of loneliness. He recalled that his mother had died in the same month, years previously, and he also recalled having been inspired by a similarly beautiful blue sky during Sabbath services when he was twelve or thirteen.

So we may infer that this spiritual experience occurred against the background of yearning for reunion with someone deeply loved, and it was triggered by the view of natural beauty, the sky and the water.

Many spiritual experiences take place against the background of natural beauty, often alongside a body of water. My friend alluded to Keats's sonnet, in which he imagines standing on a peak and viewing the limitless and boundless Pacific Ocean. He also quotes Wordsworth as he responded to a rainbow in the sky.

It is interesting that he was aware that he was living through a very unusual and "very personal" experience. He was eager to share it with someone, and he did share it with me a day or two after it happened, knowing of my interest in the subject. He probably also wished to have the lifeguard confirm whether it was consensually real or solipsistic.

Note too that motion was arrested and time stood still, a feature of some, but not all, spiritual experience. The event brought to mind a similar experience that had persisted in memory since childhood. Beauty, motionlessness, timelessness, and transcendence are all signal concepts in this account.

Let us look at another instance of spirituality.

(REPORT 2)

A woman, who considered herself "deeply spiritual" reported that she was interested in the transcendent experiences associated with great mountains. She told me that she had climbed Mount Sinai at night with the assistance of two Bedouin boys. She had prayed as she walked up the mountain, using the English version of the Catholic liturgies she had learned as a child, though she considered herself an unbeliever. At the top she was excited by the sight of "the most beautiful thing" she had ever seen, the sun coming up over the desert. At the top of the mountain she had a sense of "extraordinary alienation from the earth." She thought that the desert was so hostile, arid, and rocky, and could understand why this was the scene of the revelation of the Law to Moses. She felt wonderful for days afterward.

Again our reporter was impressed with the beauty of natural landscapes, heights, the sunrise, and a sense of "extraordinary alienation." The experience generated religious thoughts, again in the absence of belief, though she too had had a religious childhood. Again the words "beauty" and "transcendence" are used. The woman, though usually highly involved with others professionally, socially, and romantically, was virtually alone. Her guides were of no personal interest to her.

Let us look at a third example. A young woman describes a visit to a resort on the Gulf Coast of Florida for a professional meeting.

(REPORT 3)
That summer's meeting was at the South Seas Plantation on Captiva Island. I had never been on the Gulf Coast and was totally swept away. I was used to the Atlantic Ocean—cold waters and waves. The Gulf was unexpected—the water was warm and "bouncy." I could stand for an hour, with my sunglasses on, up to my neck in water and never get pulled off my feet. It was totally relaxing.

In the evening, people would go down to the beach to swim. It was hot outside and going into the water cooled us off and it was never so cold that you couldn't stay in the water. The third evening we were there we learned that there is a kind of plankton that is phosphorescent and that there was a large area of the water around the resort where these creatures were swimming. You couldn't see them, but they made the water glow. None of us really knew what that meant, but it was an interesting fact.

That night when we went down to the water, I was blown away. The effect of these creatures' being in the water was phenomenal. When I would bring my hands out of the water over my head the water dripping off my hands and arms looked like it had silver glitter in it. People were jumping up and down making splashes of glitter. Each night more and more people came down to swim and that night there must have been about fifty people in the water. The moon was full, beautiful and really bright. When I looked out over the water, I saw all of these jumping, bouncing people, silhouetted against the horizon, throwing up splashes of glittery water.

I had never experienced such a combination of things. I stood in the water, up to my neck, and felt like I stepped back and saw it all spread before me—the people (all of whom were having a blast), the glittery water, the moon, the temperature. It came to me so clearly that such a combination of wonder and beauty could only happen because of the existence of a God—of a higher being. Never had I so surely felt that Presence as I did at that moment.

Here again is a personal experience of a wonderful sight, with reference to the moon and the ocean. Although the context is different, we are reminded of the allusion to sky and sea, "wonder and beauty." This woman feels that the experience confirmed her religious belief. Although she was not alone, and the sight of many other people was important, her experience was personal. "Never had I so surely felt that Presence as I did at that moment." The first two instances occurred in virtual solitude. This one took place in the presence of friends and many others, but she was away from her family.

Awe too is an affective experience, similar to the Spiritual experience in that it is a surprisingly strong reaction to an unusually powerful impression: enormous mountains, large bodies of water, powerful storms, or even displays of extraordinary intelligence or extraordinarily stirring music. The subject is moved but feels no automatic connection to preternatural influence. Nature is not altered; time does not stand still.

In the first example, the stimulating scene was, for the observer, an ordinary one. He had been there many times before. On the occasion that he describes, this scene attained extraordinary power; time and motion stopped. It was the prepared emotion he brought to the occasion that made the view seem so impressive, rather than the view itself. In the second case, it was both the spiritual attitude of the reporter (she recited a liturgy as she walked up the mountain) and the striking view itself, the sun rising over the desert, as seen from the mountain. In the third case too, the woman was separated from her family, among a group of strangers, but also impressed by a striking natural sight—flashes of light in the water, under the moon.

We speak of awe rather than spirituality when it is the spectacle or sound alone that provokes the response, while the emotional preparation might be receptive but not specifically attuned or reaching out. We speak of Spirituality when the individual seems to invest a specific experience with a preternatural significance that moves him in a powerful and unusual way. In other words, awe occurs when a receptive mind encounters an extraordinary stimulus. A Spiritual experience occurs when a need for such an experience seizes upon a stimulus that may be unique or unusual, or might be perfectly ordinary.

The affect associated with awe has no specific name; it is a feeling of being moved, stirred. The words that come to mind are "beautiful," "stirring," "remarkable," "unusual," "impressive," usually associated with a superlative. I believe that it is accompanied also by a sense of familiarity, a feeling of belonging here.

Actually we know of two forms of awe, inviting and fearsome. One can be awed by welcome vistas, but also by frightening vistas. Most dictionaries include fear as a component of awe. Not every frightening impression is awesome. An impression is awesome if it is frightening because it is gigantic, powerful, and threatening.

A dramatic example of fearsome awe is illustrated by Munch's painting *The Scream*. A *New York Times* article (12/9/03) gives Munch's journal entry describing the origin of the image that he painted. He makes clear that *The Scream* grew from an experience he had while walking near Christiania (now Oslo) at sunset: "All at once the sky became bloodred . . . clouds like blood and tongues of fire hung above the blue-black fjord and the city . . . and I stood alone, trembling with anxiety . . . I felt a great unending scream piercing through nature." *The Times* also quotes Dr. Donald Olson, an astronomer at Texas State University, who argues that Munch saw the fallout of the volcanic explosion in the Indonesia island of Krakatoa. The awesome vision conveyed trembling anxiety and the feeling of "a great unending scream piercing through nature." The "awful" sight elicited a response of horror.

The third element in this triad, mysticism, resembles Spirituality in that it too comprises a feeling of transcendence, of being in contact with a preternatural "reality," of detachment from the here and now. It is not necessarily stimulated by, nor does it necessarily respond to, a striking encounter. Seemingly without preparation, the subject becomes aware that he is in direct contact with a supernatural entity, usually God or a semidivine creature. He may see a vision, hear a voice, and/or sense a presence.

(REPORT 4)

A manic-depressive gentleman, who was struggling with a conflict between material interests and moral obligations, sent me a long letter. In the letter he recounted the story of King David, who was punished by God for his adultery, and yet designated as the ancestor of the Messiah. (He embellished the biblical story in accordance with myth and a popular motion picture.) "What all this has to do with me, I still can't figure out, except that suddenly—and never before have I had such an experience—some power told me how to solve my present problem and not knowing exactly what to do, I went to the synagogue on the following Friday and made an anonymous offering of $1,000 with a note saying 'I thank the Lord of Israel who showed me what my tasks and solutions should be.' My spirits go up and down day by day, but on the whole, I am happy with the route I have taken, though I do not really know why I took it. All I know is that hard as it may be, it is the right thing to do."

The subject describes direct communication from "some power" later identified as the Lord of Israel. The communication was helpful, a religious revelation. Following the instruction left him with a feeling of gratification; "It was the right thing to do." The direct communication from a supernatural entity indicates a break in ego function, that is, a detachment from his sense of conventional reality, a suspension of reality testing.

The following is a description of a classical, often quoted mystical experience, described by Saint Teresa of Avila (1960).

(REPORT 5)

It pleased the Lord that I should sometimes see the following vision. I would see beside me, on my left hand, an angel in bodily form—a type of vision which I am not in the habit of seeing, except very rarely. Though I often see representations of angels, my visions of them are of the type which I first mentioned. It pleased the Lord that I should see this angel in the following way. He was not tall, but short, and very beautiful, his face so aflame that he appeared to be one of the highest types of angel who seem to be all afire. They must be those who are called cherubim: they do not tell me their names, but I am well aware that there is a great difference between certain angels and others, and between these and others still, of a kind that I could not possibly explain. In his hands I saw a long golden spear and at the end of the iron tip I seemed to see a point of fire. With this he seemed to pierce my heart several times so that it penetrated to my entrails. When he drew it out, I thought he was drawing them out with it and he left me completely afire with a great love for God. The pain was so sharp that it made me utter several moans; and so excessive was the sweetness caused me by this intense pain that one can never wish to lose it, nor will one's soul be content with anything less than God. It is not bodily pain, but spiritual, though the body has a share in it—indeed, a great share. So sweet are the colloquies of love which pass between the soul and God that if anyone thinks I am lying I beseech God, in His goodness, to give him the same experience.

She describes her experience as a vision. That word can be interpreted as implying that she knew it was not real, but she does describe the accompanying sensation as though it were real: "It is not bodily pain, but spiritual, though the body has a share in it—indeed, a great share." This experience is unlike awe in that it does not depend upon an external impression. Like a Spiritual experience, the affect is attributed to an encounter with an external agent, but the agent here does not seem to be entirely unreal. Saint Teresa had a number of episodes of illness that seem to have been psychiatric, but she nevertheless succeeded in living an active, creative, and helpful life.

I take my next example from William James's *The Varieties of Religious Experience* (1902:385).

(REPORT 6)
In that time the consciousness of God's nearness came to me sometimes. I say God, to describe what is indescribable. A presence, I might say, yet that is too suggestive of personality, and the

moments of which I speak did not hold the consciousness of a personality, but something in myself made me feel myself a part of something bigger than I that was controlling. I felt myself one with the grass, the trees, birds, insects, everything in Nature. I exulted in the mere fact of existence, of being a part of it all—the drizzling rain, the shadows of the clouds, the tree-trunks, and so on. In the years following, such moments continued to come, but I wanted then constantly. I knew so well the satisfaction of losing self in a perception of supreme power and love, that I was unhappy because that perception was not constant.

I have selected this vignette because it illustrates another aspect of mysticism. The communication with God is merely one consequence of the dissolution of ego boundaries, that is, the loss of the sense of the spatial and psychologic limits of the self. It is not merely that the mystic is touched by a supernatural entity, but that he feels united with the entire universe that surrounds him. He feels firmly at one with God and all of creation. Freud quoted Romain Roland: "The true source of religious sentiment, he says," consists in a peculiar feeling, which he himself is never without, finds confirmed by many others, and may suppose is present in millions of people. It is a feeling he would like to call a sensation of "eternity," of something limitless, unbounded—as it were, "oceanic." "This feeling," he adds, "is a purely subjective fact, not an article of faith; it brings with it no assurance of personal immortality, but it is the source of the religious energy which is seized upon by the various Churches and religious systems, directed by them into particular channels, and doubtless also exhausted by them. One may, he thinks, rightly call oneself religious on the ground of this oceanic feeling alone, even if one rejects every belief and every illusion" (Freud 1930:64).

From this quotation, the term "oceanic feeling" has become well known as a metaphor for the sense of union felt by the mystic. Because they are universal, mystical images transcend local boundaries. Moshe Idel (1988:67ff.) lists a number of examples in Kabbalistic texts that cite this metaphor, that is, that *unio mystica* can be compared to the dispersion of a drop of water in the sea.

The experience of union or reunion seems to form the core of most experiences that qualify as mystical. As noted above, all experiences of awe are initiated by some external stimulus. Most experiences that are called Spiritual need no special external stimulus to come into being, although some seemed to be aroused by a striking, especially awesome impression. But most mystical experiences seem to arise internally, without evident occasion. A few are indeed induced by a specific event. Here are two accounts of mystical experiences in which the subject feels caught up in union, elicited by witnessing examples of union in the first instance and reunion in the second.

(REPORT 7)
The speaker is a middle-aged Jewish woman.

The first time that I was in Israel was in September of 1961. The last time was last year (1998) on Yom Ha'atzmaut (Israel Independence Day), except I was here in Riverdale. I generally do not consider myself a "mystical" person. I was taught from an early age to analyze and weigh in an intellectual fashion. There have been many wonderful emotional experiences in my life—the birth of my children, a wonderful moment at the top of a mountain after a hike, and some indescribable emotional high points here and there. But last year something happened that was very different from anything that I had experienced before.

The Riverdale Jewish community had organized a parade and celebration. I went partly because I wanted to and partly because I figured I should. Well, am I glad! The parade, about a mile long, started from our *shul* and wound through the streets of the neighborhood, passed Riverdale Temple, ending up at the Hebrew Institute. The parade was OK, led by the Cathedral High School Marching Band (yes, from a Catholic school), and at the end there was the Manhattan College bagpipe band. (Only in New York?) At the final location there was a bandstand and an orchestra. They played a medley of music, people started to dance, and after a short time the program started.

First was a moment of silence with a siren blaring in memory of all of the fallen of Tzahal (Israeli army). The cantor sang a special "*El maley rachamim*" for the army dead. And then was one of the most unusual moments of my life. It is hard to describe. The cantor from Riverdale Temple sang "Hatikvah" (Israeli national anthem). She has an incredible operatic voice. But while she was singing I was someplace else and not standing on a street corner of Riverdale. Suddenly I really was in Israel, seeing again some special places. It was as if I were in the taxi in 1961, when I first visited Israel, going up the old road to Jerusalem just as the sun was coming up, and in the Emek looking out over the fields, and in Haifa somewhere, and visiting the Kotel (Western Wall) for the first time. I was in one place and in all of the places, seemingly at the same time. It was absolutely unbelievable. I don't think that I have ever had an experience just like this before. Even now, an hour or so later, if I close my eyes I can continue to see places where I have been, and some not for many, many years, so vividly. It is as if I were there right now. I left at 9 p.m. not quite waiting for the end because I didn't want it to just fade out. I needed to come home and to try to capture a little of this experience in words. Hard to believe that when I began this evening I was feeling discouraged, and not excited about the holiday at all.

I have thought about this experience a few times in the year since it happened. And I still don't understand it at all. Is that what a mystical experience means? I have actually never studied mysticism, Jewish or otherwise, preferring the safer ground of intellectual pursuit. But such an experience makes one wonder.

The last sentence of the account, "hard to believe that when I began this evening I was feeling discouraged," which seems like a postscript, tells us something important about mysticism, namely that the mystical experience may be encouraged by a feeling of discontent, a depressive unhappiness. This is what induces the wish to reunite with the mystical object. Second, the mystical transport was encouraged by the several acts of union that she witnessed: members of the local Jewish community with differing loyalties, Orthodox, Conservative, and Reform; Catholics and Jews; the assembly of large numbers of people. She was affected also by the music, the moving liturgical tribute to the fallen soldiers of the Israeli army, the singing of the Israeli national anthem. The physical and emotional assembly of many individuals creates a feeling of unity that is a source of mystical experience. As a footnote, let me draw your attention to her memory of her Israeli taxi ride. Vehicular travel is a consistent component of Merkavah mysticism (an early variety of Jewish mysticism focused on the image of God on his celestial chariot, as the scene is described in Ezekiel 1).

(REPORT 8)

A somewhat similar experience of high emotional transport was described by another woman. She was an American, studying at the Hebrew University during her third-year abroad college program in June of 1967. She remained in Jerusalem during the Six Day War. Israel took possession of the Old City of Jerusalem on June 7. The festival of Shavuot began on the evening of June 13. The following incident occurred on the following morning.

I am twenty-one years old. It is Erev (the eve of) Shavuot. I am staying with my first cousin, and his family. His parents are also here. At four in the morning he interrupts his studying to awaken us so that we can prepare for our journey, the *aliyah beregel* (festival pilgrimage) to the *Kotel* (Western Wall). First we go through the winding streets of Rehavia. Then Rehov Jabotinsky and Mamilla. Now we are joining the multitudes of Am Yisrael (the people of Israel) in a curving unbroken *shalshelet* (chain) as we climb the pathway up to Sha'ar Zion and then onward to Sha'ar Ha'Ashpatot (gates of the Old City). I looked in all directions and viewed this orderly sea of humanity. I am here with family and my people. We all say *Sheheheyanu* (a liturgical expression of gratitude upon attaining a goal) as we get our glimpse of the *Kotel*.

The young woman was overwhelmed by a feeling that, though otherwise quite articulate, she could not express in words. She felt herself almost dissolved in the mass of her people, Am Yisrael, and, at the same time, one with historical Israel, a grand unitive experience. Here too the mystical experience was elicited by the experience of being part of a group of people with a single interest and a single feeling, moving eastward into the sunrise toward reunion with a holy place, and was mingled with awe.

Following the religious scholars, we may associate mystical experience with the sense of union, a transcendence of ego boundaries.

That would include both the oceanic feeling and the sense of immediate communication with a cosmic entity. As the quote from James illustrates, these impressions can coincide in the same experience.

Religious mysticism is not confined to such phenomena, many of which can be considered trance states. In the mystical attitude, humanity, the cosmos, the deity all become one system, speculation about which becomes theosophy. Early Jewish mysticism revolves around fantasies of God in his chariot (Merkavah mysticism) or in his temple (Hekhaloth, that is, chamber mysticism), the worshipper attempting to reach him there, to see him, to be inspired by him. However, classically the seeker encounters obstacles and dangers and hostile guardians; only the best prepared, the truly pious and virtuous survive. The Kabbalistic phase of Jewish mysticism largely consists of an attempt to visualize and describe God's attributes and the reciprocal influence between God and mankind. The text of Scripture is taken as a source of that information, which is considered to be there encoded, and the Kabbalist attempts to break the secret codes. Some, proceeding from the assumption that God can be influenced by these secrets and by invocation of any of God's many Kabbalistic names, try to work magic. Idel calls this effort theurgic mysticism.

Awe, Spirituality, and mysticism constitute what might be called the spiritual triad. They share a sense of immediate experience, of a feeling for which we have no common name since it corresponds to no other feeling that is familiar to us, and to which we can refer by our conventional vocabulary. The feeling seems compelling and real, although it satisfies none of our usual criteria for reality. It cannot be dismissed. It incorporates a yearning for contact with the unattainable. And although the feeling seems real, it is accompanied by a sense of unreality.

As observed above, experiences of awe are uniformly elicited by exposure to awesome sights or sounds, as an extreme example, the theophany at Mount Sinai. Spiritual experiences, such as the one described in the letter with which this chapter began, may take place against an unremarkable background, though it is interesting that when the subject describes the event he usually starts by giving the background anyway, after emphasizing its ordinariness. Sometimes the subject will observe that he was disconsolate or disturbed before the experience, for example, the first and seventh instances. Similarly, the mystical experience seems to appear unbidden, though often against the background of conscious or unconscious unhappiness—for example, the mystical communication described by my manic-depressive patient. Often these events are prepared for and hoped for. Most, but not all, of the described spiritual or mystical experiences occurred when the subject was alone, as though they were intended to relieve the solitude.

On the other hand, many religious practices, rituals, and liturgies seem designed to evoke spiritual experiences. Mystics, whether within formal religious contexts or by idiosyncratically contrived practice, strive to make themselves receptive to mystical experiences. They cannot compel the revelation to come, but they can invite it by making themselves open to it. I shall have more to say about this subject below, when I discuss spirituality and religion.

My focus here has been upon the nature of the specific spiritual experience, and upon the circumstances of its appearance. William James, the distinguished American philosopher-psychologist of the late nineteenth century, presented in 1902 a series of lectures under the felicitous title of *The Varieties of Religious Experience*. In the book (page 31) he writes, "Religion . . . shall mean for us the feelings, acts and experiences of individual men in their solitude, so far as they apprehend themselves to stand in relation to whatever they may consider divine." That is his delineation of religion for the purposes of that discussion. He excludes from consideration religion as a group institution and practice, systematic theology, and ideas about "the gods themselves." Note that he prepares the ground for his discussion of "religious experience," which is what he calls spirituality, by including the phrase "in their solitude."

These comments were intended to introduce his defining criteria of spiritual experiences he calls mystical states of consciousness (page 31f.):

Ineffability—The handiest of the marks by which I classify a state of mind as mystical is negative. The subject of it immediately says that it defies expression, that no adequate report of its contents can be given in words. It follows from this that its quality must be directly experienced; it cannot be imparted or transferred to others. In this peculiarity mystical states are more like states of feeling than like states of intellect. No one can make clear to another who has never had a certain feeling, in what the quality or worth of it consists. One must have musical ears to know the value of a symphony; one must have been in love one's self to understand a lover's state of mind. Lacking the heart or ear, we cannot interpret the musician or the lover justly, and are even likely to consider him weak-minded or absurd. The mystic finds that most of us accord to his experiences an equally incompetent treatment.

Noetic quality—Although so similar to states of feeling, mystical states seem to those who experience them to be also states of knowledge. They are states of insight into depths of truth unplumbed by the discursive intellect. They are illuminations, revelations, full of significance and importance, all inarticulate though they remain; and as a rule they carry with them a curious sense of authority for aftertime.

These two characters will entitle any state to be called mystical, in the sense in which I use the word. Two other qualities are less sharply marked, but are usually found.

These are:

Transiency—Mystical states cannot be sustained for long. Except in rare instances, half an hour, or at most an hour or two, seems to be the limit beyond which they fade into the light of common day. Often, when faded, their quality can but imperfectly be reproduced in memory; but when they recur it is recognized; and from one reoccurrence to another it is susceptible of continuous development in what is felt as inner richness and importance.

Passivity—Although the oncoming of mystical states may be facilitated by preliminary voluntary operations, as by fixing the attention, or going through certain bodily performances, or in other ways which manuals of mysticism prescribe; yet when the characteristic sort of consciousness once has set in, the mystic feels as if his own will were in abeyance, and indeed sometimes as if he were grasped and held by a superior power. This latter peculiarity connects mystical states with certain definite phenomena of secondary or alternative personality, such as prophetic speech, automatic writing, or the mediumistic trance. When these latter conditions are well pronounced, however, there may be no recollection whatever of the phenomenon, and it may have no significance for the subject's usual inner life, to which, as it were, it makes a mere interruption. Mystical states, strictly so-called, are never merely interruptive. Some memory of their content always remains, and a profound sense of their importance. They modify the inner life of the subject between the times of their recurrence. Sharp divisions in this region are, however, difficult to make, and we find all sorts of gradations and mixtures.

These four characteristics are sufficient to mark out a group of states of consciousness peculiar enough to deserve a special name and to call for careful study. Let them be called the mystical group.

The most characteristic aspect of the mystical experience, James says, is negative, that is, that it defies expression. I see this rather as a positive quality. In essence, it is a feeling state, an affect that is specific to this spiritual experience, common in a way to all such experiences, yet slightly different from one occasion and person to another. Its inexpressibility in terms of conventional language is not a limitation, a negative, but rather a positive, a unique quality that language cannot reach.

James also speaks of the noetic quality of the mystical state. He refers to the feeling that the subject describes by saying, "Now I know why. . . ." In Report 1, the reporter does not claim any new personal insight, but finds himself repeating the opening words of Psalm 19, "The heavens declare the glory of God and the sky recites of the work of His hands." In Report 2, the speaker thinks that she now understands why this location, Mount Sinai, was chosen for the giving of the Law. In the first full mystical experience that I described (Report 4), the subject is told how he should solve his problem. And, as James continues, "as a rule they carry with them a curious sense of authority for aftertime." The terms "illumination" and "revelation" are often applied to these insights.

In this connection it is interesting that at the inception of a psychotic break, the patient will assert, "Now I see the truth for the first time. Now I see it all clearly!" What this means is that having cast off the restraints of reality testing, he assigns the sense of reality to his psychotic fantasy. The spiritual insight, the mystical revelation acquires a sense of reality by virtue of the power of the experience, irrespective of ordinary criteria for consensual reality. A wish fantasy seizes the platform of apperception and claims to be reality, even though others recognize that it is not.

The first two qualities, says James, are defining. The second two occur commonly but are incidental. All of the examples that I have cited were transient, as he says. And yet they each left an afterglow that could be retrieved in attenuated memory.

I have already commented on the "passivity" of the experience, that it seems to have occurred without having been willed, as "a visitation," so to speak, although what might be called mystical adepts or practicing mystics invite such episodes by preparatory exercises.

I have, to this point, discussed and illustrated only experiences that were described as beautiful and pleasurable. But some of the experiences that can be considered spiritual by the criteria I have listed are unpleasant, frightening, anxiety provoking, the more so because they are unnatural and cannot be expected to subside or disappear as natural events can.

There is gratifying and inspiring awe, and frightening awe; awesome and awful. The theophany at Mount Sinai was terrifying. Rudolf Otto speaks of the *mysterium tremendum*, the mystery that inspires trembling. In fact, the word "awe" is defined in the *Oxford Dictionary and Thesaurus* as "reverential fear or wonder," and "awesome" is considered synonymous with "dreadful, fearsome, frightening, horrifying, terrifying, and terrible."

In an essay entitled "Experiences of Awe in Childhood," Phyllis Greenacre (1956) tells us that:

(REPORT 9)
Albert Schweitzer (1955), writing with delightful simplicity of his Alsatian childhood, describes his first recollection of all as a most terrifying, awful one of seeing the devil each Sunday morning as he sat in his father's church listening to and thrilled by the sound of the organ. All week he looked forward to the experience, as it appears that there was some pleasure in it too. Each

Sunday he saw with terror the face of the devil appear in a metal frame beside the organ, while the positive elements of the experience were reflected in his feeling toward the organ music itself and especially toward the father whose preaching invariably announced the disappearance of the devil.

As I have observed, the vocabulary of these spiritual phenomena is less than precise. James includes awe, Spirituality, and the full mystical experience in his discussion of mysticism. Greenacre, on the other hand, includes all three varieties under the heading of awe.

The word "spiritualism" is sometimes used as synonymous with "spirituality," but I would prefer to restrict it to the realm of phenomena associated with supposed supernatural creatures or influences. One of the oldest and most widespread of these spiritualistic phenomena is the belief that the "spirits" of the dead survive and appear among the living. The Bible in I Samuel, chapter 29, reports that when Saul was alarmed by the visible power of the Philistine army, he requested the local sorceress to raise the spirit of the now dead prophet to ask for his guidance. Usually the spirits of the dead, especially those murdered, are seen as malevolently seeking revenge, or as ghosts "haunting" the living. For example, Banquo shows up at Macbeth's feast and silently unsettles him. Hamlet's dead father instructs Hamlet: "So art thou bound to revenge, when thou shall hear. I am thy father's spirit, doomed for a certain term to walk the night, and for the day to fast in fires till the foul crimes done in my days of nature are burnt and purged away" (act 1, scene 5, 8–13). Though it has roots in the period of the Second Temple and in the Gospels, the *dibbuk* (from *dvk*, to adhere) became popular in Jewish folklore of the eighteenth and nineteenth centuries as an evil spirit, often the spirit of someone dead, that enters a living person and invades his personality. James mentions the phenomenon of "spirit return." The word "revenant" appears in the literature of the nineteenth century. Today people speak of channeling. Note that these apparitions might be thought of as revisiting their old habitats or those associated with them, seeking revenge, or, in other cases, as sources of information, comforting or threatening.

Some spirits are considered benign, helpful, or playful. Such appear in *A Midsummer Night's Dream* and in *The Tempest*. Joseph

Caro, a sixteenth-century distinguished Jewish codifier of religious law and Kabbalist, reported regular visitations by a *Maggid,* a heavenly mentor, who gave him instructions for personal conduct and religious doctrine. Folklore tells of benign elves and fairies as well as goblins and witches, and ultimately the chief opponents of God, Satan and his devilish cohorts. In the religious domain one encounters both angels and demons.

All of these are spirits in the sense that they are supernatural, have no material reality, yet exert strong emotional influence upon those to whom they appear. They share these qualities with the source that is assumed to be responsible for what we call spiritual experience.

What is the essential meaning and what are the implications of the word "spirit," which has formed the center of our discussion so far? Clearly the "spirit" of "spirituality" is different from the "spirit" of "spiritualism." They have in common the quality of being disembodied, preternatural entities that usually exert important influences upon those exposed to them. The "spirit" of the "spiritual experience" is an elevating, transcendent, inspiring influence, comforting or fearsome, but attributed to a divine or cosmic source. "Spirits," on the other hand, are often small, local, supernatural creatures whose specific nature is largely defined by folklore.

The *Oxford Dictionary and Thesaurus* defines "spirit" (in part) as

1. a. the vital animating essence of a person or animal. b. The intelligent nonphysical part of a person; the soul.
2. a. a rational or intelligent being without a material body. b. a supernatural being such as a ghost, fairy, etc. . . .
3. a. a person's mental or moral nature or qualities, usually specified. b. courage; energy; vivacity; dash.
4. an immaterial principle thought to govern vital phenomena.

The creation of the concept of a spirit, which seems to have occurred almost universally, implies that we humans do not tolerate the finitude of our physical existence—neither the necessity of death nor the restriction of important influences to those associated with a physical body. So we attribute human powers, in ordinary, exaggerated, or distorted form, to other creatures, natural or supernatural, or even to entities that we imagine to possess no qualities other than spirit. Some may be revenants or ghosts; some may be independent sprites (a variant of the word "spirit"); some are assumed to possess divine qualities. In some images, God is conceived as wholly spiritual; in others, as spirit and body.

Some find it difficult, others impossible, to tolerate the idea that by our death, or the death of those whom we love, we shall ultimately suffer permanent separation. Ultimately, of course, we are alone, confined within our bodies and the limitations of our minds. We entertain and encourage the illusion of "contact" with others. Our communication may include touch, speech, music, exchange of smiles and other facial expressions, exchange of gestures and actions, and exposure to the visible presence and the bodily warmth and scents of others. All of these create the illusion of contact, even union, not being alone. It is the illusion of lovers that their spirits are united; of the religious that they achieve some form of communication with God at some variable remove; of all of us that we are literal members of our community. But in fact, we live within the limits of our skin and our brains. A communication of minds, and metaphorically of hearts and souls, is illusory but powerful. We try to undo physical separation by communication, which we have highly developed. But when someone has died, we tend to imagine some kind of persisting link. And so the concept of the spirit is created. Either it is a surviving part of a lost loved one or it fills a felt need, an emptiness.

The spiritual experiences considered so far have been unusual occurrences, some indeed singular for the individuals involved. They were reported to have been unique in the experience of each of the several individuals whom I have known personally. Saint Teresa, on the other hand, reported several mystical experiences in her autobiography. I suppose that, except in the case of individuals who are adepts and receive spiritual experiences on a regular basis, for most others who receive them, such experiences seem singular and unique. So the spiritual experience seems to be an interesting but unusual occurrence.

In fact, however, if we consider less dramatic presentations, we can find spirituality occurring far more commonly, almost as a regular part of life for many, perhaps most people in our culture.

Spirituality, of course, is induced during participation in religious services—religious spirituality is the kind most frequently encountered. Not every participant is moved by every service. The individual must be in a receptive mood and the service must be a powerful one, but if a spiritual movement did not occur regularly, few worshippers would appear. The components of the service that induce the spiritual feeling include the music, especially unison singing and antiphonic responses, moving sermons delivered by a charismatic preacher, and scriptural readings, rituals that create a sense of continuity over the generations and a magical sense of proximity to God.

The spiritual experience is ultimately an affective experience. Specifically, in religion, the affect is reaching out to God, a cultivation of a sense of closeness to him, encouraged by the fellowship of group worship and the inspiration of a sermon. When the service succeeds, it induces a truly spiritual state of mind. Of course the beauty of the house of worship, the vestments, the association of memories of religious experiences with parents, the induction of children into formal worship, all contribute to the spiritual feeling.

A man whom I had been seeing for only a few months mentioned one day that he had spent some time in a large cathedral church on a Sunday afternoon with his lady friend. I expressed surprise because he had previously disavowed religious belief and interest, though he had had a good Catholic education and had served as an altar boy and attended Catholic schools and colleges. He explained that he no longer believed any of the dogma and did not participate in the Mass or take Communion. But on occasion he liked to wander into the church and to sit there and meditate. Often, on other occasions, he found himself singing the Credo to himself at home, again without consciously taking the words seriously. These were truly spiritual experiences for him. Although he had many acquaintances and interests, professional and social, male and female, he was essentially alone, and these experiences gave him a sense of communication with a divine, transcendental entity.

Another man, a busy professional person with a reasonable degree of social activity, disclosed to me at one point that he read the Jewish prayer book for a few minutes every morning. He was not religiously observant, could not read Hebrew easily, and read without any particular system, order, or ritual, but at random. I asked where he had obtained the prayer book, and he informed me that his mother had given it to him. I think that we must infer that he created these spiritual exercises, excited by the yearnings for his mother.

Max Kadushin, a modern Jewish theologian, describes "normal mysticism," that is, a conscious awareness of religious, spiritual feelings arising in the pursuit of ordinary, everyday activities (1952). In *As You Like It* (act 2, scene 1), Shakespeare voices similar sentiments but in a secular vein. The senior Duke tries to persuade his retinue that "sweet are the uses of adversity." It is good fortune that permits the company to leave the court and its stress, to sojourn in the Forest of Arden.

> "And this our life exempt from public haunt
> Finds tongues in trees, books in the running brooks,
> Sermons in stones and good in everything.
> I would not change it."

Nature speaks to the Duke as it did to the author of the letter in the first report, who was reminded of Psalm 19: "The heavens declare the glory of God, and the sky recites the work of His hands. Day to day gives voice to speech and night to night communicates knowledge. There is no speech and there are no words whose sound is unheard." Why this message that nature communicates is important, is not evident. Shakespeare tells us that in the forest, one finds "good in everything"—that is, an ill-defined pleasure. Wordsworth, as we shall see below, writes that nature makes him feel "less forlorn."

In perhaps many cases, the spiritual experience is not acknowledged as such by the individual who experiences it. I am thinking specifically of two successful men, one in his forties, one in his sixties, who, unbeknown to their close friends and associates, would often go off by themselves, one to the seashore, the other to the woods, to enjoy their solitude there, and their surroundings. Neither associated these regular, frequent retreats with spirituality, or recognized any religious feeling. But they could not otherwise describe the pleasure that they achieved—only that they enjoyed their solitude in this specific natural background that they favored.

Deriving significant, noteworthy pleasure from exposure to nature, or even reaching out to nature to find an apparent source for feelings of warmth and belonging that could not otherwise be explained, seems to me spiritual in the sense that I have been using that term. I shall discuss the nature of this feeling and speculate about its origins below, but here will concentrate on phenomenology.

Being moved by impressions that seemingly do not relate to the sensation aroused suggests to me receptivity to spiritual experience. Responding to music, poetry, or the graphic arts often involves similar feelings, not specifically localized to any individual part of the body, not associated with any specific modality of perception, not directly assignable to such instincts as sexuality, nutrition, thermal comfort, or escape from danger. The instinct that gives rise to sensations similar to the spiritual is the attachment instinct.

But relating spiritual feelings to aesthetic experience leads to a consideration of the aesthetics of everyday life. Most of us enjoy views of bodies of water, mountains, hills, and valleys. But we also enjoy tasteful decoration of our homes, our workplaces, and the places we visit. We enjoy beautiful parks, engaging drama, pleasant conversation, amusement, well-crafted literature. All of the percepts of our daily lives contribute a sense of comfort and pleasure, above and beyond the utility of the object of attention.

While we cannot say that there is anything spiritual in a nicely decorated room, I have suggested a serial sequence that implies an ultimate continuity of behavior between a full hallucinatory mystical experience at the one extreme, and the small aesthetic pleasures of daily life at the other. I suspect that we all have experiences somewhere along this spectrum: at the one end those that clearly qualify as spiritual, in the center those merely inspiring, and at the other end those gracious and comforting. The pleasurable affect of grace and comfort is the factor unifying these various phenomena that might appear so different on the surface.

CHAPTER 3

Mind

The Psychodynamics of
Awe, Spirituality, and Mysticism

To study the psychodynamics of Spirituality and mysticism, we shall deal with developmental issues and then examine religious records for the intuitions that they reveal.

Let us start with the phenomenon of awe. We use the term "awe" when we are moved by percepts that transcend the usual range of perceptible phenomena, such as natural landmarks that are breathtakingly immense, off scale, as seen from our perspective as observers. Some panoramas are more "beautiful" than others, evoking awe not only by their size but also by their beauty. Mountains, hills, valleys, forests, deserts seem to possess a powerful ability to elicit not only aesthetic appreciation but also a sense of attraction, a wish to remain and reside there, a feeling of belonging. Often this feeling of awe is associated with a feeling of reverence. Report 2, by the woman who had ascended Mount Sinai and there witnessed the rising sun, recorded both awe and reverence. Bodies of water, oceans, lakes, powerful rivers, and waterfalls exhibit the power to move us. Two of the examples that I adduced to illustrate spirituality were associated with bodies of water. Water contained within land masses seems especially apt to convey impressions of beauty and awe.

Auditory percepts also have the power to move people emotionally. Pitch and volume extremes are often associated with traditional accounts of religious revelation—awesome thunder or, on the other hand, the "still, small voice." The power of music to move the listener emotionally needs no exposition. But among the types of emotion that music elicits are awe and especially reverence, notably in religious music, the musical settings of the mass and the requiem. I am reminded here of Sir Arthur Sullivan's "The Lost Chord," the chord that suggested "the great Amen." Certain specific sounds generated for religious purposes arouse an especially prepared audience, e.g., the early Christian chants, the Jewish *shofar*, the Australian bull-roarer. Experiences of awe may be aroused not only by simple percepts, sights or sounds, but also by complex intellectual or artistic creations—for example, the poetry of many of the psalms and some of Shakespeare's celebrated speeches and soliloquies. The Babylonian Talmud prescribes certain benedictions to be recited when confronted by these large or unusual phenomena: majestic landscapes, thunder and lightning storms, but also majesty, intellectual giants, even deformed individuals.

It is not merely being impressed by an outsized percept that creates the experience of awe. The perception induces an affective response so unusual that we have no term for it other than "awesome" or "spiritual." The affect includes components of being overwhelmed, of being "elevated," longing, a familiarity, almost nostalgia, and yet not quite déjà vu. The affect, though unusual, seems familiar, though the evocative percept may well be novel.

Cognitive psychologists argue, in a sophisticated way, that the special affect of awe is elicited as a by-product of the off-scale experience, that the unusual, unbounded quality of the experience elicits a special affective response, that the perceptual apparatus is flooded, overwhelmed. I am proposing that it is not simply the challenge to the capacity of human perception that generates the feeling of awe. The truly awesome stimulus seems to retrieve from memory a special affect that is *sui generis*. A non-awe inspiring off-scale percept will elicit only a feeling of daze, of confusion.

Of course, awe is not the only affect generated by perception. Every percept, no matter how bland or objective or abstract, in combination or even alone, elicits an affective response.

One is reminded here of the phenomenon of context conditioning. An event of serious and instinctual significance and therefore carrying important affective consequence leaves a memory trace that colors all subsequent experience with the place, season, configuration, or other quality associated with that event. Many of our neural responses are hardwired, that is, intrinsic givers of brain function, for example, the response to the rising sun, to a cloudy sky, to dark of night, to sparkling water, to sexually attractive individuals, to physical deformity, to thunder, to fearsome animals. They may be modified by experience so that their impact is dulled or sharpened. Many colors have associations, many numbers, textures, aspects of nature, the weather, kinds of people. The relevance to this discussion is that awe too can be considered an affect that seems to be generated simply by sensitivity to a special percept. Obviously also, our response to the affective potential of percepts determines our sensitivity to aesthetic experiences, from which we create a discipline of aesthetics: the study of the affects that the perceptions elicit.

I propose that the experience of awe possesses its strange power to move us because those experiences that we find awesome reproduce the experiences of early infancy, recorded implicitly as memories of the contours of the mother's body, her voice, facial expressions, skills, strengths, vigor, loving care. Iconic memories (that is, memories of the actual percepts) of these archaic experiences are no longer available, presumably because the brain was too immature to have recorded them so early, but perhaps the affects were implicitly recorded and can be elicited by current percepts. Or perhaps the affects were, in effect, hardwired, and persist in latent form, to be evoked by appropriate circumstances. Perhaps some gross traces of the early experiences were laid down, so that the congruent current representations can be recognized. Probably some or most of the effective *Gestalten* are hardwired in whole or in part, but clearly the affective response can be elicited by even the merest suggestions of them.

Since my argument in this book leans heavily on the hypothesis that memories of affects can be retrieved independently of memories of the sensory impressions that accompanied them, let me adduce some support for this idea. Initially it seemed a reasonable guess that the various types of spiritual experience could be explained by this dissociation. But then I attempted to ascertain whether the possibility of affective-iconic dissociation has been considered by others. In his book, *The Cognitive Neuroscience of Memory*, Howard Eichenbaum cites evidence that "plasticity within the same brain system (the amygdala-MO) supports emotional memory in the absence of conscious recollection" (2002:280). Also, "Via this system, it is proposed, sometimes we can feel nervous or happy or scared at an image that evokes memory, even before, or independent of our ability to declare the cause of such feelings" (262).

Eichenbaum opens this chapter with the following anecdote (261f.):

One of my favorite memory experiences began when I entered an elevator in a busy downtown office building. I stepped in at the ground floor alone and pressed the button for the sixth floor where I had my upcoming appointment. At the second floor the elevator stopped for additional passengers. There were several, so I stepped to the back of the chamber to make room. The first passenger entering was a young woman who stopped just in front of me and turned around. I immediately noticed that she was wearing perfume, and it was a distantly familiar scent. As the next few seconds went by, I began to get a great feeling of both familiarity and a sort of innocent sense of happiness. I found myself emotionally transported back to the "feeling" of high school. Within a few seconds, I began remembering girls I knew then, and then boys, too, classmates I hadn't thought of in many years. Finally I fully recognized it—"Shalimar"—a perfume that was quite popular among teenagers in the early sixties. The latter specific recollections are run-of-the-mill declarative memories. But that initial "feeling of high school" was an example of emotional memory, an emotion evoked by a past association even before the conscious recollection of the experience that provoked it.

This account reminds me of a more poetic and dramatic instance of the same phenomenon, the well-known account of the madeleine dipped in tea, given by Proust, *In Search of Lost Time* (1980):

Many years had elapsed during which nothing of Combray, except what lay in the theatre and the drama of my going to bed there, had any existence for me, when one day in winter, on my return home, my mother, seeing that I was cold, offered me some tea, a thing I did not ordinarily take. I declined at first, and then, for no particular reason, changed my mind. She sent for one of those squat, plump little cakes called "petites madeleines," which look as though they had been moulded in the fluted valve of a scallop shell. And soon, mechanically, dispirited after a dreary day with the prospect of a depressing morrow, I raised to my lips a spoonful of the tea in which I had soaked a morsel of the cake. No sooner had the warm liquid mixed with the crumbs touched my palate than a shiver ran through me and I stopped, intent upon the extraordinary thing that was happening to me. An exquisite pleasure had invaded my senses, something isolated, detached, with no suggestion of its origin. And at once, the vicissitudes of life become indifferent to me, its disasters innocuous, its brevity illusory—this new sensation having had the effect, which love has, of filling me with a precious essence; or rather this essence was not in me, it was me. I had ceased now to feel mediocre, contingent, mortal. Whence could it have come to me, this all-powerful joy? I sensed that it was connected with the taste of the tea and the cake, but that it infinitely transcended those savours, could not, indeed, be of the same nature. Where did it come from? What did it mean? How could I seize and apprehend it? (60)

And I begin again to ask myself what it could have been, this unremembered state which brought with it no logical proof, but the indisputable evidence, of its felicity, its reality, and in whose presence other states of consciousness melted and vanished. (61)

Undoubtedly what is thus palpitating in the depths of my being must be the image, the visual memory which, being linked to that taste, is trying to follow it into my conscious mind. (62)

And suddenly the memory revealed itself. The taste was that of the little piece of madeleine which on Sunday mornings at Combray (because on those mornings I did not go out before mass), when I went to say good morning to her in her bedroom, my aunt Leonie used to give me, dipping it first in her own cup of tea or tisane. (63)

Here is a most impressive dissociation between emotion and the memory of events. Proust distinguishes later between "My oldest instinctive memories, and those others inspired more recently by a taste or 'perfumes'" (263).

In these reports I find confirmation of my contention that affective and iconic memories are dissociable. I would guess that most of us can find similar, if less dramatic examples in our own lives.

But my argument requires an additional step. I am arguing that awe, Spirituality, and mysticism are affective experiences that reproduce the affects of the infant in his relation to his mother, at a time before he was neurologically sufficiently mature to acquire visual and auditory memory. In contrast to the two examples I have cited, the infant's original experience cannot be reactivated.

Notice too that in both instances odor is significant, and in the case of Proust, taste.

But when from a long-distant past nothing subsists, after the people are dead, after the things are broken and scattered, taste and smell alone, more fragile but more enduring, more immaterial, more persistent, more faithful, remain poised a long time, like souls, remembering, waiting, hoping, amid the ruins of all the rest; and bear unflinchingly, in the tiny and almost impalpable drop of their essence, the vast structure of recollection. (63f.)

Let us look more closely at the dynamics of this dissociation. It is well known that Freud thought the images and ideas available to the conscious mind represented only a small fraction of the brain activity that can become conscious. Those mental contents that can become conscious at will, though not conscious now, he called preconscious. He designated as unconscious those mental contents that cannot readily be brought to consciousness, though they might find their way into dreams and other uncontrolled expressions of mental activity. He probably thought of these as the components and representations of drives (analogous to what neuroscientists call instincts); memory associated with past gratification and frustration; memories, ideas, and plans associated with potential future gratifications and frustrations; also judgment, appraisals, and the feelings associated with all of these. He thought of complexes as groups of these components striving together to achieve some sort of gratification. But only a portion of these complexes are permitted to become conscious, whereas other elements are not permitted to rise to consciousness out of considerations of morality, realism, and/or appropriateness.

At about the same time that Freud was composing his first psychoanalytic formulations, William James wrote,

> Our normal waking consciousness, rational consciousness as we call it, is but one special type of consciousness, whilst all about it, parted from it by the flimsiest of screens, there lie potential forms of consciousness entirely different. We may go through life without suspecting their existence; but apply the requisite stimulus, and at touch they are there in all their completeness, definite types of mentality which probably somewhere have their field of application and adaptation. (1902:388)

Daniel L. Wegner in his book *The Illusion of Conscious Will* (2002) introduces his discussion of the dissociation of conscious awareness of intention and activity from the associated unconscious brain activity by referring to the work of Benjamin Libet (1992). Libet established that in the case of a voluntary finger movement, electrical potential change on the surface of the brain, as recorded from the scalp, preceded the conscious intention to move by about half a second. Wegner quotes as follows:

> The initiation of the voluntary act appears to be an unconscious cerebral process. Clearly, free will or free choice of whether to act now could not be the initiating agent, contrary to one widely held view. This is of course also contrary to each individual's own introspective feeling that he/she consciously initiates such voluntary acts; this provides an important empirical example of the possibility that the subjective experience of a mental causality need not necessarily reflect the actual causative relationship between mental and brain events. (Libet 1992:269)

Wegner quotes Oliver Wendell Holmes:

> The more we examine the mechanism of thought, the more we shall see that the automatic, unconscious action of the mind enters largely into all its processes. Our definite ideas are stepping stones; how we get from one to the other, we do not know: something carries us; we do not take the step. A creating and informing spirit which is with us, and not of us, is recognized everywhere in real and in storied life. It is the Zeus that kindled the rage of Achilles; it is the Muse of Homer; it is the Daimon of Socrates; it is the inspiration of the seer; ... it comes to the least of us as a voice that will be heard; it tells us what we must believe; it frames our sentences; it lends a sudden gleam of sense or eloquence to the dullest of us all, so that ... we wonder at ourselves, or rather not at ourselves, but at this divine visitor, who chooses our brain as his dwelling-place, and invests our naked thought with the purple of the kings of speech or song. (1877:48–50)

But my argument goes beyond the simple recognition that the contents of consciousness include only a small portion of the underlying brain activity that could become conscious under the right circumstances. I argue that at every moment in time, brain processes are accompanied by an emotion, one or more specific affective states associated with prevailing instincts, or a mood reflecting an anticipation of one form or another of gratification or frustration. Just as there is no dream without emotion, there is no conscious state without emotion. Except in the presence of pathologic dissociation, as in hysteria, or numbing, as in post-traumatic syndrome, the emotional component of the mental state comes through. And that, I believe, is what happens in the case of spiritual experience. In response to instinctual needs, usually attachment needs, appropriate memories, however fragmentary, are activated but find limited access to consciousness for reasons mentioned above. But the associated instinctual affect and mood can be retrieved under appropriate circumstances. The spiritual experience is the experience of the emotion associated with the retrieval of an infantile or childhood longing for attachment to a maternal object, expressed in whatever form, but associated with little or no memory of the circumstances of the original experience.

If that is so, one may ask which of the myriad experiences of the infant's reaching out to the mother is immortalized in the spiritual experience. In the absence of knowledge, one may guess that it was an especially vivid experience that is recollected, or perhaps a kind of composite. It is this dissociation between emotion and iconic memory that the anecdotes of Eichenbaum and Proust illustrate.

It is interesting that almost immediately after the madeleine-tasting incident, Proust begins extensive discussions of religious memories. The infant's earliest attachment to the mother ordinarily relies on impressions of both taste and smell, probably before vision and audition—perhaps coordinate with touch. Yet, though spiritual and religious experiences will on occasion invoke taste and smell, these do not occupy a central place in conscious description of the experiences. The minimizing of taste and smell may have something to do with concepts of purity and holiness. (I discuss these issues below in my consideration of religion.)

To return to the psychodynamics of awe, that the affect arises in the mother's arms or in her lap accounts not only for the formal characteristics of the affectively stimulating percept but also for the nature of the affect, namely, the feeling of being in the presence of a *Gestalt* that is overpoweringly beautiful, large, forceful, or fascinatingly attractive. What is seldom expressly noted is the feeling of being welcome, belonging. Nostalgia is part of the experience of awe. We yearn to reach out or to be reached out to by an inconceivably attractive, transcendent influence that we seem to know well, although we do not recall from where or when.

As noted above, most dictionary definitions of awe emphasize its awful, fearsome aspects more than its awesome, inviting aspects. One thinks of the awesomeness of the thunder and lightning of the storm, especially the storm at sea, and of the frightening aspects of great masses of people. Not every fearsome experience is awesome; some are just fearsome and frightful. What makes the experience awesome is its magnitude, its overwhelming quality, or some otherworldly component. The compounds of Auschwitz, the ovens and chimneys of Birkenau are awesome, not because of their natural qualities but because of their off-scale, horrid, historic associations; their apocalyptic associations; the suggestion of the frightening, open mouth of a violent, gigantic, wild animal; perhaps the image of the angry mother.

The mother's frown, her angry outbursts, her brief periods of turning away—as if abandoning the infant—all form the ultimate paradigms for frightening awe. When, as adults, we see our universe collapsing, we reexperience the affects that persist from early childhood experiences of being briefly abandoned or attacked by the individual, or rather the giant, whom we count as our principal protector.

Whereas awe is elicited in the presence of percepts that move us because they elicit similar affects first experienced early in childhood, either hardwired or implicitly recorded, Spiritual experiences usually arise from inner need. It is true that moving experiences may elicit Spiritual responses. For example, in Report 2, the woman was moved by the awesome experience of sunrise as seen on Mount Sinai. The exultation she felt exceeded mere awe. Similarly in Report 3. But in Report 1, what the subject saw was something he had seen almost every summer for years without having experienced the same response. Evidently, in these cases, the inner need was strong enough to permit a response to be triggered either by a truly awesome experience or by a visual percept not truly awesome but suggestive, or by a percept not intrinsically suggestive, or by no percept at all. Many or most Spiritual experiences appear without evident external stimulus. If we take Report 1 as the paradigmatic case, this man's surprising and remarkable experience expressed his loneliness and his wish to be comforted, bereft now of the companionship of his beloved wife, his intimate companion of perhaps seventy-five years.

There were two components in his response. The first was a change in his perception of the real world, an alteration of ego function (that is, the function of the executive agent of the personality and the agent of conscious appraisal) in the sense that he perceived colors more vividly than before, that his surroundings seemed preternaturally still, quiet, and stationary. Second, verse 2 of psalm 19, which he had perhaps not thought of in years, spontaneously came to mind. It told him that the aspect of the skies that so moved him actually was revealing a comforting communication and the presence of a God whom he no longer took seriously, but who had presumably been a reassuring figure of his early childhood. He reverted to religious imagery, which he had long abandoned. Psalm 19 records God's response to a yearning, the communicating voice of the heavens, just as my friend, in the illusory silence of his experience, perceived the otherworldly response to his yearning for his wife, for his mother, for whatever he had sought in the synagogue community of his childhood.

This vivid example illustrates my contention that the Spiritual experience, characterized by the affect of yearning and by perceptual illusion, expresses the desire for reunion with each individual's first object, the mother. In fact, when the baby is briefly abandoned, he will exhibit discomfort and cry for his mother; the adolescent will avoid protracted solitude. And the adult will marry or arrange for other continuing companionship, and ultimately, when bereaved, mourn and yearn for renewal of his stabilizing attachments. In a way, then, the Spiritual experience may be understood as an illusory device for gratifying the instinctual need for attachment. But people who do enjoy attachments may seek and enjoy Spiritual experiences as well. So we must conclude that they still feel something missing from their lives, a gap that real, current attachments do not fill.

The attachment instinct differs from others. When the sexual, nutritive, self-protective, or thermal stability instinct is gratified, the consummation extinguishes the need until it is aroused again. But when the attachment instinct is gratified, the search terminates but the attachment is actively maintained. The Spiritual aspiration consists primarily of affect, but little can be done in the real world to effect the gratification. Gratification, as in our example, is illusory in the sense that there is no physical, objective partner, and it may not preclude the continued wish and hope. The Spiritual approach toward life, therefore, may be phasic, or it may be a continuing attitude. One may lead a Spiritual life.

We ordinarily use the term "regression" to refer to disturbed function of the ego. The term implies that the disturbance represents a reversion to its function at an earlier stage of development. While that is not necessarily always correct, it may very well be in the case of awe and Spirituality, if it is true that the entire experience reflects a regression to a childhood, if not infantile state of mind. Since awe reflects only an altered affect and Spiritual experience often includes an illusion, we may say that the ego disturbance is greater in the latter case than the former and that perhaps an earlier phase of development is fragmentarily resurrected.

Just as it is difficult to draw a sharp dividing line between awe and Spirituality at one end of the spectrum, so it is difficult to draw a line between the Spiritual and the mystical at the other end. I have described the characteristics of each and the differences between them in chapter 2. The dynamic mechanism of mysticism is a further regressive step backward, to hallucination and the full loss of reality testing. It would not be improbable that the infant, in a state of relative deprivation, hallucinates gratification, as Freud guessed (1911b:220n4). And that is what happens in the mystical experience. My patient (Report 4), seriously troubled by a problem that arose from a seemingly insoluble conflict, hallucinated a resolution in the form of "some power that told me what my course should be." Carrying out that resolution terminated his obsession and brought him some temporary peace of mind. Note that the form of the hallucination was determined by two influences: a film that he had recently seen and his recollection of biblical history as influenced by the film.

But there is another component to the mystical experience and the mystical disposition, that is, the sense of union—union with the lost object, union with the supernatural informant, union with everybody, everywhere, and union with the universe. I discussed the "oceanic feeling" in chapter 2 as an expression of the sense of union. If our thoughts about regression are correct, then the oceanic feeling may reproduce the feeling that the infant has lost when he begins to appreciate that he and his mother are two separable individuals. The mystic's yearning for union then expresses the wish to reunite with the mother into a symbiotic unit (Freud 1930:64–72). Perhaps it is not yearning; perhaps the illusion of union satisfies the regressive need.

In addition to the hallucinatory wish fulfillment and the illusory sense of unity, a third feature characterizes virtually every mystical experience: the revelation. This is what James called the noetic quality. In the example I cited, the revelation was the solution to his problem. In general, there are two kinds of revelation in mystical experience: the solution to a problem and the appearance of the individual or a deity longed for. We find such instances in religious revelations, considered below. In a dream related to me recently by a friend, I encountered a composite.

(REPORT 10)
At a vulnerable moment, when I was all of nine or ten years old, I dreamed that I was sitting outside in the grass on the front lawn of my house, at night. In the dream I was looking up at the moon when all of a sudden, writing appeared on the moon. In the dream I felt that this was some type of proof that God existed and had made this direct attempt to communicate to me and was watching over me, and I felt intense relief, gratitude, and, of course, when I woke up, much troubled puzzlement about what this experience really meant.

Sitting on the grass on the front lawn I interpret to mean sitting on his mother's lap. The moon I interpret to be his mother's face and the writing, the revelation in this mystical dream. The dream indicated a desire to see his mother's face and to scan it in order to ascertain whether she was smiling or frowning upon him. That was the revelation that he longed for at the time. The boy grew up to become a distinguished scientist, still searching for revelations.

In Report 5, Saint Teresa's experience was not only an affective experience but also a revelation. In Report 7, the woman saw in her mystical vision not a person, but places. Jerusalem, for the observant Jew, is always seen as the mystical mother.

For reasons that I do not quite understand, accounts of experiences in the three categories considered here are seldom reported in psychotherapy or even in psychoanalysis. Awe is reported more frequently than the other two. Perhaps the frequency and intimacy of the therapeutic relation alleviates the sensation of loneliness and separateness that induces Spiritual and mystical experiences, and perhaps the truly Spiritual life does not invite psychotherapy.

Spiritual yearnings are expressed often in literature, and especially in poetry. Among the familiar English poets, Wordsworth expresses such sentiments clearly and beautifully, voicing the exhilaration that can be obtained from contemplating nature and looking to it for inspiration. Note that it is to Wordsworth that the reporter of Report 1 turns to find words to express his feelings. In Hamlet's vision of the ghost of his father, we see a literary example of a mystical vision, combining the image of the recently lost father with the answer to the question about his murder and a recommendation of a course of action that Hamlet is to follow.

What is the difference between a mystical experience and a fantasy? Both fulfill wishes. The mystical experience has a fairly specific form: one encounters in hallucination a longed-for object, generally a parent or parent surrogate, and sees or hears him or her more or less clearly and often sees or hears a message that solves the problem or gives instruction, and the vision may ultimately convey the feeling of union. The fantasy, on the other hand, does not conform to any such stereotype. It does not achieve hallucinatory representation. It merely gratifies in imagination wishes not otherwise readily gratified.

Edgar Allan Poe wrote masterfully of situations in which longing led to fulfillments that were perverse and horrifying rather than gratifying. William Blake in "Tiger, Tiger" wrote of surprising synaesthesias in a way that created a surprising, unnatural unity of natural elements. In "Kubla Khan," Coleridge achieved a mystical effect by describing a scene commonly encountered in mystical visions, namely, a mystical chamber in which the ultimate gratifying vision is encountered. In Dante's *Paradiso* and *Inferno*, there are descriptions of trips to realms outside the earth, to heaven and to hell respectively, in which the author makes us familiar with events in these other worlds and the implications for worthy and unworthy behavior on earth. Extraterrestrial travel is a common feature of mystical visions, as is the converse, namely the earthly visit of extraterrestrial beings and the vehicles that bring them. The frequently reported unidentified flying object (or UFO) exemplifies this category (cf. Halperin 1995).

Derivatives of instinctual needs in the form of wishes make their way into dreams, whether during periods when the threshold for conscious representation is lowered, as it is in rapid eye movement sleep or in toxic states, or when given special impetus by temporal lobe irritation.

Purely Spiritual longing is not likely to find expression in a dream because the dream sees the wish as fulfilled. By the same token, images that find expression in mystical experiences find expression more easily in dreams. Therefore mystical dreams occur not infrequently. The dream of the moon that I reported just above illustrates that point. Bilu (2000) reports a series of visitation dreams circulated among Moroccan Jewish immigrants to Israel. In the typical dream a *tsaddik* ("saint"), who had been venerated at his local memorial site in Morocco, appears to the dreamer and instructs him to construct a sanctuary for him in Israel. Had these dreams appeared as waking hallucinations, they would qualify as mystical experiences. Of course they express the longing for the parent or ancestor surrogate to accompany the immigrant to his new home. These dreams are strikingly congruent with the visitation dreams of the patriarchs in Genesis, and share some characteristics of the images of classical Merkavah and Hekhaloth mysticism, in which God is visualized, sought, or approached in his chariot (Ezekiel 1) or in his heavenly chamber (Isaiah 6).

If one attends to hypnagogic hallucinations, they seem to represent visually current impressions and hallucinated gratification of impulses. However, they are quite fragmentary and fugitive. The dream seems to be a coordinated scenario creating a relatively organized story that incorporates these elements. But of course it ignores considerations of reality, consistency, and logic. That being the case, wishes and impulses that are strong enough to achieve hallucinatory representation, such as mystical experience, can certainly achieve dream representation. As a hallucinated representation of the gratification of a distinct wish, the mystical experience strongly resembles the dream. In fact, many such mystical experiences could be called dreamlike states.

In the early parts of the Book of Genesis, God introduces himself to the patriarchs in visions that are called dreams. Presumably the similarity between actual dreams and mystical experiences was known to the composers and editors of the Bible, so that dream mysticism became almost conventional. Since, in the visions, God promises a land, progeny, and prosperity to his favored, dreams could be interpreted as anticipating the future. Prophecy was, in each case, the revelation that accompanied the mystical experience. Relatively few dreams in the Bible are not mystical experiences, and most of those are attributed to gentiles rather than to Jews. The biblical text reports variously that God appeared to a specific person, or appeared at night, or appeared in a dream, or appeared in a vision whether *mar'eh laylah* or *mahazeh laylah*, both expressions meaning a nocturnal vision. In the ancient Mediterranean world, in the practice called incubation, the worshipper would go to a holy site, usually a temple, and sleep there in the hope that he would be granted a divine revelation that would solve a problem for him.

In sum, one might say that the dream facilitates the mystical vision and provides the abrogation of reality testing without requiring the ego distortion of waking hallucination.

I have argued in this chapter that all of spiritual experience—awe, Spirituality proper, and mystical experience—is created by the regressive retrieval of the states of mind of infancy. All three types represent a yearning for the mother, a strong wish. In the mystical experience, the wish is gratified by hallucination. In the Spiritual experience proper, one has the feeling of a preternatural contact with a transcendent being or force. The awesome experience seems partly to fulfill the wish, partly to strengthen it, as if partial gratification encourages the hope.

The fourteenth-century German mystic, Suso, correctly recognized the affect.

Thus it grew into a habit with him, whenever he heard songs of praise, or the sweet music of stringed instruments, or lays, or discourse about earthly love, immediately to turn his heart and mind inwards, and gaze abstractedly upon his loveliest Love, whence all love flows. It were impossible to tell how often with weeping eyes, from out the unfathomable depth of his outspread heart, he embraced this lovely form, and pressed it tenderly to his heart. And thus it fared with him as with a sucking child, which lies encircled by its mother's arms upon her breast. As the child with its head and the movement of its body lifts itself up against its tender mother, and by these loving gestures testifies its heart's delight, even so his heart many a time leapt up within his body towards the delightful presence of the Eternal Wisdom, and melted away in sensible affections. (see Underhill 1964)

We have to examine also the ego change that occurs as a central component of all spiritual experience. Recall that in each of the exemplary reports that I have cited, the reporter mentions a change in the way he or she regarded the world of reality, a change in ego state.

In ordinary daily life, we attend to our proper business, and, except when we abandon ourselves to reverie or fantasy, try to be realistic, logical, and consistent. We acknowledge feelings when they occur and automatically relate them to our recent or current experience, or what we expect. We seldom acknowledge that we don't know the source of a feeling. Psychoanalytic exploration or dream interpretation or some experimental procedures will usually disclose that, preconsciously or unconsciously, we record percepts outside our area of conscious interest. Also, we ordinarily maintain the distinction between figure and background fairly consistently.

In the spiritual experience, all of these conditions fail. Our consciousness is seized by percepts or images other than the figure before our eyes. We pay more attention to the background and especially to its affective qualities. The ordinary parameters of our perception are altered. Objects are preternaturally large or small, bright or dim, loud or soft; time passes slowly or rapidly or stands still; similarly with motion. And the whole experience is pervaded with affect, specifically the affect of longing, yearning, union, or even ecstasy. The sense of reality preempts reality testing and the subject volunteers that the otherwise highly unlikely scenario seems hyperreal. The prevailing affect is not linked to any specific percept or modality of perception, or mode of instinctual gratification— other than attachment. The change is a change in ego function. It seems reasonable to interpret that change as a regressive reversion to the form of ego function that prevailed during early childhood (assuming that we can apply the concept of ego at that early age), when that was the age-appropriate *modus operandi* of the ego or of its precursor.

Students of infant behavior acknowledge that no one can ever know what the infant is feeling or thinking. Do the various spiritual experiences recapture these very early mind states of the child? My argument in this chapter has been that the various kinds of spiritual experience can be understood as the result of regression to very early childhood, in imaging, affect, and mode of ego function.

CHAPTER 4

Religion

Spirituality and Religion

The concepts of religion and spirituality overlap, though they do not coincide. The word "religion" implies a certain kind of experience that is perhaps usually spiritual, but also a system of worship, a set of myths, and a kind of communal organization. Not everything that is spiritual is necessarily religious, nor is everything that is religious necessarily spiritual. Most of the examples of the spiritual that I have given could be considered religious, and in fact most spiritual experiences that are reported fall within the rubric of religious, but not all.

Wordsworth espoused a spirituality of nature.

THE WORLD IS TOO MUCH WITH US

The world is too much with us; late and soon,

Getting and spending, we lay waste our powers:
Little we see in Nature that is ours;
We have given our hearts away, a sordid boon!
The Sea that bares her bosom to the moon;
The winds that will be howling at all hours,
And are up-gathered now like sleeping flowers;
For this, for everything, we are out of tune;
It moves us not.—Great God! I'd rather be
A Pagan, suckled in a creed outworn,
So might I, standing on this pleasant lea,
Have glimpses that would make me less forlorn;
Have sight of Proteus rising from the sea;
Or hear old Triton blow his wreathed horn.

He deplores our being out of touch with nature. "It moves us not." Yet, employing "Great God" as an expletive, he opts for a "creed outworn" and would be moved by glimpses and sounds of pagan deities. In other words, though he prefers nature, he finds himself resorting nevertheless to religious images to illustrate his preference for nature. The terms "bosom" and "suckled" remind us of spirituality's focus on the mother.

What is the basis for the affinity between spirituality and religion? Spiritual experiences essentially reach out to an imagined transcendent presence that seems so compellingly inviting that it challenges our notion of reality. An actual mystical experience usually presents itself as real; one may sense its unreality at the time, or only in retrospect. That being the case, it is inevitable that images will be contrived to serve as virtual sources of the spiritual feeling, or that real objects will be endowed with the power to induce the spiritual feeling.

Religion, of course, is much more than the construction of a divinity or a collection of divinities. It involves social organization, approach to the problems of life, morality, magical protections against illness and death. But psychologically it is based ultimately on the updated yearning for the earliest infantile experience of the mother's comfort. I shall consider several aspects of the spiritual basis of religion.

A proper understanding of the concept of spirituality invites an examination of the implications of the word "spirit" in its classical sources. "Spirit" obviously derives from the Latin *spiritus*, which, in turn, is derived from *spirare*, to breathe. Spirit is associated with breath, and breath with life. Chapter 2 of Genesis states that "YHVH, the God, formed man from the soil and He blew into his nostrils the breath of life and so he became a living soul."

The word "spirit" appears at the very beginning of the King James Bible as the translation of the Hebrew word *ruah*. That and its Greek equivalent, *pneuma*, may denote spirit, breath, or wind, depending on the context. Breath and wind share the allusion to movement in response to some often invisible influence. Presumably spirit too denotes a perceptible but invisible movement, and in that sense, corresponds to the object of "spiritual" desire. The fact that *ruah* or *pneuma* may signify any of these three items tells us that in biblical times, these three were strongly related conceptually, perhaps almost identical. It is worth examining scriptural literature for the intuitive knowledge implicit in the usage.

God's spirit hovers over the primordial waters from which the universe was fashioned. Let us assume that the sequential account of creation in chapter 1 of Genesis recapitulates the mental development of the infant as it must have seemed to the ancient observer—and to us. Chaotic darkness precedes the awareness of welcome light and its differentiation from unwelcome darkness. The infant becomes aware of sky, up and down, wet and dry, water and solid ground. Then vegetation, that is, green versus brown. And so on, sun, moon, and stars. Also animate creatures, small and large, among which humans are differentiated and these ultimately differentiated by gender.

Ruah in this context is translated as spirit or wind by many translators of the biblical text. I have not seen it translated as breath. Yet this is the comment to that verse by Rashi (Rabbi Solomon ben Isaac), the celebrated eleventh-century Jewish scholar of Troyes:

> The throne of the divine glory was standing in space, hovering over the face of the waters by the *Ruah* of the Mouth of the Holy One Blessed Be He and by his command, even as a dove hovers over its nest.

Obviously, in this context he interprets *ruah* to signify breath. He has invoked one of the central symbols of early Jewish mysticism, the divine throne, and suggests that the force of God's breath supported it in the air. By bringing in the mystical image, he directs the reader's mind to archaic images and to the mother's breath. For him this combined image means spirituality. That concept brings me back to my suggestion that the essential spiritual experience consists of the retrieval of very early, implicitly recorded memories, emphasizing now, not only the appearance of the mother and her voice but also the sounds of her breathing, which are comforting to the infant. It is generally argued that the word "spirit" is derived from *spirare* because it is associated with the breath of life. The original Hebrew quotation from Genesis 2 reads that God blew into man's nostrils *nishmath hayim*, which means the breath of life, from the verb *nasham*, to breathe. However, even in the scriptures, it acquires a secondary meaning of soul, in the sense of the living person. The verse continues that the man became a living *nefesh*, that is, a living being. It also implies breath, specifically the breath of life of all creatures. So that the biblical account states that God's breath is transferred to man and God's life or spirit is transferred to the human as well.

Rashi alludes to the word *merahefet*, which he translates appropriately as hover. The same verb appears in Deuteronomy 32:11, which says that God protects Israel as an eagle hovers over its young. The analogy here is mother and child. The primordial spirit in the Genesis mythology is the mother's breath as perceived by the newborn or perhaps even by the late fetus. I am arguing that in its psychic as well as etymologic origin, the concept of the spirit goes back to the mother's breathing.

Presumably the spirit of a person is that quality that resembles or perhaps reflects the divine spirit, or responds to it. The term Holy Spirit, *ruah hakodesh*, is used in both Christian and Jewish theology, but with different meanings. However, both usages refer to the Divine Spirit, the contemporary image supplementing the archaic one. The minor spirits, sprites, ghosts are given that name only to indicate their ethereal quality.

As I have argued here, the spiritual experience is essentially an affective experience. But naked affects strive to actualize themselves, not only in cognitive images but also in action. The actualization of spiritual affect gives rise to religious systems, beliefs, myths, magic, prayer, religious poetry and song, and ritual. Spirituality is an essential motivating force of religion.

The concept of a god satisfies the need for a being, an entity, the virtual object of spiritual aspiration, yearning, and a current representation of what the mother was to the infant. Most of the spiritual experiences described above took place in a religious context, oriented to both God and the religious community. Awe lends itself to association with religion but is not necessarily associated with it. Spirituality, in its narrow sense, is more commonly linked to religion, while mysticism is almost always associated with religious imagery and religious interpretation. The quotation from Romain Roland, reported by Freud (page 000), makes the association between the oceanic experience and religion explicit. The tenacity with which many people cling to religious beliefs reveals the power of the spiritual need, which may even ultimately lead to violence, suicidal, internecine, or international.

The three varieties of spiritual experience with which we have been concerned invite or even demand some completion.

The situation is least imperative in the case of simple awe. This is the feeling of yearning, of belonging, sometimes but not consistently leading to a reference to God. The author of Report 2 experienced a religious sense of awe and spirituality.

God's awesomeness is attested, for example, in Psalm 29. While we may experience awe in a nonreligious frame of mind, it lends itself easily to religious application. Here is an example.

PSALM 29

A Psalm of David.
Ascribe to YHVH, you divine creatures, ascribe to YHVH glory
    and strength.
Ascribe to YHVH the glory of His name; bow to YHVH in the
    presence of the splendor of His holiness.
The voice of YHVH sounds over the waters; the God of glory
    thunders;

The voice of YHVH is heard over the sounds of mighty waters.
The voice of YHVH is heard in power; the voice of YHVH is
heard in splendor.
The voice of YHVH shatters the cedars; YHVH splinters the
cedars of Lebanon.
He causes Lebanon and Sirion to skip like a calf, like the young
of the wild ox.
The voice of YHVH splits flames of fire.
The voice of YHVH makes the wilderness tremble; he makes the
wilderness of Kadesh tremble.
The voice of YHVH causes the hinds to calve, and strips the for-
est bare, while in His Temple all say "Glory."
YHVH sat enthroned above the flood, YHVH sits enthroned as
King forever.
YHVH will give strength to his people; YHVH will bless His
people with peace.

The many powerfully impressive natural phenomena are here attributed to God; their power is a manifestation of his power. When
the same divine powers were exhibited on the occasion of the
theophany at Mount Sinai, the people retreated, fearing that they
would perish under the impact of God's voice (Exodus 20:15). We
use "awesome" in the positive sense and "awful" in the negative.

The Spiritual experience proper, as illustrated in the first example, demands an other, a transcendental object, more definitively.
Note how "a complete unbeliever" automatically reverts to religious memories. "The heavens declare the glory of God, and the
sky recites the work of His hands." In the words of Yehuda Halevi,
the eleventh-century Jewish scholar-poet of Toledo, "Going out to
meet You, I found You coming toward me" (Carmi 1981:338).

Although mystical experiences may occur in an entirely secular
context, we almost always hear of them against a religious background. The two most striking mystical experiences appearing in
Scripture, and the paradigms for all subsequent Jewish mysticism,
are Ezekiel's vision of God's chariot (the account of the Merkavah)
(Ezekiel 1) and Isaiah's vision of God seated on his throne in his
celestial chamber (Isaiah 6).

In the thirtieth year, on the fourth day of the fifth month, when I was in the midst of the exile on the river Chebar, the heavens were opened and I saw visions of God. On the fifth of the month—that was the fifth year of the exile of King Jehoiachin—the word of the Lord came to Ezekiel the son of Buzi, the priest, in the land of the Chaldeans, on the river Chebar. And the hand of the Lord came upon him there.

And I looked and here was a stormy wind coming out of the north, a great cloud and a flaming fire, and a radiance surrounded it, and from within, the appearance of hashmal [amber?]—that is, from within the fire. And from within it, the image of four creatures, and this was their appearance: they each resembled a man in appearance. And each had four faces, and each one also had four wings. And as for their legs, the leg was straight, and the foot resembled the foot of a calf, and they gleamed like the appearance of polished brass, and there were human hands under their wings on each of their four sides, and their faces and their wings were the same for each. Their wings were joined one to another; they (the creatures) did not turn as they traveled, each could proceed straight ahead. And as for the appearance of their faces, each had a human face, and on the right side, each of the four had the face of a lion, and on the left side, each of the four, of an eagle. That, with respect to the faces; and their wings were separated above; two of the wings of each were joined each to its fellow and two covered their bodies. And each individual could proceed ahead; wherever the spirit went, they went: they did not turn as they moved. And with respect to the image of the creatures, their appearance resembled burning embers of fire and the appearance of flames moved among the creatures, and the fire emitted radiance, and from the fire, lightning [or sparks?] emerged. And the creatures darted up and back so that they appeared like lightning. And as I looked at the creatures, there was a wheel on the ground alongside the four faces of each creature. The appearance of the wheels and their structure resembled tarshish [beryl or chrysolite], and each of the four had the same appearance, and their appearance and structure suggested a wheel within a wheel. On each of their four sides, when the creatures went, the wheels went, and they did not turn when they moved. And as for their rims, they were tall and frightening, and the rims of the four were covered with eyes all around. And when the creatures traveled, the wheels traveled alongside them, and when the creatures were lifted above the earth, the wheels were lifted. Wherever the spirit was inclined to go, they went; there the spirit traveled; and the wheels were lifted alongside them, for the spirit of each of the creatures was in the wheels. When the one went, so did the other and when the one stopped the other did too, and when they were lifted above the ground, the wheels were lifted next to them, for the spirit of the creature was in the wheels.

And the image of an expanse, resembling the appearance of the awesome crystal, was stretched above the heads of the creatures. And under the expanse their wings were extended each to its neighbor for each creature, and each of the creatures had two covering wings, that is, covering their bodies. And I heard the sound of their wings, like the sound of rushing waters, like the sound of Shaddai, as they moved, the sound of tumult, like the sound of an army; when they halted, they dropped their wings. And there was a sound above the expanse above their heads; when they halted, they dropped their wings. And above the expanse above their heads, there was the image of a throne resembling sapphire in appearance, and above, upon the image of the throne, an image that resembled a human form. And I saw the gleam of hashmal, like the appearance of fire within a surrounding frame that extended from what appeared to be its loins upward, and from what appeared to be its loins downward, I saw the appearance of fire surrounded by radiance. Like the appearance of the rainbow that one sees in the clouds on a rainy day, that was the appearance of the surrounding radiance; that was the image of the appearance of the glory of the Lord; I saw it and I fell on my face and then I heard a voice speaking.

In the year of the death of the king Uzziahu, I saw the Lord sitting on a high and lofty throne, and his skirts filled the chamber. And seraphs were standing in attendance, six wings, and six wings to each. With two each covers his face, with two he covers his legs and with two he flies. And each calls to the other and says "Holy, holy, holy. The Lord of hosts. The earth is filled with His glory." And the doorposts were moved at the sound of Him who called and the building was filled with smoke and I said, "Woe is me because I am undone. For I am a man of unclean lips and I reside among a people of unclean lips. For my eyes have seen the King, YHVH Zevaoth."

And one of the seraphs flew toward me with a live coal in his hand which he had removed from the altar with tongs. And he touched my mouth and said, "This has touched your lips and your sin will depart and your transgression forgiven." And I heard the voice of YHVH saying, "Whom shall I send, who will undertake this for us?" Then I said, "Here I am. Send me," and He said, "Go and say to these people, 'You may listen but not understand; you may see but not comprehend.' Dull the heart of this people and stop its ears, and close its eyes, lest it see with its eyes and hear with its ears, and comprehend with its mind, and relent and find healing." And I asked, "Until when, YHVH," and He said, "Until cities become desolate without inhabitants, and houses without dwellers, and the ground lies waste. YHVH will banish the population and the deserted spots will multiply in the midst of the land. And a tenth of the abandoned area will survive and repent. It will be burned, so that, like the terebinth and the oak, a stump survives their destruction; the holy seed will be the stump."

In each of these theophanies, the prophet finds himself face to face with God and is overwhelmed by the experience. But in the end he is authorized to embark upon his prophetic enterprise with assurance of divine support and with a specific message. If the account is at all veridical, that is, if the prophets did indeed experience the mystical transport, then I would infer that in each case, the prophet yearns for encouragement, authority, and reassurance for his proposed endeavor: namely, preaching basic morality within the community and political wisdom in external affairs.

The Human-Divine Encounter:
A Developmental, Epigenetic Scheme

Religion may perhaps be described as a social system in which the spiritual drive is channeled into a set of modes of worship, a set of beliefs, and a set of behavioral imperatives and prohibitions, all within a social structure. Typically the religious individual lives with one foot in the world of religious spirituality and one foot in the world of consensual reality.

The spiritual drive craves the gratification of spiritual experience, and religion provides a set of devices intended as means to achieve that gratification, one of which is worship. If Spirituality expresses the instinctual need for attachment, as I have argued above, and if religion provides modalities and methods for Spiritual gratification, then we may see worship as a method of inviting spiritual experience and the conviction of attachment that it conveys.

The need for attachment that is present immediately after birth and persists throughout life is an instinctual need. It differs from other instincts in that it is tonic rather than phasic. That is, whereas the sexual instinct, the nutritive instinct, the self-protective instinct, and so on, are released by appropriate stimuli, and the gratification of the instinct extinguishes it, the attachment instinct seeks continuing affection and contact with the object. Gratification does not extinguish it. However, the instinct does require maintenance and recurrent reinforcement, otherwise it attenuates over time. The individual spiritual experience, whether deliberately induced or spontaneous, creates a feeling of attachment to a transcendent other. As noted above, James observed, "Mystical states, strictly so-called— are never merely interruptive. Some memory of their content always remains, and a profound sense of their importance. This modifies the inner life of the subject between the times of their recurrence."

Since religious Spirituality, in the monotheistic religions at least, hopes to achieve the sense of attachment to God, each religion has devised a set of procedures by which the devotee may attain that end. The sense of fellowship that accompanies communal worship should not be considered a secondary aspect of the worship service, rather than a primary aim; mutual communal love and the social, political, economic, and military activity that facilitate it importantly are effective in the outer world.

What I propose here is that each of the various forms of worship offered by the different religions is derived from and symbolically replicates a specifiable stage in child development.

The epigenetic scheme I offer is not the first attempt to comprehend religious attitudes with respect to behavioral and conceptual development. It is obvious that religious attitudes mature with age as do all other attitudes, and several scholars have attempted to catalogue these successive stages. That proposition is reasonable, and reasonable too is the effort to coordinate the schedule of religious development with other schedules of behavioral development. The scheme of Piaget appeals most to the religious scholars, but they turn to others' as well.

James W. Fowler's scholarly *Stages of Faith* (1981) attempts to describe the synthesis of the various aspects of personality development so as to determine successive stages in religious attitudes. This schema is sophisticated, complex, and epigenetic. It starts with a prestage of undifferentiated faith based upon trust and mutuality with the major caretaker. Stage 1 is called Intuitive-Projective faith, in which the child's attitudes are primarily influenced by the visible faith of "primally related adults." Mythic-Literal faith, Stage 2, is associated with narrative myths and observances of the child's own community. In Stage 3, Synthetic-Conventional faith (associated with adolescence), the faith "must provide a coherent orientation in the midst of a more complex and diverse range of involvements" and "provide a basis for identity and outlook." Stage 4, Individual-Reflective faith, takes form in early adulthood. "The person must face certain unavoidable tensions: individuality versus being defined by a group . . . ; subjectivity and the power of one's strongly felt but unexamined feelings versus objectivity and the requirement of critical reflection; self-fulfillment or self actualization as a primary concern versus service to and being for others." Phase 5, Fowler calls

Conjunctive faith. It "involves the integration into self and outlook of much that was suppressed or unrecognized in the interest of Stage 4's self-certainty and cohesive, cognitive and affective adaptation to reality." He continues, "importantly, this involves a critical recognition of one's social unconscious—the myths, ideal images and prejudices built deeply into the self-system by virtue of one's nurture within a particular social class, religious tradition, ethnic group or the like." Finally, he calls Stage 6 Universalistic faith. This is nothing less then full commitment to "a particular vision of reality" that its bearers call "the coming Kingdom of God."

This is little more than a set of chapter headings of a complex and sophisticated argument. But the study of developmental religious personality changes is not my concern. I am looking to the stages of development, especially in childhood, to understand why God is worshipped in particular ways.

More relevant here is a careful, scholarly study done by Ana-Maria Rizzuto (1979), a psychoanalyst, on the developmental sources of images of God that each individual constructs. The major thrust of her argument is that "God, psychologically speaking, is an illusory transitional object." She refers here to the work of Winnicott (1953), whom she quotes as follows.

"Transitional objects and transitional phenomena belong to the realm of illusion which is at the basis of initiation of experience. This early stage in development is made possible by the mother's special capacity for making adaptation to the needs of her infant, thus allowing the infant the illusion that what the infant creates really exists.

"This intermediate area of experience, unchallenged in respect of its belonging to inner of external (shared) reality, constitutes the greater part of the infant's experience, and throughout life is retained in the intense experiencing that belongs to the arts and to religion and to imaginative living, and to creative scientific work."

Rizzuto also conveniently summarizes her own arguments (1953:177–179):

God is a special type of object representation created by the child in that psychic space where transitional objects—whether toys, blankets, or mental representations—are provided with their powerfully real illusory lives.

God, like all transitional objects (Winnicott, 1953), is located simultaneously "outside, inside and at the border." God "is not a hallucination" and "in health . . . does not 'go inside' nor does the feeling about it necessarily undergo repression. It is not forgotten and it is not mourned."

God is also a special transitional object because unlike teddy bears, dolls, or blankets made out of plushy fabrics, He is created from representational material, whose sources are the representations of primary objects.

God is also a special transitional object because He does not follow the usual course of other transitional objects. Generally, the transitional object is gradually allowed to be decathected, so that in the course of years it becomes not so much forgotten as relegated to limbo. . . . It loses meaning . . . because the transitional phenomena have become diffused . . . over the whole cultural field.

God, on the other hand, is increasingly cathected during the pregenital years and reaches his most appealing moment at the peak of oedipal excitement. God, according to Freud, is to become the object of sublimated libido after the resolution of the oedipal crisis. But God's presentational characteristics depend heavily on the type of resolution and the compromises the child has arranged with his oedipal objects.

Throughout life God remains a transitional object at the service of gaining leverage with oneself, with others, and with life itself. This is so, not because God is God, but because, like the teddy bear, He has obtained a good half of his stuffing from the primary objects the child has "found" in his life. The other half of God's stuffing comes from the child's capacity to "create" a God according to his needs.

The psychic process of creating and finding God—this personalized representational transitional object—never ceases in the course of human life. It is a developmental process that covers the entire life cycle from birth to death. Winnicott says:

The task of reality-acceptance is never completed.... No human being is free from the strain of relating inner and outer reality, and ... relief from this strain is provided by an intermediate area of experience which is not challenged (arts, religion, etc.) (1953:13).

God is not the only mental representation used by children and adults alike as a transitional object. Many others are available. In our culture, however, God has a special place, because he is the cultural creation offered to men for their private and public (in official religions) reelaboration of those primary ties that accompany each of us "unto the grave" (Mahler, 1972).

The child's and the adult's sense of self is affected by the representational traits of the individual's private God.

Rizzuto speaks of her own approach and Winnicott's as dealing with object relations rather than drives or instincts. I find it difficult to think of human behavior without reference to what Freud calls drive and what we now, especially with reference to neuroscience, speak of as instincts. The term "object" refers here to the person with whom the subject has a powerful emotional relation, that is, the object of the instinct. The object relation is motivated by an instinctual tendency. With respect to the relation between mother and child, the instinct is the attachment instinct. The transitional object or concept is then a substitute for the mother, who, as the child matures, only gradually comes to occupy less and less of the child's central field of motivational interest.

Winnicott's transitional object then becomes a material or conceptual or affectively appreciated object to which the individual attaches in a state of loneliness or deprivation, the object of the attachment instinct that was originally addressed to the mother and subsequently addressed to substitute objects.

My schema addresses not the various images that are created to represent God, but the several worshipful attitudes and behaviors that are employed in that engagement.

In 1984, William W. Meissner, a Jesuit and a psychoanalyst, published a book, *Psychoanalysis and Religious Experience*, that dealt with, among many other subjects, "developmental aspects of religious experience." Like Fowler and Rizzuto, he attempted to relate phases of development of religious attitudes to the psychological development of the child:

> The first mode of religious experience is a primitive and/or deeply regressive state that is dominated by the conditions of primary narcissism. . . . Faith cognition at this level is entirely undifferentiated, functioning in terms of a preconceptual and prelinguistic disposition to accept the conditions of life. This relates to the conditions of basic trust that characterize symbiotic union of mother and child. The religious experience at this level would presumably involve merging the boundaries between self representation and God representation.
>
> The second mode of religious experience follows differentiation of a grandiose self from perception of another as an idealized parental imago. . . . The God-representation at this stage is built on the omnipotence and omniscience of the perfected and idealized imago.
>
> The third mode of religious experience is conditioned by the highly significant developmental achievement of the integration of a cohesive self. . . . The greater and more consistent delineation between inner and outer worlds allows for increasing differentiation of verifiable facts and claims from speculation or fantasy. Matters of belief or valuative judgment are determined primarily by an appeal to trusted authority, although in areas of judgment and action the capacity for using resources of inductive and deductive thought processes increases.
>
> A fourth mode of religious experience is articulated around the formation and consolidation of the superego. . . . The internalization of ideals and values means the organization of conscience. Consequently, danger is henceforth experienced mainly as moral anxiety, or as a sense of failure to attain and satisfy the demands of the ego ideal and the internalized value system— whereas previously the child responded to extrinsic threats and to primitive expectations of retaliation.
>
> The fifth and last modality of religious experience is characterized developmentally by a number of significant achievements, which include the integration and structuring of drive derivatives

with relatively autonomous functions of the ego . . . the religious belief system and its tradition are seen in increasingly realistic terms that affirm their inherent tensions and ambiguities and accept the relativity, partiality, and particularity of the beliefs, symbols, rituals and ceremonials of their religious community.

Meissner, as did Fowler and Rizzuto, has tried to understand stages of development of religious attitudes as determined primarily by ego function in its various aspects but also in terms of the forms of narcissistic primacy of superego function. Again, this differs from my approach of trying to understand the various forms of divine service and efforts to make contact with the divine, which, I believe, are based upon early phases of the child's behavior.

I have tried earlier in this chapter to demonstrate that some basic religious concepts, especially those directly associated with the image of God, can be seen as elaborations of spiritual elements, and that these, in turn, can be associated with attachment behavior relating the child to the mother. At this point let us try to approach the same problem from the other direction, by listing the various stages in the child's attachment to the mother and father and trying to ascertain which modality of the human-divine encounter can be attributed to each phase.

I assume an undifferentiated phase, that is, an initial phase when the infant does not yet recognize that he and the mother are distinct individuals. I referred in chapters 2 and 3 to the "oceanic feeling" as a regressive reevocation of the sense of symbiotic union, and noted that Freud (1930) had associated this undifferentiated phase with the mystical experience of union.

Following Spitz (1965), I would guess that the next recognizable phase would be characterized by the smiling response: between ages two to six months, the infant smiles in response to a moving face, in practical terms, the mother's face. The mother will usually respond with a reciprocal smile or vocal expression, or some other gesture of recognition and reciprocation.

Given the heartiness of the normal smile, it is difficult to imagine that it is not accompanied by some pleasant affect, perhaps the initial, prototypic form of the affect that accompanies successful attachment. Is there a religious or other spiritual experience that would seem to build on this primitive exchange of beneficence and good will? Consider the biblical priestly blessing (Numbers 6:24–26):

> May YHVH bless you and protect you
> May YHVH cause his face to shine upon you and be gracious
>   to you.
> May YHVH turn his face to you and give you peace.

This formula tells us the meaning of the word *berakha*, which is usually translated as blessing. I interpret the shining face of YHVH as a current representation of the mother's smile that is affectively equivalent to it. The parallel term, "be gracious to you," I interpret as implying that God's grace repeats the mother's grace. I find support for my interpretation in the interpretation of Rashi (Rabbi Solomon ben Isaac), the celebrated Jewish exegete of the eleventh century. Rashi says that the verse means, "May God greet you with a smiling face."

"May YHVH turn his face to you" could be understood with reference to its opposite. One turns one's face away from someone to express anger, so turning toward someone expresses love. Rashi says that the verse means, "May God refrain from displaying an angry face." And the result of the blessing will be tranquility. There are many citations in the Bible of the expression *hestaer panim*, hiding one's face. God's hiding his face is given as a punishment for misbehavior. Turning one's face toward a person then is the opposite of rejecting.

When we bless God, we are reciprocating the divine blessing of man, just as the infant reciprocates the mother's smile. The baby's presumed primitive affective response to the mother is now reflected back to her, so that the expression of love reinforces the attachment bond on both sides.

Rabbinic literature employs the concrete expressions of a "smiling face" (i.e., a happy mood) and a "gloomy face" (i.e., a sad or angry mood) to contrast the various emotional tonalities of different types of sacred literature. . . . Furthermore, not only were contrasting genres of literature characterized by a wide range of facial expressions, but the inner moods of the divine Person Himself—His joy and His sadness—were boldly described in a similar fashion. (Muffs 1992:146)

Let me be clear about these arguments. I am not suggesting that the childhood experience discussed here is essentially religious or even potentially so. Rather, I am suggesting that on occasion, later in life, when current attachments and prospects seem to wane or leave a defect in our view of our opportunities for maintaining a sense of composure, when current opportunities for gratification fail to protect against depression or despair, we seem to be able to reactivate a complex of affects and dispositions that prevailed early in childhood. These present themselves as the seemingly transcendent affective experiences that we call spiritual. For people concerned with the human-divine encounter, conventional religion provides a variety of patterns, each of which corresponds to and may be derived from these early childhood forms of attachment behavior.

And so I have proposed that the several forms of primary spiritual experience—mysticism, Spirituality, and awe—are based upon the earlier affective experience of the infant, rather than cognitive processes, and the concept of blessing corresponds to the exchange of smiles between mother and infant.

It does not seem a great leap to infer that the first and most enduring and impressive of the infant's early memories are the experiences of the mother's body, the body that warms, comforts, cradles, and feeds him. The sights and sounds of this enormous structure are recaptured in the feelings of awe.

Perhaps the earliest experience that the infant and mother share after birth is mutual touching. The mother touches and strokes the infant, who visibly enjoys the experience, and who, seemingly automatically, reaches out to and touches the mother's face and body and breast—sometimes licking the areola before beginning to suck. Lower mammals do more licking, though it is not clear how much touching they do. Jaak Panksepp suspects that they do more touching than we imagine. Perhaps kissing amounts to a combination of touching and licking. Touching in lower animals becomes grooming, which sometimes functions as an introduction to mating.

If we look for touching and kissing in religious behavior, we find relatively little. Occasionally the prophet feels "the hand of the Lord upon him." Authority or religious power is transmitted by placing one's hands upon the head of the object—for example, in transferring sins to a sacrificial animal. And one accompanies a blessing by placing one's hands upon the head of the individual to be blessed.

If it is correct that spiritual and religious behavior is derived from infantile or childhood behavior, then we should expect more derivatives of touching in the former. I believe that we don't find them because after the early years, children do not wish to be touched by their parents, and especially during adolescence. At that time, touching is preempted by the sexual instincts so that it becomes an introduction to the sexual act, ultimately foreplay. During the transition from parental touching to sexual touching, especially in this prurient age, strokes of parental affection may be misinterpreted as inappropriate sexual advances or even "sexual abuse."

I argue below that religious impulse sometimes recruits sexual behavior—see, for example, Saint Teresa's fantasy in Report 5. The easy invoking of sexuality in what is intended as a religious act results in careful ritual circumscription of the latter. What starts out as social warmth in a religious congregation occasionally grows into flirtation and then sexual attachment. That is why Jewish and Islamic orthodoxies carefully segregate the genders during services and discourage touching.

As adults we suppress our memories of odors, and even mask many odors with fragrances and deodorants. But odors are important to infants; they can and do distinguish between the scent of their own mother and that of other lactating women. To my knowledge, odors do not play a large part in the worship practices of modern Western religions. To be sure, God is said to have enjoyed the pleasant aroma of Noah's sacrifice, and subsequently, of the many Temple sacrifices. But the smell of temple sacrifices was masked by incense, for there is reason to believe that it was not pleasant to human sensitivities. Song of Songs, in many different verses, tells of the fragrance of the lover, of the lover's perfumes, of clothing, of surroundings. But I cannot recall any accounts of spiritual experiences of any time in which odor was noted. Incense is used in some current church services. In the Havdalah service terminating each Sabbath and holiday in the Jewish religion, each of the senses in turn is celebrated, including the ability to perceive fragrance.

Of course, the visual appearance of the mother's body and the sounds of her breathing and voice leave profound impressions. The hope to revisit the earliest impressions of the bodies of both parents often finds expression as the desire and attempts to see God or his pagan predecessors face to face. In the scriptures, that is sometimes completely prohibited, sometimes permitted to a limited extent, and sometimes permitted without comment. Visions of God are commonly reported in medieval and especially mystical literature. However, formal religious services do not purport to disclose an image of God, although depictions of Christ and of the saints, are common in many Catholic places of worship. Idols were plentiful in the ancient world.

Because of his awesomeness, the possibility of being confronted by God may be frightening. Moreover, looking at him may imply the utmost disrespect. The problem is complicated by the fact that visualizing God may involve at least two different elements. The earlier is the revisualization of the parent's body. The later involves recognizing a parent as a sexual person with genitals and other sexual characteristics. Seeing God as a sexual object is a gross violation of his holiness and otherness. Note that Noah's son Ham observed his father lying naked in a drunken stupor, whereas Shem and Japheth modestly covered him without looking at him. Ham was punished for his presumption.

Many revelations and theophanies are, in religious literature, prized experiences. In the unconscious, this is as close to the return to the mother as is possible after infancy.

The mother's voice and doubtless the father's voice are somewhat easier to reproduce, that is, sounds that would seem to possess the power to elicit significant responses. Scripture tells of the awesome thunder and lightning as well as the sounds of the *shofar* at the theophany on Mount Sinai (Exodus 19:16 ff.). Actually the word translated as thunder in this context is *kol*, which can also be translated as voice (cf. Psalm 29). On the other hand, in Kings I, 19:12, the voice of the Lord is a *kol demamah dakah,* a thin, small voice.

That sounds have the power to move strongly is evident. That music simulates the human voice in exerting that power is almost equally obvious. I propose that the similarity to the memory of the mother's voice gives musical and voice sounds that power, and many students of the subject concur (Panksepp and Bernatzky 2002).

The search for the mother's presence through the medium of voice finds expression in several ways. Unison singing induces cohesion among the members of the religious congregation, a sense of lateral attachment that reinforces a sense of vertical attachment to the transcendent, divine entity. Each of the various religious musical modalities contributes its own spiritual signature: deep, reverential voices, soaring soprano voices, solemn voices, plaintive voices.

Antiphonic singing would directly convey the impression of conversation with the divine. Music may also find expression in religious chanting, a kind of structured musical speech. Perhaps pure music and pure speech are modalities differentiated out from an evolutionarily earlier undifferentiated vocal expression. Chanting classical religious Scripture before the congregation suggests hearing God's voice directly. Most Jewish services incorporate chanted or read selections. Many Christian services also incorporate "The Word of God." The poetry of the Hebrew prophets touches one as powerfully as music and certain forms of inspiring speech. Some of the beauty comes across in the King James translation.

I have long pondered the biological significance of the concept of redemption and salvation. Panksepp (1995) suggested that sad music may achieve its beauty and its chilling effect as a symbolic rendition of the separation call in the emotional context of potential reunion and redemption. He pointed out further that one could speak of redemption when the young mammal or bird has wandered or fallen away from the mother or nest and then is retrieved. This is a powerful image. It suggests that when the human infant feels abandoned or lost and its cry brings the mother to find it, the situation is the paradigm for the concept of redemption.

Shortly after the middle of the first year, most infants display a fear of strangers. This anxiety varies from child to child in intensity and circumstances, as do most functions. It is influenced by the behavior of the stranger and by the proximity of the mother (cf. Bowlby).

The concept of the stranger enters the Bible in two contexts. In the earlier books, especially in the Pentateuch, Israel is frequently reminded to treat strangers who live among them with equity and compassion, reminding Israel that they were strangers in the land of Egypt, from which they were redeemed. The word "redeemed" brings us back to Panksepp's suggestion that ultimately, redemption consists of returning the abandoned or lost infant to the mother. Affectively, redemption parallels the establishment of Spiritual contact with the transcendent other. While redemption may be given specific meanings and placed in specific contexts in the various religions, I accept Panksepp's idea that psychologically the experience can be understood as the return of the lost infant to the mother.

A man in his fifties, the son of a Protestant minister, when depressed, spoke of himself as "little boy lost." He dreamed that standing in his crib as a baby, he saw his mother's face alongside the face of the baby Jesus. He hoped for the redemption that he could obtain from his father's religion, but also from psychoanalysis. I believe this vignette illustrates Panksepp's suggestion nicely.

But the word "stranger" appears in a different context in the later prophets. There it denotes a vicious enemy whose work will be feared because he is a stranger. "Your land is laid waste, your cities are burnt down before your eyes, the yield of your soil is consumed by strangers" (Isaiah 1:7). "I shall bring against you strangers, the most ruthless of the nations. They shall unsheathe their swords against your boasted wisdom, and strike down all your splendor" (Ezekiel 28:7).

The enemy is more fearsome if he is unrecognized and unknown. Guerrilla fighters often wear masks. The alien is a common subject for horrifying science fiction. The concept of an enemy is basic for both individuals and communities. The attack of September 11, 2001 upon the World Trade Center traumatized America by demonstrating that we have active enemies and rectifying the concept that we need fear no one.

Many of the Psalms, especially those attributed to David, ask for protection and rescue from enemies. I suggest here three sources of the psychologic concept of enmity. First, reality. There are enemies in this world, arrayed against us as individuals and societies. One may attribute enmity to rivalry, envy, jealousy, arrogance, and cupidity.

Second, paranoiac enmity. Almost all paranoiacs fear enemies. Often there are no enemies, or the enmity of unfriendly forces may be greatly exaggerated. My understanding of this phenomenon is that depressive influences, often in the service of mood regulation (which I shall take up below), are projected out, externalized, and attributed to an external enemy. Anti-Semitism is a classic example. The internal depressive forces are projected out onto the Jews, sometimes taking advantage of a real but trivial offense (Ostow 1995).

But third, the fearsome "stranger" of early childhood might be seen as the original paradigm of the enemy upon which the other two instances are based.

To return to the subject of spirituality, I am suggesting that when we feel lost, abandoned, like a stranger in an unfamiliar society, we hope to establish contact with a transcendent other, usually divine, to be rescued. But also when we are frightened by actual strangers arrayed against us, we may turn to our God or other source of salvation with praise, propitiation, or petition.

The infant desires comfort from the mother's body through each of the senses, though obviously sensations from all of them are combined to create an integrated impression. In the individual's subsequent attempt to reproduce the pleasures of the mother's body, the image one strives to retrieve seldom includes all of these dimensions, but focuses on one or a few of them.

Since among the first interactions of mother and infant is her feeding him, it is not surprising to find ritual meals among the common forms of religious worship. For example, in anticipation of his rendezvous with God on Mount Sinai, Moses, accompanied by Aaron, Nadab, Abihu, and seventy elders of Israel, ascended the mountain; there "they saw the God of Israel and under his feet the appearance of a sapphire pavement, pure as the sky itself. Yet he did not raise his hand against them, and they beheld God and they ate and drank" (Exodus 24:10, 11). In the modern world, family and communal meals become forms of worship, being so designated by the preliminary recitation of an appropriate liturgical formula. In Jewish practice, the meals celebrating the inception of religious holidays are preceded by the formula, "Blessed are you, YHVH, our God, King of the Universe, who has sanctified us by his commandments and granted us" whatever the Sabbath or holiday might be. In the Christian Communion, the church ritualizes the meal with wine and wafer, and interprets these as the blood and body of Christ.

In the ancient world, the animal sacrifice was a form of mutual feeding between God and man. After the Flood, Noah sacrificed a few of the ritually clean animals that he had saved on the ark with him. The text states that God enjoyed the aroma of the burnt flesh and resolved that he would never again curse the earth nor attack every living creature (Genesis 8:20, 21). The word the text uses is *reah*, literally odor. God inhales the odor of the sacrifice and finds it pleasing. But the word is cognate with *ruah*, breath, spirit, discussed above. Sacrifice of the animal brings man into spiritual communication with God by the medium of the fragrant aroma of the burnt offering. In addition, in many kinds of ritual sacrifice, much of the meat of the animal was consumed by a community of priests and/or worshippers. So the sacrifice provided a medium by which man and God shared a meal. Further, the Hebrew word for sacrifice is *korban*, which literally means a gift, an offering, and is derived from the verb *krv*, to approach. The *korban* therefore is the medium that brings man and God together. In many instances in the ancient world, the sacrifice was performed by burning the animal on an altar, where the flame was maintained constantly. Fire is a symbol for love as well as for destruction, but also for spirit, so that the lighting of candles became an expression of ritual devotion.

Because the feeding experience is so vital to the child's survival, we tend to focus on the nutritive need as primary. Freud spoke of the anaclitic instincts; that is, he argued that the child's love for his mother is based upon his need for the mother's nourishment. Yet we have noted the importance of the mutual smiling response between mother and child, which is vital for the child's flourishing, if not for his actual survival. I would surmise that feeding provides not only physiologic, caloric substance but also the affective gratification that accompanies it. This is what causes the child to suck upon a pacifier, and as an adult, to cultivate the various oral pleasures, whether or not they result in actual nutrition.

To retrieve, in a search for a spiritual experience, the gratification of the feeding situation, it will not suffice just to eat something, anything, no matter how tasty. The goal is to approximate, as closely as possible, what must have seemed the overwhelming pleasure of the experience of the mother's overflowing breasts. They are symbolized in the ceremonial eating and drinking at the various religious services. These are clearly not thought of as fulfilling nutritional needs. They may be said to be symbolic of nutrition. Presumably we view "blessing" the bread and wine, rendering it fit for sacred use, as expressing gratitude for the food. I am suggesting here that the ceremonial consumption of bread and wine, accompanied by the appropriate benedictions, inspires the spiritual feeling desired. The infant loves—if we may use the word at that early age—the mother, not because the mother feeds him but because he enjoys the affective experience of being fed. It is that affective experience that the ceremonial food is intended to reproduce.

The spiritual celebration of nature to which I have alluded previously can be seen as the spiritualized retrieval of the affect associated with the contours of the mother's body. This type of experience comes to mind spontaneously in the presence of natural beauty without any necessary association to religious ideas.

I have been describing infantile experience in the presence of the mother, and the spiritual and religious attempts to recapitulate it. But at a given point, the child starts to become aware that the enjoyment of the mother's bounty is not automatic, but contingent upon the mother's readiness to bestow it. The infant becomes able to distinguish between the good mother and the disappointing mother. The expectation of a good mother gives rise to a religious optimism. God is the ready source of sustenance and of grace and will provide for all our needs. But contingency means that God cannot be relied upon to be consistently available. God will occasionally turn his face away or even express anger or threat.

The child learns that virtuous behavior will maximize parental attention, and propitiates with gestures of gratitude, with primitive speech responses clearly aimed at pleasing the parent. The religious derivatives of these attempts at propitiation take the form of verbal prayer and ritual gesture. Prayerful expressions of praise and gratitude fill large proportions of any prayer book. Much of the Psalter consists of hymns of praise. Praise of the reigning deity occurs prominently in virtually all worship.

The word "pray" itself is derived from the Latin *precari*, to en-treat. What is the relation between spiritual connection and en-treating? On the surface it would appear that asking for favor is the primary purpose of prayer. But I argue that that is secondary to the establishment of the spiritual connection. Entreating derives from a later phase in child development. The child learns to exploit the attachment for practical advantage. He or she wishes for not only a smile or a sweet but also a gift or a privilege. The adult worship-per calls God's attention to his acts of piety, or makes promises to exhibit piety in the future. But the request and counteroffer are based upon affective attachment. This is not simply a transaction of convenience. It is considered a mark of a greater degree of spiritual elevation if the worshipper neither requests nor expects tangible reward. For the spiritually religious, God's favor is an expression of God's reciprocal affirmation of the attachment, rather than a re-ward. For the less spiritual, praying for a favor becomes instrumen-tal, theurgic magic, coercing God to do your will by using religious ritual or verbal formula.

Jewish prayer and some Christian prayer softens the entreating element by three devices. The formula may recite God's capacity to heal the sick, to resurrect the dead, or to send a redeemer without directly calling for that favor, merely hoping that God will take the hint and deploy his powers. Second, prayer is in the plural, asking that God favor the entire community, rather than the individual, with whatever is desired. Third, God is blessed in the second person and his powers described in the third person. "I will extol you my God the king, and I will bless your name forever and ever. I will bless you every day, and I will praise your name forever and ever. The Lord is great and worthy of prayers; there is no discerning his greatness" (Psalm 145:1–3). "YHVH is good to all and his mercies extend to all his creatures. All of your works will praise you and your righteous ones will bless you" (145:9–10).

I have observed above that spiritual experience may be associ-ated with a positive affect, spiritual elevation, or with a negative affect, spiritual anguish. The prospect may be awesome or awful. The essential Spiritual experience may be sublime or disheartening. The god encountered in the mystical experience may be benign and loving, or angry and threatening. When one opens oneself to and invites spiritual experience, one cannot know in advance what that experience will be—that is, from the psychologically naïve point of view. But from the psychodynamic point of view, one can predict that the outcome will be determined by the mood of the worshipper at the moment. The chapter on mood regulation will explain that mood controls the affective valence of experience.

Accordingly, we find that much of prayer is propitiatory. The seemingly excessive expression of praise is not meant only to reciprocate favors already received or hoped for; nor are the self-imposed restrictions meant merely to prevent punishment or encourage favor. They are meant to encourage a positive outcome of the spiritual quest rather than a depressing or frightening one. Propitiation includes obedient accommodation to the parent's indicated wishes. Expressing thanks is also meant to encourage a beneficent response. But we must keep in mind that prayer may have no selfish motive at all. It may just be the spontaneous influence of love and appreciation. We may say "I love you" to someone we love, merely because we do and wish to express it, without any direct expectation of a reward.

The religious expressions of propitiation, praise, and ritual thanksgiving are all either verbal or given by behavioral signs that are generally understood. Obviously the infant in his first few months is incapable of this type of behavior. But I am arguing that the propitiatory behavior of the adult can reproduce propitiatory feelings and rudimentary acts and gestures of the infant in the same mood. The purpose in each case is to maintain the parent's and later God's committed attachment to the infant or himself as adult.

At this later stage in the development of the child, he can conceive of a kind of a transactional relation with his parent. The parent says, usually explicitly, "If you will obey, I will reward you, and if you misbehave, I will punish you." Reward and punishment here refer to the behavior that is appropriate to the stage of development at which this transaction takes place. No matter when it actually appears in early childhood, it is reproduced later and into adult life in the same simple way.

The Psalter is one book of the Jewish Scripture in which man talks to God, whereas in most other books God talks to man. In the

Psalms, the singer praises God, gives thanks, and hopes for reward for good behavior. Deuteronomy records the promise of generous reward for exemplary behavior and harsh punishment for misbehavior. The prophets interpreted Israel's history in terms of reward and punishment.

At least a word should be inserted here about the posture of prayer. The classical prayerful posture is eyes raised toward the heavens, often with hands held upward as well. In the dream and fantasy imagery of Holocaust victims during their travail, similar images appear frequently. In a dream recorded in chapter 6, a similar image is given, representing the state of depression of the dreamer, looking for help from above. The basis for this behavior can only be the child's upward gaze and upward reach toward the mother, when the child needs to be picked up, rescued. Help comes from above.

PSALM 121

A Song of Ascents.
I shall lift my eyes toward the mountains.
From whence my help shall come.
My help comes from YHVH
who made heaven and earth.
He will not permit your foot to stumble.
Your guardian will not sleep. . . .

This is clearly the petition of an adult who feels the kind of helplessness that a small child would, and prays for rescue and protection. As I observed elsewhere, many of the cult sites of the ancient world were situated in high places, the prototypical locus of the protective parent.

The other classical posture of prayer is bowing the head, while kneeling or in full prostration. These positions simulate the fact that the child is lower then the parent, but I suspect that the posture derives from early biology rather than from human childhood. Konrad Lorenz (1974) clearly describes the posture of the defeated animal in intraspecies combat: it presents a vulnerable part of the body, often the nape of the neck, to the victor, thereby signaling submission. I am not claiming that humans imitate animals, but that a similar instinctive mechanism favors exhibiting submission to more powerful force in this way.

Here is Panksepp's view of the posture of prayer:

> Religious feelings have two postures—One, praying with clasped hands with head down (seemingly the posture of an infant in despair after social separation, hoping, praying no doubt, for reunion). Two, arms uplifted in an open gesture of reverential awe, wonder and desire toward the sky (seemingly the posture of an infant eager to be picked up by a loved one).

Muffs (1992), a distinguished contemporary student of ancient Near Eastern religion, describes transactional worship and its theoretical basis in the following terms:

> The religious life of the ancients—Mesopotamian and Hebrew alike—was less a quest for salvation or union with a metapersonal godhead than an ongoing personal relationship, of different degrees of stability and intimacy, between man and his god(s). Like most personal relationships, the divine-human encounter, once formalized, was often experienced in legal terms, as a covenant: between overlord and vassal; between father and son; or between husband and wife. Furthermore, the religious covenant, exactly like its societal analogue, was created, sustained, and renewed by a continuous exchange of gifts and favors—the tangible signs of the mutual good will and loyalty of the parties. Thus, without denying the importance of divine service and the more numinous aspects of ancient religion, there can be little doubt that the normal everyday intercourse between man and his god(s) was reflected in this ongoing exchange of gifts: the gifts—in religious language, "the blessings"—of life and wealth, healing and assistance bestowed by divinity on everyman; the authority bestowed as a gift to kings, especially in Mesopotamia; and in Israel—at least according to the midrash—the gifts of the land, the Torah, and the Sabbath, granted to the people for all time. In return for these blessings, man reciprocated with his contributions to the temple and with the payment of his vows:

in Mesopotamia with his food-offerings to the gods; and in Israel with his tithes, first-fruits and sacrifices, and later, with his prayers. And even if his sacrifices were formally considered as divine demands rather than spontaneous donations, nevertheless—at least according to a rabbinic tradition—if offered with a full heart and with enthusiasm, they were accepted as free-will offerings. (165 f.)

In this connection, Muffs argues that the smile that reflects the inner joy of the individual and the frown that expresses his inner sadness have striking legal implications: the smile is a poetic but nonetheless legal expression of willingness, while the frown, as the outward reflection of inner sadness, is a dramatic indication of unwillingness and inner reservation.

This brings us back to our earlier discussion of the power of the smile in mother-infant relations—and thereafter as a social gesture. Parenthetically, we may note that at later phases of development, we may revert to and integrate more archaic behavior. This principle recurs in the incorporation of individual items of behavior into group behavior.

What I am describing here is transactional worship. But to revert to its spiritual paradigm, we seem disposed to encourage spiritual experience, when we do, by exhibiting qualifying virtuous behavior, however that may be understood. The classic mystics learned how to encourage mystical experience by such practices as excluding the normal sounds and sights of the environment, by self-denial, and by obedience of various kinds, but also by extremes of virtuous behavior.

Transactional worship gives rise to rules, codes, obligations, and religious systems. Every religion has its sets of behavioral codes, some involving cultic worship, some civil behavior. In the ancient world, animal sacrifice was widely employed as a means of influencing divine mood and intent. And so was human sacrifice, though there the violation of ordinary human sensitivities seems to have required one or more other contributing components such as oedipal rivalry, sibling rivalry, sadism, or intertribal hostility.

To the extent that the small child learns that he can influence his parent's behavior, it must seem to him that he possesses power over the parent. In a way, he learns that he can control the parent by his behavior. In the context of reward and punishment, that power is real and reasonable. But the child is also likely to generalize that experience to the idea that his gestures and actions can control the parent. In the religious context, transactional worship may and often does degenerate to performance worship and magic, as though the gesture, rather than the mind-set, is effective (Isaiah 1:10–17).

Penitence is not often given as a component of nonreligious spirituality, but becomes a common theme in religious worship. It represents the child's attempt to regain the parent's good will when that is withdrawn following misbehavior. In worship it is intended to deflect punishment or to make restitution.

So far we have been considering the experience of attachment to the parent and the infant and small child's need to maintain it, as well as the method the child may use to maintain or refresh it. But around the fourth year a complication enters. The child begins to become interested in sexual and gender issues. Mother and father are now not simply separate individuals, but individuals whose bodies look different from each other, and attract a new kind of interest. Children become aware of the difference between the sexes, the fact that they relate to each other in mysterious ways that require the use of these gender-specific structures, and ultimately they wonder and speculate about what all this has to do with the birth of babies.

Freud saw this genital interest as a late element of the epigenetic series of general libidinal interest, following oral, anal, and phallic. More recent behavioral research differentiates between filial-parental attachment needs and sexual needs. Among most lower animals, the young leave the parental nest when their gonads begin to mature. Sexual interest and parental and affiliative attachment are incompatible except in those few species that are monogamous. Human monogamy is expressed in marriage or lasting attachment, requiring the ability to direct attachment behavior and sexual orientation to the same individual. In people lacking that ability, we encounter the well-known Madonna-whore syndrome. For a man with this problem, each woman is seen as either a Madonna or a whore, so that he cannot enjoy a sexual relation with the woman he loves. Two peptide hormones are relevant here. Oxytocin mediates the mother's attachment to the young and briefly, postcoitally to a sexual partner, but plays no role in sexual instinctual behavior. Vasopressin plays an analogous role in males (see Panksepp 1998).

When the individual regresses to an earlier phase of development in search of spiritual sustenance, he may find himself attracted to this early phase of genital sexuality, that is, about age four. A religion based upon such images will be a sexually oriented religion. Early pagan religions had ithyphallic idols as well as female idols with grotesquely large breasts. Even the premonotheistic mythologies include gods who are sexually active, who ignore the rules of human sexual morality, and who can be engaged by sexual acts in a social context. The Pentateuch and later Jewish scriptures describe the seduction of Israel by sexual cults and the struggles of the prophets against them.

Pure monotheistic religion rejects sexual behavior as a mode of worship. Sexuality is incompatible with holiness, since the latter requires an absence of materiality. Yet practical religion must make provision for normal sexual behavior, so it is generally permitted but ringed with restrictions. Extramarital intercourse is discouraged or forbidden, homosexuality is disdained, the clergy may be required to be abstinent, intercourse may be limited to only a certain portion of the menstrual cycle. The aim is to prevent simple sexual excitement from being conflated with true spiritual arousal, though to be sure, one may facilitate the other. In some religious systems worship may recruit sexual energy to reinforce it. In the account of Saint Teresa experience (Report 5) we see a plainly mystical experience recruiting sexual arousal.

The phase of phallic genitality gives way to a phase of latency during which the child begins to attach laterally. That is, the vertical attachment to parents is gradually replaced by a greater and greater degree of attachment to contemporaries. The child becomes integrated into a society of his peers, and as he develops, he becomes more and more integrated into his community, at first locally and then more broadly.

The religious parallel to this transition is the development of a religious society. The mythological and historical accounts of the inception of new religions start with the formation of the community.

The initial approach of the divinity is to the prophet, who is expected to mobilize his community. Abraham, Isaac, and Jacob are engaged by God, and they commit their progeny. Moses is selected as the prophet to the Israelites of Egypt but also to transmit divine instruction to the people. In each case a covenant binds the people to God and determines their obligation to him. The prophet communicates God's moral demands to the community and demands that they observe this morality in their relations with one another. In the ancient Near East, covenants or arrangements setting out mutual obligations of partners were voluntarily entered into, usually between a superior and an inferior. In the scriptures, God establishes covenants with Israel on a number of occasions.

At the height of the socializing tendencies of adolescents, they organize themselves into teams, fraternities, gangs, secret societies. The members bind themselves to one another by specific mutual obligations.

The religious community too becomes a source of mutual emotional support for its members. There may be no formal covenant respecting membership, but the community as a whole often sees itself as in a covenantal relation with God. This kind of relation provides both horizontal social attachments and the vertical attachments to the divine entity. I would guess that this dual attachment provides the major motivation for religious affiliation. But so it is also for the cultic forms of religion, the nonreligious or antireligious movements, and even political movements. In these, social attachment complements commitment to the cause and to the leader.

The basic point is that when realistic daily life leaves gaps in satisfaction or contentment, or when extraordinary stress makes the usual sources of emotional supply inadequate, many people search for supplementary gratification in the form of spiritual experience. The most common and successful forms of spiritual experience are religious, but nonreligious attachments can be equally gratifying. Regression to the period of establishment of the covenantal group is less dramatic than regression further back to early childhood models, and the group spiritual experience is also less dramatic, but by the same token, more accessible.

The child's socialization involves first siblings, then classmates and other friends, subsequently adolescent groups, then community, nation, and sometimes supranational entities. Religious communities are prominent among them. In a sense, soliciting or accepting membership in any of the groups entails accepting the terms of the written or implied covenant. That set of terms becomes the moral covenant of the society, and morality then refers to the readiness to comply with it. In this way, moral behavior becomes a feature of spirituality. It brings a person into the orbit of this spiritual group.

The readiness to accept moral obligations is attributed by psychoanalysis to a special intrapsychic agency, namely the superego. The superego can be said to take over the role of the authority behind the movement, the inspector and the enforcer. It acts to restrain individual impulses that are inconsistent with group mores.

Freud attributed the formation of the superego to the conquest of the Oedipus complex. By foregoing his sexual interest in his mother and identifying with his father, the child acquires the ability, in fact, the need to repress the inadmissible impulse, that is, to refuse to acknowledge it, but more generally to resist inappropriate desires and impulses so as to submit to social morality.

Mystical literature describes methods for preparing oneself to invite a mystical experience. Stringent moral behavior is always one of the elements. Not only does moral behavior favor spiritual gratification, but immoral behavior precludes it.

Of course there are the antinomian groups whose *raison d'être* is to defy conventional morality. Creating a group with a different, in fact opposite set of rules will make it possible to enjoy a spiritual experience by virtue of immoral behavior. Perversity is the determining factor. Here the spiritual, transcendent affect is attached to a diabolic entity.

Most of the statements in this epigenetic scheme relate to positive experiences. But in reality we often encounter disappointments. The hoped-for maternal smile may be replaced by a scowl; the mother may be absent when we need her to be there; misfortune may be interpreted as punishment; a bad mood may make even propitious circumstances seem unkind. A number of psychic rationalizations may then be invoked: punishment for misbehavior, a diabolic agent.

During adolescence, the young person continues to transfer attachment needs to contemporaries and attenuate attachment to parents, though these never really disappear. During adolescence, the person continue to vacillate between attachment and autonomy or even rebellion. Sometime during the third decade, a satisfactory compromise may be reached, which persists with some stability. It is for this reason that young people who had distanced themselves from formal religion may return. The return is conventionally explained as intended to prepare for the religious education of the children, but I surmise that it is the final resolution of the religion–antireligion struggle.

At this point, I would enter a modifying commentary in my remarks about modes of worship and their origin in childhood behavior. I have spoken of central tendencies, as though behavior and the entire population were essentially uniform. Obviously, a more realistic view of the subject requires acknowledging that, as is the case of all behavior, religious behavior differs from individual to individual. It is true that attachment instincts govern very much of childhood behavior, and the religious behavior that I assume develops therefrom. However, observation discloses a variety of forms of attachment behavior (Bowlby; Ainsworth) and of intensities.

Perhaps it would be more helpful to think not simply of variant intensities of attachment behavior, but of the action of a second, opposed factor, namely, a tendency toward autonomy. The result would then be the outcome of contention between these two tendencies. From the point of view of nosology, we tend to think in terms of rubrics like oppositional behavior, antisocial behavior, or psychopathic behavior. I am addressing behavioral variants well within the normal spectrum. Some of us are joiners, others independent; some are compliant, others deviant; some more social, others less so. Accordingly, in any religious community some will be more observant, others more free thinking; some will join, some remain aloof. (I owe this emphasis to Peter B. Neubauer.)

One of the areas of concern for tightly organized religious communities is marriage out. Its prevalence generally reflects the security of the group. Obviously a community under attack is more cohesive, and one more generally accepted by its neighbor is more adventurous. The issue is complex. As I commented above, the familial attachment instinct and sexual instinct are partly independent, but also partly concordant. Incest is not only proscribed but also usually unattractive. However, marriage outside the coherent religious community is also proscribed, leaving as the universe of potential mates those outside the immediate family but inside the community. I observed above that when the sexual attachment is incompatible with familial attachment, that is, attachment to a new, extrafamilial partner, starting a new family, we encounter the Madonna–whore syndrome. But these sexual attachment tendencies are not always orderly or compliant with familial community expectation; that is, they are autonomous. Then they lead the individual outside his religious community with a resulting diffusion of its boundaries. Scripture reports the recurrent threat to the biblical community of "whoring after" other gods.

Let me call your attention to another aspect of the epigenetic scheme of patterns of the human-divine encounter. We have traced a series of such patterns starting from the infant's earliest awareness and continuing through to early adult life. Each pattern relates to the behavior of the individual, and the spiritual experiences built upon these pieces of behavior have been individual experiences.

However, starting with the social instincts, we observe the behavior of the individual within the social group. But at no point have we dealt with behavior of the society as a group. I am not qualified to discuss group behavior, in early or late forms. I do wish to call attention to the fact that, with respect to purely spiritual experience and especially to its religious variants, groups can experience the same manifestations of spirituality as individuals. In fact, as a member of the group, the individual feels the exaltation more intensely than when he is alone. Partly this intensification can be attributed to the fact that active membership in the group is itself spiritually gratifying, but in addition, the participation of the group seems to validate the experience of the individual and so permits him to abandon resistance to being incorporated. In the individual spiritual experience, the subject discards the self-consciously critical attitude that prevents his relaxing his adherence to reality except in a limited and clearly defined way, for example as part of the audience of a theatrical performance, or being moved by music. Even the individual's spiritual experience requires opening up to primitive affects that are not governed by considerations of reality, logic, or consistency. However, when the group as a whole enters into the spiritual venture, it seems to validate throwing off reality constraints and thereby intensifying the spiritual experience.

Awe, for example, is ordinarily an individual sensation, but a group can open its members to an intensified feeling. A group may be induced to participate in the hallucinatory vision of a member. Group passive messianism takes the place of the individual who hopes for redemption. Group prayers of praise, propitiation, and petition seem more cogent than those of individuals.

Since drug addiction and spirituality can, in many instances, serve the same function, it should not be surprising that they can replace each other. From that point of view, conversion from one to the other should not seem surprising, though on the surface, the fact that one is deplored and the other laudable causes astonishment and suspicions of hypocrisy. Some earnest men of religion are spoken of as "God intoxicated."

Juxtaposing immoral behavior and self-righteousness is always cause for self-righteous gloating. And in many, perhaps most cases, censure is warranted. But I am arguing that the perverse or immoral or disappointing behavior has the same function as the engagement of the Spiritual experience, namely to substitute for inadequate gratification in social life, family life, vocation, or self-esteem of whatever origin.

Our discussion sheds some light on the strange relation between addiction and spirituality. Alcoholics Anonymous provides a two-pronged approach for the alcoholic who is trying to overcome his addiction. One element is the encouragement of the fraternal relationship among a group of hitherto unknown others who share the subject's problem. Public confession within the group invites mutual identification and group solidarity, replacing shame with fraternal loyalty. This socialization procedure compensates for the typical subject's difficulties in object relations and combats the low self-esteem that brought about the social avoidance in the first place, or that followed the addictive behavior.

The second element of the Alcoholic Anonymous cure is the encouragement of a spiritual attitude and orientation for both the individual and the group. Spiritual experience is sought to replace or to supplement or reinforce inadequate attachments or attachments that need to be strengthened in the presence of some challenge that demands extraordinary resources of morale.

Transactional worship becomes, for the group, covenantal religion. In group religion, individual lustful thoughts or impulses become orgiastic worship.

To summarize, I have tried to demonstrate here that many of the experiences of the young child can be recaptured as the spiritual or religious experiences of an adult when the affective situation seems to require it. These are all variants of emotional attachment, as are the spiritual experiences based upon them. The lateral social attachments and the vertical parental attachments at times replace each other, and at other times reinforce each other. In the end, the very earliest childhood affective experiences are probably the most powerful feelings of our lives. When troubled, we hope to recapture them, or at least the positive experiences among them. We can recognize a childhood experience in each of the types of spiritual and religious states of mind that we try to achieve.

The Qualities of God

The Image of God

The image of God, as it appears in the Bible, is fairly consistent: male, omnipotent, omniscient, ubiquitous, exhibiting both love and justice. In Exodus 34:6–7 God is described as compassionate, gracious, slow to anger, kind, faithful, extending kindness to the thousandth generation, forgiving iniquity, transgression, and sin, yet he does not remit all punishment, visiting the sins of the fathers upon children until the fourth generation. And in Chronicles I 29:11 David describes God as great and strong, splendid, triumphant and glorious, Author of everything in heaven and earth, King of the kingdom and Sovereign over every leader. In Christianity, God the Father shares divinity with Jesus the Son and the Holy Spirit, which brings us back to the subject of spirituality. Mary, the quintessential mother figure, was added subsequently to the divine retinue.

Note that at the beginning of the account in Isaiah, we are told that the theophany appeared soon after the death of King Uzziahu. We may guess that this is not only a date stamp but also a cause-and-effect relation: that is, having lost the mortal king, Isaiah aspired to reach the divine king.

But these are late images. Many of the early deities of the Near East were female, and their cults persisted, overlapped, and competed with the cult of the Jewish God. It would be interesting to reconstruct the social and political forces that determined the transition from the predominantly female to the predominantly male pantheon, evidently representing the mother, then the father with a collection of sibling gods associated with them.

Since affect strives to achieve actualization in association with an image and with action, the infant's yearning for the mother may likely be associated with a hallucination of her face and body, voice and odors, and with actions appropriate to eliciting her appearance, smile, and beneficence. Accordingly, it is not surprising if the images of the gods that are created to satisfy the adult's yearning to secure the mother's return resemble the features of the mother that were most prominent to the infant's sensibilities. So the off-scale aspect of the mother's body is represented especially by suggestive features of the landscape, hills, mountains, crevasses, ravines, thunder, forest sounds such as roaring, that elicit feelings of awe. These features are not consciously recognized as belonging to the mother, but they seem to reside in what neuroscientists call nondeclarative memory, if in memory at all. Yet they can create the illusion of familiarity even though not retrieved iconically. The various goddesses and gods exhibit similar qualities, often in exaggerated form. The cultic idols that have been retrieved from antiquity surprise us with their protuberant breasts and buttocks, as do the ithyphallic gods among the male divinities. They reproduce the naked bodies of the parents, the object of every small child's curiosity.

In the full Spiritual experience, images do not necessarily play an important role. In Report 3, a woman's voice singing religious and patriotic melodies triggered the experience for which the circumstances had prepared the subject. But the pure Spiritual experience contributes little to our image of a god. Rather, the full mystical experience provides the images to which we are accustomed, as suggested above. How did the image of the divine mother give way to the image of the divine father? Repeated biblical affirmations of the uniqueness of the single, monotheistic, male God warn against being seduced into the worship of pagan gods, multiple, and variously female and male. These accounts doubtless reflect a developmental history.

Does that transition reproduce and resemble the transition from the young child's emotional involvement with the mother to involvement with the father? That transition does not take place at a uniform age. It depends upon the involvement of the father in the infant's feeding and care, play and education. Moreover, the transition is more complete for boys than for girls. Possibly the transition in each culture reflects the child's awareness of the sources of beneficence, protection, and power. The images that appeared in the mystical experience reflected the circumstances of promise and threat that the child—and the adult—perceived in the immediate surround.

I find it interesting that in many of the best-known mystical images, such as those cited above (Ezekiel 1 and Isaiah 6), God is perceived on or in a container. In Isaiah, he is on a throne, within a chamber. In Ezekiel, he is on a platform. Later mysticism refers to the image of the platform borne by four semidivine creatures, as a chariot, elaborating the container *gestalt*. I see that feature as a symbol for a male God within a female body, a phallic creature within a maternal surround.

That interpretation brings the maternal deity back into the picture. The Kabbalists did much to restore what was probably the original female participation in the Godhead. They developed a theosophy of a Shekhinah that was used in the Pentateuch to allude to an immanent presence of God, for example, as He came to reside in or above the desert tabernacle. In the Talmud, the Shekhinah becomes a less grand entity, but often rewards individual virtue with its presence. For the Kabbalists, the term was associated with one of the *sefiroth* (a set of God's emanations), called *malkhuth* or kingdom, which signified the feminine principle or component. The aim of the Kabbalist is through his own merit to facilitate the connubial union of the masculine God (the Holy One blessed be He) with his Shekhinah. Various qualities are attributed to her, giving her aspects of a maternal divinity. It's as though the transition from female to male divinity is never complete, the female persisting in one form or another, whether as the container for the male or as the female Shekhinah in her different manifestations. In Christianity the female persists as the return of Mary. This residue, I believe, attests to the primacy of the mother as the basis of the concept of a god. Gershom Scholem (1941) acknowledges, "Dimly we perceive behind these mystical images, the male and female gods of antiquity, anathema as they were to the pious Kabbalist."

In the following excerpt from St. Augustine's *Confessions*, it is difficult to ignore the hints of maternal qualities in the image of God.

> What then do I love, when I love Thee? . . . I love a certain light, and a certain voice, a certain fragrance, a certain food, a certain embrace when I love my God: a light, voice, fragrance, food, embrace of the inner man. Where that shines upon my soul which space cannot contain, that sounds which time cannot sweep away, that is fragrant which is scattered not by the breeze, that tastes sweet which when fed upon is not diminished, that clings close which no satiety disparts. This it is that I love, when I love my God! (Underhill 1964:69)

In the popular mind, God has assumed the image of a bearded old man with a beneficent or stern visage, depending on the mood of the worshipper. Gnostics, on the other hand, dismissed the anthropomorphic God of Israel and elevated above him a god devoid of any animal or material qualities, a purely spiritual entity. The creator of heaven and earth they dismissively called the Demiurge (Greek for craftsman). Gnostic theosophy includes two other features that relate to our argument. It attributes an androgynous quality to the supreme God and to certain subordinates, especially Sophia (wisdom). Thereby it reflects the bisexual nature of the parent couple, which permits the archaic maternal deity gradually to be replaced by the paternal deity. Second, gnostic mythology says that the soul within the human body is exiled from its place of origin, its home, and longs for return to its noncorporeal origin. I read in this an allusion to the virtual localization of the spirit, in the case of the individual Spiritual experience, to a point outside and beyond the current surround (see Filoramo 1990).

Of course these images of the bodies of the parents have been recorded in retrievable memory at a point later than the point of origin of the primordial precursors of the Spiritual experience. The later images were then superimposed upon the original affect, so that the images we have of God are condensations of the retrieved images from childhood together with the affect that accompanied them, and now in retrieval, along with the original affect. Religion seems to recapitulate the child's relation to his family, whereas pure spirituality recapitulates the infant's relation with his mother.

The Name of God

If the concept of a god arises in response to a spiritual need to make contact with a transcendental other, then that god cannot be apprehended, engaged by the same means as fellow humans or other physical creatures. While the name under ordinary circumstances serves to designate a specific individual and to suggest certain relationships such as family of origin or family by marriage, or gender, or birth community, it also serves as a kind of handle by which the individual can be called, that is, invited or attracted. In the case of spiritual beings whom we ordinarily can't perceive, the name is the only means by which we can call upon them. Even when we try to influence God by prayer, we need his name to engage him in our address or conversation.

In the history of all religions, the gods have many names. In the ancient Near East, a common name was *El*, associated with the idea of power. It also expands to *Eloha* and its plural *Elohim*. These terms are used in the Bible either as a proper noun, the name of God, or a common noun, a god or other authority.

The definitive name of the biblical God was YHVH. Since the name is not to be pronounced, the devout Jew will use a substitute, *Adonai*, sometimes spelled YY and meaning my Lord. The pronunciation was said to have been lost, but L. F. Hartman, who wrote the article on the names of God for the *Encyclopedia Judaica*, reports that according to ancient Greeks, it was pronounced *Yahweh*.

The etymology is obscure, but it seems to be derived from the root *Hvh*, the verb to be. The folk etymology suggested in the Bible in the story of Moses at the burning bush is *ehyeh asher ehyeh*, which translates to "I shall be what I shall be." These terms all point to existence as the essential attribute of God, denying his abstractness or nonexistence, that is, he is not merely a reification of a transcendental hypothetical entity. Combining forms are *yah* and *hv*. I wonder whether it is fortuitous that the sound *h*, a fricative, that is, a sound created by the friction of breath forced through the larynx, appears in all of these forms. The word *ruah* ends in a fricative. Do the H (heh) and Ḥ (het) sounds remind us of the respiratory etymology of the word "spirit"?

In Kabbalistic theosophy, God has many names, one of which is *ayin*, meaning "nothing," that is, God is above and beyond anything that can be conceived in the terms of worldly reality. He is also spoken of as the *ayn sof*, the infinite or boundless, another allusion to his transcendence.

In Jewish tradition, God is referred to as *Hamakom*, the Place (that is, the world is his place) and *Hakadosh Barukh Hu*, the Holy One blessed be He.

An interesting and puzzling biblical name for God is *El-Shaddai* or simply *Shaddai*. A number of etymologies have been suggested, but I wish to point to two. The Hebrew word *sheyd* means demon, that is, a demonic God. But *shad* means breast. The words *sheyd* and *shad*, though vocalized differently, are spelled in Hebrew identically, that is *shd*. So *shaddai* may allude to a full-breasted matriarchal divinity, a mythical precursor of the biblical God, and derive from the child's memory of his first contact with the mother. While I argue that the concept of spirit derives from noniconic affective memories, iconic memories from a slightly later period may be retrospectively condensed with that primordial affect.

To make it unnecessary to use God's name in profane context, the word *Shem*, meaning name, is often substituted. YHVH is called *shem hameforash*, that is, the explicit name of God. But *Shem* is not simply a verbal symbol; it carries a sense of mystical potency despite its origin as a simple substitute. When we use the English phrase, "In the name of God," we are claiming divine authority for what we are about to do. The concept of a god provides a referent for the object of spiritual yearning, and giving the god a name makes him accessible. Invoking that name creates the feeling of intimate contact. It contributes to the mystical experience.

Yet we read in scriptures and mystical documents that direct confrontation with God is awesomely frightening. Using his name is one step removed. But even the use of his name, YHVH, involves a considerable degree of awe and trembling. The use of the word "name" itself, *Shem*, rather than the actual name increases the distance from the actual presence of God to a manageable degree, that is, two degrees of separation.

Both in the Lord's Prayer and in the Kaddish, it is the name that is hallowed, rather than God himself. I assume that the reason is that God is beyond magnification and sanctification. The recognition of his qualities has to be amplified, what people think of him. His reputation among men, his name requires constant refurbishing.

Moshe Weinfeld in the Anchor Bible for Deuteronomy 1–11 (vol. 5, 1991) writes that "Deuteronomy defines the Sanctuary as 'the place where YHVH chose to cause *his name* to dwell there.'" "The expression 'to cause his name to dwell' reflects a new theological conception of the Deity, and that the repeated consistent employment of this and similar expressions ... by the author of Deuteronomy and his followers is intended to combat the ancient popular belief that the Deity actually dwelled within the Sanctuary. The Deuteronomic school uses this 'name' phraseology in a very consistent manner and never made the slightest digression from it." The idea, according to Weinfeld, is that God is not to be pinned down by the cult to a specific locus, so the Sanctuary was built not for him but for his name. It follows that the use of the name is an attempt to combat the idea of God's residing within temporal precincts rather than heaven and earth.

The Visibility of God

The subject of the visibility of God includes two separate issues. In the first place, God is invisible. He may not be seen by humans. In the Bible, God is rarely seen. He is heard; his messengers (called angels) are seen. His presence (the Shekhinah or the *Kavod,* glory of God) may be seen, as a cloud or as a ball of fire, or he may become manifest in thunder and lightning. Moses saw God, as did Isaiah and Ezekiel, but others saw only indications of his presence. No human, in the biblical account, may look at him and survive. (In Exodus 24:9 there is an exception.) In the case of the theophany of Isaiah 6, the prophet says that "His skirts filled the chamber," and the room was filled with smoke, presumably obscuring vision to a certain extent. In Ezekiel's theophany the image of God is clothed in fire and therefore invisible.

Classical Jewish mysticism describes tension between the individual's wish to see and the danger incurred in doing so. A full and detailed description of these matters is given in chapters 4 and 5 of my book, *Ultimate Intimacy* (1995).

To quote from one of the Merkavah mystical texts:

The Holy Living Creatures do strengthen and hallow and purify themselves, and each one has bound upon its head a thousand thousands of thousands of crowns of luminaries of divers sorts, and they are clothed in clothing of fire and wrapped in a garment of flame and cover their faces with lightning. And the Holy One, Blessed be He, uncovers His face. And why do the Holy Living Creatures and the Ophanim of majesty and the Cherubim of splendor hallow and purify and clothe and wrap and adorn themselves yet more? Because the Merkabah is above them and the Throne of Glory upon their heads and the Shekhinah over them and rivers of fire pass between them. Accordingly do they strengthen themselves and make themselves splendid and purify themselves in fire seventy times and do all of them stand in cleanliness and holiness and sing songs and hymns, praise and rejoicing and applause, with one voice, with one utterance, with one mind, and with one melody. (Hekhaloth Rabbati) (Scholem 1960:29)

Rabbi Ishmael said, this is what Rabbi Nehunya ben Hakanah said: "In the seven hekhaloth (palaces) Tutrasi'i (probably a reference to the Tetragrammaton, the four-letter name of God, YHVH) the Lord God of Israel sits in one chamber within another, and at the entrance of each palace, eight guards stand, four on each side of the door. (Hekhaloth Rabbati) (Jellinek 1967:vol. 1)

One of the most intriguing stories of rabbinic mystical literature is the following.

Four entered the garden, namely, Ben Azzai and Ben Zoma, Aḥer and Rabbi Akiva. Rabbi Akiva said to them: When you arrive at the (place of the) stones of pure marble, don't say, Water, Water! Because it is said: He who speaks falsehood will not stand before my eyes (Ps. 101:7). Ben Azzai looked and died. Scripture says about him: Blessed in the eyes of the Lord is the death of his righteous (Ps. 116:15). Ben Zoma looked and was afflicted. Scripture says about him: If you have found honey, eat (only) your fill, because if you become surfeited, you will vomit (Prov. 25:16). Aḥer cut the shoots. Rabbi Akiva departed in peace. (Babylonian Talmud, Ḥagigah 14b)

The story is intriguing on many accounts, but what is relevant here is the need to look and punishment for looking. What the garden symbolizes is obscure. Scholars have offered a number of reasonable conjectures, such as the garden in which the disciples of Epicurus assembled. Whatever the case, this garden is something that is supposed to be off-limits to the observant Jew. (To the psychoanalyst, a garden is a symbol for mother's genitals.)

Where the English text says "looked," the Hebrew is *hezit* or glanced, emphasizing that none of the four actually looked in a studied way. But observe the consequences. Ben Azzai died. Ben Zoma "was afflicted." Rabbinic scholars interpreted his affliction as mental illness. Aḥer is a pejorative epithet for a distinguished scholar whose name was Elisha ben Abuya. "Aḥer" means "something other," and it alludes to his having been excluded from the community because he rejected his faith. "There is no justice and there is no Judge," he declared upon hearing of the death of a man in the course of performing a good deed. The unknown author of the story refers to his apostasy in the strange phrase, "cut the shoots." Rabbi Akiva, one of the most revered rabbinic scholars of the period around the turn of the first century C.E., is reported to have "departed in peace." Well, not quite! Knowledgeable scholars were aware that his mystical tendencies led him to hail his contemporary, Bar Kokhba (Bar Koziba), as a messiah, thereby encouraging all of his own disciples and then the armies and the people who responded to him to revolt against Rome in 132. They suffered the greatest destruction and loss of Jewish life before the modern Holocaust.

The point of the story then is that excessive involvement in mystical speculation, in looking at God, incurs dangers of insanity, death, loss of faith, and tragically poor judgment (see Ostow 1995:130 ff.). Interpreted in this way, the story sounds to me like a reasonable statement of the situation. A mystical trance state or even serious mystical theosophic engagement is a state of mind that involves a marked detachment that, in susceptible individuals, might easily pass over into a psychotic state with any of the consequences enumerated above.

Probably as result of such observations, rabbinic scholars of two thousand years ago and religious leaders during the millennia that preceded and followed them discouraged mystical engagement. The Talmud (B. T. Ḥagigah) limits the teaching of mystical subjects to selected small audiences and discourages cosmologic speculation.

What we discover then in Scripture and in subsequent classical Jewish literature is a tension between the eagerness of the individual to seek the ultimate spiritual gratification, encountering God face to face and even being touched by him, versus fear that transgressing beyond a certain boundary will bring dire consequences. Even in Scripture itself, there is both the prohibition to visualize God and examples in which celebrated figures actually do so. In Exodus 9:21 YHVH said to Moses, "Go down and warn the people less they break through the bounds to YHVH in order to see Him and many of them will perish." In Exodus 33:18–23 Moses said, "Do let me see Your glory." And he replied, "I shall pass all of my magnificence before you and I shall announce my name YHVH before you and the grace that I shall bestow and the mercy that I shall show." And he said, "You will not be able to see my face because no mortal may see me and survive." On the other hand, in Exodus 24:9–11, "Moses and Aaron and Nadav and Avihu and seventy of the elders of Israel ascended. And they saw the God of Israel, and beneath his feet they saw what seemed to be a pavement of sapphire as pure as the very sky. And He did not raise his hand against the elite of Israel and they saw Him and ate and drank." In Exodus 33:11 YHVH spoke to Moses face to face the way one man would speak to another. Ezekiel 1 and Isaiah 6 again give accounts of God's visibility to humans. This tension, I believe, represents the tension between the child's wish to see the unclothed body of the parent(s), and the prohibition against doing so.

I mentioned above that when the subject is in a depressed or fearful mood, the prospect of spiritual gratification may become threatening, a reminder of the contrast between awesome and awful. Below we shall see that there is danger too in excessive enthusiasm.

Religion and the Universe

Where is God to be found? If we were to ask a theologian, he would reply, "Nowhere." As a nonphysical being, God cannot be located in the physical universe. Above I quoted a Jewish scholar poet, Yehudah Halevi, specifically his poem, "Lord where shall I find You?" It begins, "Yah, where shall I find You? Your place is elevated and invisible. And where shall I not find You? Your glory fills the universe." However, the conventional view is that God is to be found in heaven. In rabbinic literature, the term "heaven" is sometimes used as an allusive name for God. Our daily language includes phrases such as "for heaven's sake," and "in the name of heaven." Children are told that after death, people's souls go to heaven.

Religion has commonly associated the gods with heaven and with heights in general. Many of the premonotheistic religions worship sun gods and moon gods. The expression "YHVH Zevaoth" occurs commonly in the Bible, where it is usually translated as Lord of hosts, presuming that "hosts" refers to celestial bodies.

In the ancient world, religious sites were often set up on hills, for example the Acropolis and the Jerusalem Temple. These places seem to be endowed with an immanent spirituality, often awesome. I believe the reason is that the small child always needs to look up to the mother's face and cries to be lifted in her arms to her shoulder. Above, for the child, is the source of salvation. Demons lurk in the chthonic depths, as the child on the floor is vulnerable to strangers and to animals.

In the ancient world and today, religion is sited in temples and caves, enclosures, which represent, I believe, the mother's lap, and symbolically the interior of her body. The child, when not carried aloft, will often try to burrow onto her lap or into her belly. Again it is the yearning for closeness to the mother that gives rise, in subsequent memory, to feelings of spirituality.

We build religious structures with spires that point upward. The word "spire" reminds us of the word "spirit," aspiration, and alternatively, as observed above, respiration. In fact, various dictionaries state that it relates to the root *spir*, an old English and Scandinavian root referring to a blade of grass or a stalk, the word ultimately yielding "spear" and "spike."

Let us look back to the opening account in this book, "The heavens declare the glory of God, and the sky recites the work of His hands." One aspect of the spiritual experience was the man's appreciation of a "special arrangement" of the clouds. He focused on the heavens. He saw there a communication, the revelation that accompanies most mystical and many Spiritual experiences. Psalm 19 continues with a description of the course of the sun through the heavens. Then it dwells on the Bible as the ultimate revelation.

Why is God everywhere? Because the transcendent object of the spiritual wish is not limited to a particular place. It is an object that one is almost in contact with, but not quite. If God is the entity imposed upon the imagined object, then God too exists neither everywhere nor nowhere, but beyond place and beyond time. The affective memory is based upon the experience of early infancy, but it floats freely, not fixed in space or time. "Omnipresent" and "eternity" are words that occur frequently in liturgy.

Fellowship

I have so far spoken of Spiritual experience as an experience of the individual, and religious ideas as ideas of the individual. In fact, though, religious spirituality often appears within the religious community. Religion is a group phenomenon. Religious worship is optimally community worship. The members of the community see themselves as brothers and sisters, worshipping God the Father. Much of the feeling of spiritual gratification obtained in the process of worship comes from the feeling of fellowship it entails. The spiritual endeavor seems to be facilitated when the members of the community engage in it together. Is this phenomenon just a matter of group contagion? Does it depend upon normal and ordinary modes of group attachment, the basis of the organization of a society? Is it ultimately derived from basic family relations? Of course, there is a tension between family cohesion and sibling rivalry. The more intense the cohesion, the stronger the reactive rivalry. Fundamentalist religious movements are more inclined to splintering than mainstream movements, and despite religious ideals of brotherhood of man, religions vie with one another for political, military, and economic power.

The average community in our society is ordinarily not cohesive. However, when some critical threat supervenes, community feeling is strengthened and individuals and families become more supportive of each other. Also, the more homogeneous the community, especially when it differs in a significant way from its neighbors, the more it coheres. Yet on occasion, patriotic fervor appears, for example, when a national issue looms large—a crisis, an anniversary, a celebration. Something different happens. The ordinary social instincts seem to be reinforced in a special way. If we look for a developmental origin of this phenomenon, it would seem reasonable to assume that when family loyalties come into play, they lend a stronger and less restrained tone to the community mutual attachment.

The members of a religious congregation, even though they often conflict with others, and although some are less than admiring of others, tend to cohere more closely than other communities, especially if surrounded by members of other communities.

The mutual attachments within the religious congregation suggest the pattern of the childhood family as well, but with an additional dimension. In the case of the surge of patriotism, the government and the flag become central. Yet the individual leadership may or may not be idealized. But in a religious community, the lateral attachments to fellows are complemented by an intense attachment to the deity, that is, the object of worship. In childhood too, the lateral sibling attachments are complemented by the vertical attachment to the parents. This twofold direction of attachments strengthens family integrity.

Of interest here, though, is the feeling accompanying the attachment. Presumably the lateral attachments in the religious congregation reproduce the feelings of lateral attachment that prevail among the child and siblings or other roughly contemporary family members. Indeed, in psychoanalytic experience, in dreams, fantasies, imagery, associations, the images of the group often symbolize the mother (Scheidlinger 1974). The adult may seek refuge in the group when he craves maternal protection, as he did as a child, when feelings were primitive and strong. Although the experience of adult attachment probably reproduces, in some altered form, the childhood experience, it does not necessarily revive these memories. But the memories might be available and could be retrieved at least in part if the occasion arises. On the other hand, if we credit our earlier discussion of the subject, the vertical attachment to the deity is derived from the spiritual longing and yearning and love that reproduces the very young child's experience of longing for the mother, the literal memory of which is not retrievable.

Even within religious communities, more intensely spiritual groups often assemble. These may take the form of mystical movements. By attracting members' loyalty to their usually deviant beliefs and practices, they present a challenge to the parent community. After a period of conflict, they may then be incorporated into the latter. The seventeenth-century Sabbatian mystical movement among the Jews attracted many adherents but was never incorporated into mainstream Judaism. The Frankist movement that followed shortly thereafter remained a deviant movement and ultimately abandoned Judaism. The Hasidim, on the other hand, who appeared in the late eighteenth and early nineteenth centuries in Eastern Europe, were first severely criticized and rejected by the mainstream, but in the latter half of the twentieth century, that is, after the Holocaust, they have been tolerated, if not welcomed alongside their right-wing orthodox (haredim) brothers. In Israel, and even to a small extent in the United States, they constitute a politically significant voting bloc.

Individual mysticism is seen by the community as deviant and challenging because the mystic lives by the rules of his own personal revelation. Even the privacy of the sexual couple is limited by the demands of the community for control and compliance. While mysticism is usually an individual phenomenon, not infrequently mystics will assemble into fraternities that keep themselves separate from and often depart from community norms. Some mystical fraternities cultivate secrets because the secrecy unites them and constitutes their own private revelation. Knowing the mystical secrets that clear the way for approach to the Godhead reinforces cohesion among the members. Others are secret because they are rejected and held in contempt and as outlaws by the host community. Still others seek every opportunity to spread their views widely and to proselytize.

For a further discussion of the subject of mystical groups and their relation to the community, see my introduction and chapter 8 of *Jewish Mystical Leaders and Leadership in the Thirteenth Century* (Idel and Ostow 1998).

Morality

Morality is a central component of probably every religion and especially of the three major monotheistic religions. And, in most minds, it is associated with religious spirituality.

In the earliest phases of childhood behavior from which we have derived the spiritual experience, morality has not yet begun. Perhaps the earliest expression of deliberate obedience and disobedience occurs during the second year, that is, after the very early precursors of awe and essential Spiritual experiences, and perhaps contemporaneous with the precursors of the images incorporated into the mystical experience. So awe is not necessarily associated with religious morality, the essentially Spiritual experience is more so, and mysticism is usually. The opportunity to connect with God is contingent upon moral behavior and piety; immorality may preclude that connection or invite punishment for the effort, or both.

The religious mystical revelation is almost always a moral one. For example, in Psalm 19, to which I have referred, even the Spiritual awareness of God's presence is followed by a recitation of the virtue of Scripture and the hope that the psalmist will be prevented from sinning. The mystical theophanies of Isaiah 6 and Ezekiel 1 are followed by instructions to the prophet, in each case, to teach the lessons of virtue and sin, reward and punishment. On the other hand, some mystical accounts, such as that of Saint Teresa (Report 5) and our other examples, do not convey moral messages although they occur in a religious context.

The Hebrew prophets deemphasize the mystical element of the cult in favor of morality. From beginning to end, the emphasis in the Hebrew Bible shifts from cult and direct communication between God and man to prophetic religion, that is, morality, civility, and ethics, and then to "wisdom," which emphasizes the last two. This reflects the history of the composition of the component books. Yet the major prophets each sought authentication by citing an initial mystical initiation, followed by the moral preaching to the people.

My point is simply that morality is not an intrinsic component of spirituality, even of religious spirituality. Developmentally, spirituality arises before the child has learned good and evil. The concept of obedience and disobedience appears somewhat later and becomes obligatory as the child emerges into participation in family and certainly social life. Religion, as a social institution, must necessarily include morality as a practical matter. Morality is central to religion, although the affective motivational basis of both arises in spirituality. In each of the two central mystical experiences to which I have repeatedly referred, Ezekiel 1 and Isaiah 6, the arresting experience is the mystical one. Immediately after the direct theophany, the moral message commences, and moral behavior is the subject of the rest of the prophecy.

Holiness

Holiness is a central element of most religions. It is generally seen as an attribute of a deity, but it may attach also to the objects associated with divine worship, to sites, to the cult professionals, and to those worshippers who satisfy certain religious requirements. In the monotheistic religions especially, it is consistently associated with morality, with virtue, with purity. All these associations can easily be illustrated by many verses from Scripture. The classical terms that designate holiness are *kadosh* in Hebrew, *agios* in Greek, and *sacer* in Latin. However, the unifying concept around which all of these qualities cluster is not evident. What is the essence of holiness? Most of the criteria allude to contact with or association with divinity and separation from the profane.

Rudolf Otto, a German theologian, suggested an original approach in a book that has been widely celebrated in the field, *The Idea of the Holy*, first published in 1917 (English translation 1923). He proposed "to invent a special term to stand for 'the holy' minus its moral factor . . . and . . . minus the 'rational' aspects altogether. Further this holy represents the gradual shaping and filling in with ethical meanings of what was a unique original feeling-response which can be in itself ethically neutral and claim consideration in its own right." It "cannot, strictly speaking, be taught, it can only be evoked, awakened in the mind; as everything that comes 'of the spirit' must be awakened." The term he suggested for the essence of the holy was "numinous," derived from *numen,* a Latin word defined as "a presiding deity or spirit." The "deepest and most fundamental element in all strong and sincerely felt religious emotion" he called the "mysterium tremendum." "Mysterium" "denotes merely that which is hidden and esoteric, that which is beyond conception or understanding, extraordinary and unfamiliar." The term "numinous" includes elements of awesomeness, majesty, and energy, but also fascination. Further, "The 'holy' will then be recognized as that which commands respect and as that whose real value is to be acknowledged inwardly" (51).

Clearly, Otto proposes that appreciation of the holy is an emotional experience of a spiritual quality, in the sense that I have been using the term "spiritual." In this he was anticipated by the medieval Jewish philosopher and poet Judah (Yehudah) Halevi, quoted above. Eliezer Schweid writes in the article on *kedushah* (holiness) in the *Encyclopedia Judaica*, "Holiness according to Judah Halevi, is a power that engulfs the soul which unfolds toward it." To repeat the quote from his poem: "And when I went out towards You, I found You coming towards me, and when I was astounded by Your power, I saw You in Your holiness."

Max Kadushin (1952) a modern scholar, differed from Otto in that according to rabbinic usage, he writes, "The concept of *kedushah* (holiness) has connotations which project it onto the sphere of the normal and practical." But he does agree that "Holiness is not something that is a product of intellectual ratiocination; it is either felt, experienced, or it is nothing. . . . The concept *kedushah* is a value concept, not the type of defined concept with which philosophy must operate."

These observations lead to a psychologic discussion of holiness. Whatever theologians might say of the sources and carriers of holiness, it seems clear that its apprehension is an affective, spiritual experience. The religious, spiritual experience probably always includes a dimension of holiness. As observed above, it usually includes an element of religious morality, which I interpret as a component of postinfancy childhood psychology, and grafted upon the infancy, premoral Anlage of the nonmystical spiritual experience. To come back to Otto, "When once it has been grasped that *qadosh* or *sanctus* is not originally a moral category at all, the most obvious rendering of the word is 'transcendent.' But, 'transcendent' is a purely ontological attribute and not an attribute of value; it denotes a character that can, if need be, abash us, but cannot inspire us with respect" (1952:52).

The holiness experience, stripped of its moral component, then seems to be an aspect of the purely spiritual. We attribute holiness to the object of infantile longing, that is, the nurturing parent. I would argue that the infant, without much analytic scrutiny, associates that object with power for good and evil, with cleanliness and purity, with the capacity to transfer its essential wondrous qualities to individuals and objects that come into contact with it.

Psalm 24 reads:

The earth belongs to YHVH, and the fullness thereof,
Cosmos and its inhabitants;
For he has founded it on the seas and set it up on the water
  courses.
Who shall ascend the mountain of YHVH

And who may stand in His holy place?
He who has clean hands and a pure heart,
Who has not taken my name for falsehood,
Nor sworn deceitfully;
He shall receive a blessing from YHVH
And kindness from God his deliverer.
This is the generation of those who seek Him
Who solicit His presence, O Jacob. Selah.
Lift your heads you gates and be elevated
You entrances of the world;
So that the King of Glory may enter.
Who is the King of Glory? YHVH powerful and mighty,
YHVH is mighty in combat.
Lift up your heads you gates and be elevated you entrances of
    the world,
So that King of Glory may enter. Who is the King of Glory?
YHVH Zevaoth,
He is the King of Glory.
Selah.

The psalm is introduced by the dominion of YHVH over the universe, land and sea, earth and cosmos. The infant's cosmos is his
parent's body, solid flesh and fluids. But in this entire structure, one
place is holy, the high place, "the mountain of YHVH."

What is now the mountain of the Lord was once the mother's
shoulder. His holy place was once the mother's close presence. The
very young child who has not yet acquired the capacity to disobey
or deceive parents can enjoy their close affection. The parent is
clean and the child must acquire the ability to keep himself clean.
He must not lie or dissemble. Only then will he be granted the
favor of immediate closeness to their beneficence and to God's. The
image in the psalm is readily transposed to the child's world, his
image of the magnificent father and mother, that is, the pregendered
parent. The quality of awesome size is again recognized. Taller then
the gates of the world and larger than its entrances, he displays
glory and majesty and power. He is YHVH Zevaoth, the God of his
retinue, that is the totality of the inhabitants and component parts
of the cosmos. (Scholars interpret this psalm as a song intended

to accompany the installation of the Holy Ark on its place in the Temple Mount, in the ritual of an annual festival; therefore its allusions to "the mountain of the Lord," "His holy place." Lifting the gates are elevation of the entrance [Sarna 1993].)

God sanctifies us and we sanctify God.

Our Father Who art in heaven,
Hallowed be Thy name. (The Lord's Prayer)

May His great Name be magnified and sanctified. (Kaddish)

In other words, as Halevi said, as we go out to find God, we encounter Him coming toward us. The infant yearning for the mother hopes to find her coming to him.

God designates the Sabbath and so sanctifies it. We sanctify it by observing it.

Of course, the epitome of the concept of holiness is found in Isaiah 6. Looking at it again, you will see that the first clause does not give merely a date stamp. Uzziahu reigned for perhaps half a century. and during that time he established trade routes, strengthened fortifications, and expanded his kingdom. When a long-lived and effective king dies, the people mourn. It was during this period of mourning that Isaiah recorded his mystical vision. Here he again sees a king seated upon his throne, but the divine King. The impression is of an awesomely large image in a gigantic chamber filled with sounds, activity, and smoke, awe inspiring, and reminding us of the experience of the small child in the presence of the gigantic parent. When that emotion is experienced later in life, it is called awe. Note the layers of images here. The earliest is the affective memory of awe in the presence of the gigantic parent. Superimposed upon that is the memory of the actual parent, remembered vaguely as an awesome, impressive figure, commanding and protective and irascible, corresponding to the image found in Isaiah and similar scriptural texts. The conventional image of the refined, noncorporeal, "spiritual" deity is then superimposed, and incorporates all of these perceptible components and the powerful qualia accompanying them that elicit the spiritual affects we recognize as religious feelings.

The throne is elevated, reminding us of the religious high places noted just above in the comments about the mountains of YHVH. Then we read about the seraphs, fiery angels. *SRF* in Hebrew means to burn. They probably accounted for the smoke in the chamber. Burning is a method of purification. They each have six wings, only one pair of which they use to fly. That is, they can ascend without difficulty to the divine high places. With another pair they cover their faces so they do not look at God. With another pair, they cover their legs, legs being a euphemism for genitals. Note the extreme modesty. One may not look at God nor permit one's genitals to be seen, and God's own garments fill the gigantic chamber.

God, in the image, is surrounded by an immense retinue. Perhaps they symbolize the children whose divine father is God. It has been suggested, in *Veteris Testamenti Libros* (Lexicon Koehler, E. J. Brill, Leiden 1958), that the expression "YHVH Zevaoth" is a contraction of "YHVH *Elohey Zevaoth*," that is, YHVH the God of hosts. The referent for "Zevaoth" is obscure; it may include the soldiers of God, military forces, the stars and planets of his universe, or his infradivine agents such as the angels, here the seraphs. The relation of the divine father to his host obviously suggests the relation of the idealized human father to his family.

In Isaiah's vision, the seraphs antiphonically call out to one another, "Holy, holy, holy, YHVH Zevaoth. The world is filled with His glory." Their worship consists of acknowledging his holiness and his glory. Holiness and glory are closely associated in Psalm 24 as well as in this section from Isaiah. From the context it seems that the element common to all of these accounts, as well as to "glory" in Psalm 19, is the awesomeness of the universe. That is the numinous to which Otto refers, the "mysterium tremendum" and "fascinans." The theme of awesomeness is continued in the next verse in Isaiah 6, with respect to the sounds of the antiphonic worship and the smoke emanated by the seraphs.

The prophet, by contrast, speaks of himself as unworthy and subject to punitive destruction because he is a person of "unclean lips" and because, as such, he has seen the inscrutable divine King. A seraph, a fiery angel, cauterizes his mouth with a live coal and thereby overcomes his iniquity. It would seem then that unclean lips are a metaphor for sinfulness. The sinner cannot stand before God, and may not look upon him. The eyes of the seraphs who address God, and their lips that utter the trisagion (thrice holy) are pure. Having been purified, the prophet is now qualified to carry God's message. He has become holy. The cauterization of the lips and the removal of sin is not what makes him holy. This only makes him eligible to acquire holiness from God. As Otto tells us, holiness is a different dimension, a different category from innocence. However, we see here that the individual becomes able to acquire holiness once he becomes innocent.

The attribute of holiness and its requirements are emphasized repeatedly in the Bible, especially in Leviticus. But there is a note in Deuteronomy (23:14) that deserves attention. Among a long series of cultic, civil, and criminal regulations is a directive requiring soldiers about to embark upon a campaign against an enemy to provide for the hygiene of the camp. Namely, provision is to be made for the orderly separation and covering of excrement. "Since YHVH, your God, moves within your camp to protect you and deliver your enemies to you, therefore let your camp be holy; let Him see nothing unseemly among you, lest He turn away from you."

If we ask what in the experience of the young child this concern would suggest, we must conclude that it corresponds to the child's obligation to keep himself clean by proper toilet hygiene. One aspect of holiness then would be cleanliness and self-control. And derived from that would be nonmateriality in general, pure spirit. Consistent with this idea would be Psalm 24: "Who shall ascend the mountain of the Lord and who shall stand in His holy place? He who has clean hands and a pure heart." "Clean hands" here asks to be understood metaphorically, but it also has a literal meaning.

I am reminded of a fantasy given in Ḥagigah (16a), a tractate of the Babylonian Talmud that deals largely with mystical ideas.

Six things are said of human beings: in regard to three, they are like the ministering angels, and in regard to three, they are like the beasts. "In regard to three, they are like ministering angels": they have understanding like the ministering angels; and they walk erect like the ministering angels; and they could talk in the holy tongue like the ministering angels. "In regard to three, they are like beasts"; they eat and drink like beasts; and they propagate like beasts; and they relieve themselves like beasts.

In other words, humans resemble the angels in their holiness in that they have understanding, walk erect (so that they do not sniff excreta), and speak the holy tongue. These are potentially spiritual qualities. But in three respects humans resemble beasts, namely, they eat, propagate, and relieve themselves, and thereby compromise their potential holiness.

So what can we infer about the nature of holiness? It seems to be a quality (quale) inherent in the divine image, including its awesomeness, its grandeur, its majesty, its mysteriousness, its inscrutability, its power, and its purity. Purity refers here not only to speech but also to qualities of ritual and physical cleanliness, extended by the prophet and the psalmist to moral cleanliness. Perhaps holiness is coterminous with divinity, though it can be acquired by humans who qualify for it by personal and moral purity and respect for God.

CHAPTER 5

Brain

In recent years the popular press has reported "scientific findings" claiming that imaging procedures demonstrate that one or another area of brain is active at the time that spiritual and religious feelings are experienced. The frontal lobe, the parietal lobe, the temporal lobe, the amygdala, the hippocampus, and the cingulate cortex are the structures most frequently identified. Some have inferred that "science" has demonstrated the "reality" and validity of religious belief. More careful thinkers acknowledge only that the brain is responsible for all feelings no matter how they are generated, and therefore that these images tell us nothing about their external source.

Joseph (2001), D'Aquili and Newberg (1999), and Austin (1998), among others, have described spiritual experiences induced under observation, and they described the brain events that accompanied them. Although they and almost all others who have contributed to the field that has been called neurotheology acknowledge that they are recording only what happens in the brain concurrently with these experiences, nevertheless, some of these authors permit themselves to go beyond the facts. D'Aquili and Newberg (1999:193) for example, tell us, "since it is in principle impossible to determine which starting point is more fundamental, external reality or the awareness of the knower, one is forced to conclude that both conclusions about God are in a profound and fundamental sense true—namely, that God is created by the world (the brain and rest of the central nervous system) and that the world is created by God." And Joseph (2001:283) says, "However, trance states, isolation, fasting, prayer, meditation and LSD can free the mind of inhibitory restraint, producing not just dreamlike hallucinations, but by opening the mind to the full range of experience, so that what is concealed may be revealed."

What is clear is that spiritual experience, like all other experience, is accompanied by brain changes that some investigators consider specific and characteristic. These may occur spontaneously or they may be induced. What the data cannot tell us is whether these experiences put us in touch with a true external "reality" as the religious would like to believe, or reveal nothing about the "truth" of religion. It seems clear that one would have to go beyond the data to ascertain whether the experience and the brain changes that accompany it permit any inference whatever about an ultimate reality.

The problem of localization of brain function is a difficult one. Individual components of mental function and behavior are executed in fairly specific structures and known locations: speech in Broca's area, fine motor movement in the motor cortex of the contralateral cerebral hemisphere, primary visual reception in the occipital areas, long-term memory in the dorsolateral prefrontal cortex, and so on. However, any complex piece of behavior—and I would include spiritual experience in that category—involves much of the brain. For that reason, imaging studies are difficult to carry out and to interpret. While the dramatic component of the mystical exercise may be the hallucination, the full experience includes the process of instigation, usually internal; experiencing the affect; becoming aware of the hallucination or illusion; creating the specific image by condensing several old memories; perhaps some motor activity, such as assuming a prayerful posture, weeping, laughing, or smiling; sustaining autonomic changes such as alteration of heart rate and blood pressure; perhaps sexual feeling associated with the experience of love. Obviously large reaches of the brain participate in the total experience. Any imaging procedure that demonstrates that only one region is involved must be flawed and misleading.

If, as I contend, the spiritual quest expresses an instinctual need, in this case the need for emotional attachment, then the instinctual apparatus of the brain, involving some fairly archaic structures, must be active. The activation of instincts is influenced by what Panksepp (1998) calls the seeking system, which involves elements at the base of the brain, phylogenetically old, the limbic system. Cortical areas play roles such as reflection, self-observation, general sensation, vision, and hearing. The hippocampus contributes affective memory; the amygdala signals affect changes; the cingulate gyrus expresses affective activity and probably attention; the temporal lobe controls the degree of illusory distortion; and the ventromedial frontal lobe supervises realism and rationality. The idea of "localizing" spiritual experiences is itself illusory. In other words, the impetus for a spiritual quest arises in the motivational activities of the most archaic brain structures, either autonomously or in response to external stimulation or to internally felt needs associated with deprivation. Seeking appropriate gratification, the instinctual impulse engages sequentially those neural systems—each of which usually comprises several separate structures—that must be activated to secure gratification. So if an artificial, unnatural, or pathological impulse is applied to some responsive points along the path, the illusion of a spiritual experience may be created. Notice that this is different from the statement that the normal spiritual experience itself is an illusion. Whether one regards it as such depends upon belief in the objective existence of an external source—such as a divine entity—for the excitation of the experience. What I am describing is the illusion of a veridical spiritual experience elicited unnaturally by irritation or stimulation of the pathway that might appropriately lead to its realization, beyond the initial point of origin.

For example, Wilder Penfield and Herbert Jasper in their magisterial work, *Epilepsy and the Functional Anatomy of the Human*

Brain (1954), recorded the mental productions of epileptic patients whose brains they had stimulated during surgery. One patient, following a spontaneous seizure, stated that he was dead, that he was in the House of the Lord, and that he saw saints who were both violet and blue. He repeated a prayer over and over and subsequently recalled having had this impression and interpreted it as a dream that he was in heaven. He had been said by his father to have a tendency toward religious and "mystical" thinking. Another patient during her seizures would "dream" that she was in church or in a convent and hearing a song.

Similarly, Bear and Fedio (1977) have described interictal (between seizure) behavior in temporal lobe epilepsy. From reports of a number of investigators, they have put together a list of eighteen qualities that were said to have been observed more often as personality characteristics of patients with temporal lobe epilepsy. Among these are *"religiosity* which is defined as holding deep religious beliefs, often idiosyncratic, multiple conversions, mystical states; *philosophical interests* defined as nascent metaphysical or moral speculations, cosmological theories; and *dependence*, positively defined as cosmic helplessness, at the hands of fate, protestations of helplessness."

In Report 4 a man related that "some power" told him the solution to his problems, relieving him of his worry. He had not been particularly susceptible to spiritual experiences previously. Yet this experience exhibited the earmarks of having been genuine. It appeared against the background of a mild to moderate depressive state and resulted in a significant and appropriate act, a philanthropic contribution. But shortly thereafter he began to suffer almost constant, severe déjà vu experiences, which at times created delusions. He wrote to a newspaper columnist, asking why he had repeated columns that he had published previously, and did not believe him when the columnist denied that he had done so. He believed that he could predict stock market behavior since he remembered having seen the current market situation previously. Déjà vu phenomena often result from temporal lobe damage. Because the patient was suffering from a serious dry eye problem, otherwise unexplained, Sjogrens syndrome was considered. It is often accompanied by cerebral lesions. Although no evidence of brain damage could be found on clinical, radiologic, and electroencephalographic examination, the severe déjà vu phenomenon raises a serious question about structural damage. Was the mystical experience nothing more than the manifestation of abnormal brain function, or, in view of the depressive background and appropriate subsequent behavior, was the mystical experience generated naturally? Given the data, my best guess is that both may be true, namely, that given a difficult problem during a depressive state that might have favored a spiritual resolution, the brain lesion reduced the threshold for the initiation of the mystical experience. A few weeks after the first experience, the man described a second mystical experience of lesser intensity.

The individual personality disorder associated with temporal lobe epilepsy, mentioned above (see also Schomer, O'Connor, Spiers, Seeck, Mesulam, and Bear 2000), suggests similarly that damaged temporal lobe structures that can sometimes give rise to seizures may in the interictal state influence personality on a continuing basis, including the favoring of "religious" behavior and interests.

Persinger (1987), for example, argues for the idea that what he calls the God Experience, is nothing but the consequence of transitory, random, electrical stimuli, eliciting responses from those temporal lobe structures that give rise to the perturbations of the parameters of space, time, and reality that are generally associated with spiritual experience. I find that kind of argument unacceptable.

First, we do not infer that the precentral motor cortex (the area on the surface of the brain that lies just in front of the major fissure that divides the front of the brain from the back, the Rolandic sulcus) is the source of the initiative to move one's limbs, just because stimulation of points in that region elicits muscle movement. We understand that wherever motivation originates, it engages the motor cortex on its path to execution. The same argument applies to the temporal lobe. That stimulation of points on or in the temporal lobe yields phenomena that we associate with spirituality means only that the neurons of that region lie on the path to execution of the spiritual endeavor.

Second, spiritual and religious experiences play an important role in the lives of many individuals and cannot be thought of as epiphenomena without instrinsic meaning—as a seizure is. Of course, it is well known that experiences determined by autonomous activity or the consequences of brain damage are often misinterpreted as volitional. But these are interruptive segments that intrude into psychic life and are easily recognized by the observer as extraneous. Spirituality, for the susceptible individual, may occupy a central place in conscious life. It is imbricated in the whole personality and can no more be thought of as an epiphenomenon than the rest of conscious life and personality. There is, after all, a certain solace in spiritual retreat from reality; it is a comforting experience.

Persinger lists the several conditions that favor spirituality: physiological stress and dysfunction, the low oxygen level associated with heights, the low blood sugar associated with fasting, dysregulation of endocrine and autonomic systems, changes in lifestyle. Mystical adepts know about the physiological stresses that favor mystical experiences and use fasting and isolation to invite mystical transport. "Changes in lifestyle" include important separations, frustrations, threats, and discomforts, which are usually the circumstances that trigger spiritual experience. And I would argue that they do so because they disrupt important emotional attachments and frustrate other instincts—not because they generate hypothetical "electrical transients" in the temporal lobe. These changes require compensatory repair such as what the spiritual can bring.

At the same time it is necessary to reject the claims of those who would see the hallucinatory mystical states described in the Bible and other classical religious literature as nothing more than temporal lobe seizures or even psychosis. I refer especially to the vivid phenomena described by Ezekiel and Isaiah and by medieval and modern mystics. Authentic mystical experiences, initiated by the deep sources of the attachment instincts, may achieve expression by activating temporal lobe mechanisms naturally, without the assistance of seizure activity.

To summarize, we don't have much to say that is specific about the brain's creation of the spiritual experience. Arising as an expression of the attachment instinct, it must originate in the instinctual apparatus, which presumably is mediated in the brain stem, a small, crowded area that creates motivation, but relatively nonspecifically. From there the pathways ascend to the limbic area, that is, the phylogenetically old region of the brain, where they engage the affective apparatus that brings the instinctual tendency into fulfillment, providing felt affective desire and affective caution and inhibition. But before execution, the stream of instinctual activity rises to the neocortical, the most advanced level, where it receives relatively sophisticated, detailed information about the environment and is subject to practical, social, or moral authority, encouragement, and restraint. From the temporal lobe it seems to receive the specific illusory qualities of space, time, reality, and familiarity. The activation of these parameters by appropriate displays and perceptions creates or contributes to the experience of awe, and thence to reverence and thence to spirituality.

Nothing in this process is specific to spirituality except that the instinct involved is the attachment instinct, the earliest instinct to appear that engages another person, and the specific quality of illusion contributed by the temporal lobe. The overlay of religious mythology, belief, and social and cultural organization are probably contributed by the prefrontal areas of the neocortex. The areas designated as cingulate and ventromedial cortex are always active in conscious affective experience, but at this point we can't say what they contribute specifically to the spiritual.

In a very recent report of some experimental data relating to the neuroscientific basis of spirituality, Borg et al. (2003) claim that "the serotonin system may serve as a biological basis for spiritual experiences." The authors speculated that the several-fold variability in 5-HT 1A (serotonin) receptor density observed may explain why people vary greatly in spiritual zeal.

While the method is questionable and the argument is not very powerful, the strength of the reported correlation seems impressive enough to be taken seriously, and the proposed hypothesis, whether or not validated, leads to interesting conclusions.

I find two major problems with the study. First, the presence of "spirituality" in the fifteen male subjects was determined by their responses to a "Temperament and Character Inventory," a self-report questionnaire. A "self-transcendence" scale was strongly influenced by one of its components, the "spiritual acceptance" scale, which measures a "person's apprehension of phenomena that cannot be explained by objective demonstration." "Subjects with high scores tend to endorse extrasensory perception and ideation, whether named deities or a commonly unifying force. Low scores, by contrast, tend to favor a reductionist and empirical worldview." I quote the original essay to make clear that the concept of "spirituality" the author employs is fairly fuzzy by contrast with the sharper, more precise descriptions I have introduced.

The other variable, "the serotonin system," is equally problematic. The study investigates the activity of serotonin at its 1A receptor in the brain, only one of fourteen serotonin receptors. Further, what is measured is the 5HT 1A binding potential in each of three regions of the brain (dorsal raphe nuclei, hippocampal formation, and neocortex). The problem is that the functional significance of receptor density is obscure. "In subjects with high spiritual acceptance scores, a key question is whether the observation of low 5HT 1A receptor levels corresponds to low or high activity in serotonergic cortical projection areas. Currently the literature provides support for both interpretations."

The reason I describe the drawbacks of the study is that the results, if they can be duplicated and if they are powerful enough to overcome the handicaps, are both interesting and instructive. The authors report an impressive inverse correlation between the degree of "spirituality" as they define it and serotonin receptor density. What does it mean? As the authors note, we don't know whether a high receptor density means a high or low degree of serotonin activity.

They remind the reader, however, that many hallucinogenic drugs "cause perturbations of the serotonin system in several brain regions." "On a behavioral level these drugs elicit perceptual distortions, illusions, a sense of insight, spiritual awareness, mystical experiences, and religious ecstasy. Of interest, such pharmacological effects induced by hallucinogens resemble the extrasensory perception and ideation endorsed by subjects scoring high on the spiritual acceptance scale." So these chemical agents that are known to influence brain serotonin activity can induce sensations, perceptions, and thoughts that remind a person of the experiences that may be grouped under the general heading of spiritual.

Why do I find these proposed correlations so interesting that I am willing, provisionally at least, to overlook the limitations of the experimental observations and the conclusions drawn from them?

Because if the correlation is valid, then we learn something important about the state of the ego that is associated with spiritual experience.

The brain is constantly active. When and where brain neural activity becomes conscious, it induces mental imagery. Perception is a process, not simply of recording what is there but also of searching in the environment for percepts of instinctual interest; the more salient the instinctual need, the greater the sensitivity to such stimuli. So when the need for the comfort of the earliest maternal love becomes strong, the individual will become sensitive to whatever might reproduce that experience. The stronger the instinctual claim, the more sensitively will the perceptual apparatus search the environment. We begin by responding to percepts that only approximate those we seek. We may mistake a passerby for someone we miss. But when the pursuit becomes strong enough, we see images and perceive objects even in their absence: we hallucinate. Spiritual and religious experiences are either perceptions of divine influence—as the religious world declares—or purely illusory, hallucinations, as the secular world claims. In either case, an unusual perception is recorded in response to an unusually strong need or desire.

The experiment I have described encourages us to add another dimension to the parameters that determine the individual's openness to spiritual experience. The authors argue that individuals vary in their sensitivity to percepts in general; in their readiness to create illusions or hallucinations. That seems a reasonable argument, and it suggests that as individuals vary in their perceptual sensitivity, so they vary in their sensitivity to spiritual experience. That conclusion stands, whether or not—as the authors claim—it is the availability of serotonin at the 1A receptor that determines perceptual sensitivity and therefore spiritual inclination. Note that in most examples of spiritual experience that I have given, there is some comment on the vividness of the percepts associated with the feeling of spirituality.

To quote the authors further, "a common view is that variability in religious behavior among people is determined by environmental and cultural differences. However a twin and adoption study has reported that genetic variation contributes about fifty percent of individual variation in religiosity, thereby suggesting a biological underpinning. The findings of the present study may provide support for biological underpinnings specifically related to the central serotonergic system."

The reference is to a paper by Bouchard et al. (1990). Bouchard and his associates examined 35 pairs of monozygotic twins reared apart and 37 pairs of dizygotic twins reared apart, with respect to traits that they call intrinsic and extrinsic religiousness. They found "significant heritability (0.43 and 0.39 respectively). In other words, their data suggest that religious interest, whether personal and spiritual or community affiliations, are communicated from parent to child on the basis of genetic as well as environmental influences.

I have attempted to establish that the biological basis of spirituality and therefore of religion resides in the attachment instincts. But we can say more about how the attachment system functions. Not all instincts are active all the time. They have to be activated and released and they are usually extinguished with consummation. Sexual and nutritional instincts, for example, remain extinguished until the need for reactivation reaches a threshold. The inactive instinct may be reactivated by a disturbance of the appropriate homeostatic equilibrium, for example, hunger, and the instinctual need to eat is activated by low blood sugar. The sexual instincts are activated by the influence of the sexual hormones. The attachment instinct clamors for satisfaction when the infant is separated from his mother. Panksepp (1998) has established that desperate separation cries are emitted by lower mammals and even young chicks.

Attachment is necessary for humans of all ages. After infancy the need for it is not quite so desperate, but important nevertheless. Parental attachment, filial attachment, social attachment are ultimately independent needs, but often combine so that husband and wife, over the years, adhere as they play the role of parent, child, and friend to each other. The sexual instinct also drives attachment behavior intensely. But by itself, it is extinguished with each consummation and does not establish enduring connections. Lasting attachments that are also sexual are created when the sexual attachment and social, friendly attachments are combined. Absent that combination, monogamous attachments, marriage, could not survive.

If my argument that the spiritual experience strives to reproduce the infant and young child's experience of being attached to the mother or later, the father or siblings is accurate, then the spiritual experience must be seen as the expression of an instinct and therefore characterized by the usual properties of instinctual behavior. Since attachment need is activated by separation and isolation, it is reasonable to expect that spirituality will also be encouraged by separation, as many of the case examples have shown.

The activation of an instinct differs from its release. Activation means readiness, and an instinct may be primed and ready for discharge, but ordinarily the discharge will not occur except in the presence of an adequate releaser. For example, an individual may be sexually motivated, but except under unusual circumstances, will not attempt sexual contact except in the presence of an attractive and available partner. But sometimes, when the individual has had no opportunity for sexual activity for a relatively long time, discharge will occur nevertheless, on a physiological level, for example by nocturnal orgasm (usually accompanied by an appropriate dream), or on a behavioral level, for example by masturbation. Spiritual expression may be compared to overflow discharge of sexual and other instincts. Separation, literal or figurative, releases the attachment instinct, which is always ready to be active in subjects in good health, or in good enough health to respond to separation with eagerness to attach. In the case of an awesome experience, the vista is enough to release the instinct and create the feeling of being attached to a giant, inviting, maternal body. However, the spontaneous Spiritual experience or the mystical hallucination can be compared to an overflow phenomenon. The need is so strong that, in the absence of an adequate releaser, the individual generates a feeling, image, or voice that seems to fulfill his desire. This is where serotonin comes in—if it does. That is, low serotonin level in the relevant portion of the brain facilitates oversensitivity so that the subject feels, perceives, believes that his attachment needs are being met. This is a descriptive view. The religious individual will see the phenomenon as the result of being sensitized to authentic, divine communication.

Since I have been arguing that the spiritual need is driven by attachment instincts, it would be appropriate to say a few words about the biology of attachment. In 1969, Bowlby described attachment behavior in the context of psychoanalytic theory, and the behavioral results of separation in 1973. These two volumes may be consulted for the theoretical psychoanalytic background and the relevant observations. The brain events that yield this affiliative behavior are no clearer than the neural activity that gives rise to other instincts. Although Bowlby and later students of the subject promoted material attachment to designate the existence of emotional ties, those ties had been mentioned frequently in psychoanalytic literature previously, in *Inhibitions, Symptoms and Anxiety* (1926). Freud's understanding there is that the anxiety that appears when the child is separated from the mother signals helplessness and the loss of access to supplies (168 ff.). Bowlby's contribution is the idea that attachment itself is an instinctual need, not simply a device to prevent helplessness (see Ostow 1955).

Alternatively, attachment behavior may be regarded, not as an independent instinct, but as appetitive behavior intended to facilitate the execution of true instincts. No instinct that requires the cooperation of two or more animals (including humans) can be gratified unless they are brought into approximation, usually by instinctive attachment. It would make sense therefore to regard attachment as a kind of platform that brings the actors together so that the prevailing instincts can be successfully executed. For example, the mother-infant attachment is vital because it permits the fulfillment of the appropriate instincts of both the infant and the mother to be gratified. Similarly, erotic attachment permits the complete gratification of the erotic instinct. From this point of view, attachment can be considered an enabling appetitive device that functions to facilitate the proper fulfillment of those instincts that require approximation for their gratification.

A relevant observation has been reported by Panksepp (1998). Opiates are derivatives of opium that are used clinically to reduce pain in illness. Panksepp has administered opiates to young mammals and birds and demonstrated that these substances diminish separation distress vocalization. Presumably opiates diminish emotional distress much as they diminish physical pain. Substances chemically similar to opiates, called opioids, are found in the brain. While it has been conventional among those experimenting with these substances to assume that stress itself elicits secretion of opioids, Seeger et al. (1984) have demonstrated that the opioid secretion comes with the offset of the stress, i.e., that the release of the opioid contributes to the reward that the animal experiences for escaping the pain. Opioids, in other words, signal relaxation, a reduction of effort. Panksepp (personal communication) wonders whether they "may denervate one's spiritual resources, leaving only coarse feelings of dominance and pleasure. Opioid antagonists may open up the gates of submission to more spiritual points of view."

If we cannot say more about the brain specifically, we can say more about the biology of behavior that is associated with spirituality. In the section on religion above, I mentioned the instinctual basis of some religious behavior, sacrifice, submission, prayer, and blessing. Even raw instinct can give rise to fairly complex behavior, and when that is refined, carefully directed and fine tuned, the result can appear so complex as to seem calculated and contrived rather than instinctual. In *The Creation of the Sacred*, Walter Burkert (1996) has attempted to discern "tracks of biology in the early religions." It is difficult to imagine that awe, Spirituality proper, or mysticism has any biological survival value. Not every biological function has survival value. Does aesthetic sensitivity? From deprivation experiments we know that both slow wave sleep and rapid eye movement sleep accomplish necessary functions, and we know that the experience of dreaming is physiologically necessary, but we don't understand its specific function. The experience of each of the spiritual states is usually associated with either positive or negative affect. What prevails is what is determined by prevailing mood. But we don't know that the experience in either case confers significant physiological or psychological advantage. There are claims that religious commitment improves physical health and augments life expectancy (see Koenig 1997). However, there are as many counterclaims, and those who claim a wholesome effect do not take into account the *post hoc propter hoc* fallacy. It is only reasonable to expect that seriously ill people who maintain morale are more likely to exhibit interest in religion than those who become demoralized and despairing. Also, the misanthropic, the paranoid, those who live a solitary life probably enjoy a shorter life expectancy than others and are less likely to become committed members of a religious community.

But religion is a culturally constructed system, voluntarily accepted by large masses of humanity, so we must assume that it is at least gratifying and possibly also useful from the point of view of biological advantage. However, we do not have to infer that all of its manifestations and practices are equally useful. Some may be survivals of archaic mechanisms visible in lower animals; others may be only symbolically useful. Does praying for a long life actually result in greater longevity?

What benefit, if any, accrues from participation in the religious enterprise? As we have seen, religion comprises many different elements. We may ask that question with respect to individual spirituality in each of its variants. And we may ask it about the communal aspect of religious participation. The element of benefit too must be understood in terms of simple pleasure, relief from distress, or ultimate evolutionary value.

The professionals of religion would like to encourage religious feelings and participation purely out of spiritual wish and yearning for religious gratification. And yet the scriptures encourage us by the prospect of reward and punishment. While many religions promise healing, some movements even encourage the belief that they actually achieve healing.

Pargament (1997), in *The Psychology of Religion and Coping*, presents an extended and sophisticated review of the literature on the usefulness of religion in daily life together with many quotations from that literature and from his own private practice. He includes an appendix summarizing the results of about 250 studies of the effect of religion on people coping with various stresses. Some results were clearly negative, other clearly positive, and most positive with respect to improvement of morale but with little evidence of objective improvement.

Burkert (1996) suggests that ritual sacrifice is a practice intended to propitiate an angry deity, as though he were a pursuing, vicious predator. That explanation would apply to human sacrifice and animal sacrifice, but also to semisymbolic rites such as ritual circumcision, which replaces ritual castration and was practiced by special *galloi* of the ancient Near East, and perhaps infanticide. Recall the story of the circumcision of Moses's son by his wife Zipporah to save the child from the wrath of YHVH, who is described as though he were a desert demon (Exodus 4:24–26). That story resonates with the account in Genesis 17, in which God establishes his covenant with Abraham (then Abram), promising him progeny and protection and expecting in return ritual circumcision, subsequently known in Jewish tradition as the sign of the covenant. This covenantal pericope is inserted between the account of the birth of Ishmael and the birth of Isaac, soon after Abraham's circumcision. The circumcision of the covenant is not merely apotropaic; it secures God's favor, namely the promise of progeny. Nonetheless, Isaac's life is later threatened by God's demand that he be sacrificed. The sacrifice is aborted as God relents and, in return for Abraham's willingness, again promises flourishing progeny (which would have had been precluded by Isaac's death) and possession of the land. This theme is developed further in chapter 8.

A hierarchy of authority prevails among men and the higher primates. Authority is granted to the largest members of the society, to the most powerful, and to those who are close to them. God and the ruler are praised as powerful, mighty, long-lived, omniscient, and omnipotent. Authority is symbolized by height and erect posture, whereas the commoner is seen as smaller, weaker, and submissive, bowing and genuflecting. In Isaiah 6, God sits on an elevated throne. Praising the god, offering submissiveness and subservience, and singing to him are all means of soliciting His favor and precluding divine wrath.

Gestures and postures of submission are seen in intraspecies combat where one animal is about to be vanquished by the other. The surrender arrests the attack. Very similar behavior occurs among humans.

As noted above, the adult parent presents an awesome aspect to the infant, whether gratifying or frightening, and becomes a prototype and paradigm of all authority to the infant grown to adulthood. The infant yearns to be raised to the mother's shoulder, to look into her face. For this reason the gods are seen as enormous, and their customary abode is the mountains or the heavens, or—referring to the mother's lap and her body—the cavelike temple.

Without being able to be too specific, we can say that our brains are so constructed as to resonate to facial expression, glances, voice, gesture, and music with the brains of those around us, so that we tend to cohere into groups and societies. The need to reach out to others is so strong that it extends to animals and upward to virtual companions, spiritual entities, the images of ancestors, and even at times to mythological spirits. The coherence of many minds in a grand cooperative endeavor mobilizes powerful energies and subjective exhilaration. However, as is the case with all other instinctually driven activities, intrinsic braking mechanisms come into play at a certain point and result in self-destructive overreaching, group fragmentation, leadership disputes, and so on that have, at least up to this point, prevented any unimpeded domination of the planet. The story of the Tower of Babel in Genesis chapter 11 (1–9) illustrates both the power of the fantasy of collective endeavor and its limits.

CHAPTER 6

Mood Regulation

Let us examine another aspect of my claim that spirituality has an affective basis. Its evocation depends upon, and in turn influences, mood. Mood is the affective background of all conscious experience. We usually take it for granted and don't notice it unless it draws attention by unusual intensity, inappropriateness, or duration. Mood may be overridden by affect that is elicited by an external event or by an internal need, and in turn, the mood may favor a congruent affect. My intention in this chapter is to describe mood fluctuation and how it influences susceptibility to spiritual experience, and especially how it is influenced or corrected by spiritual experience.

(REPORT 11)

A spiritually sensitive Protestant minister complained, while he was depressed, that he felt "screwed into the ground," expressing metaphorically the sense that his spirituality was arrested or, as I

understand it, that he was no longer sensitive to spiritual experience. When, as a result of treatment, he began to recover, he felt
his spirituality liberated. However, when he felt fully recovered
from depression, he again complained of a lack of spiritual sensitivity. Months later, when the effects of the medication began
to subside, he observed a return of spirituality, at least until he
relapsed fully, at which point he felt once more "screwed into
the ground."

From this and other similar instances, one may infer that susceptibility to spiritual experience is a function of mood. Let's
check this observation against the examples in the earlier chapters
of this book. In Report 1, the paradigmatic example, the subject
was surprised by what happened. He had been feeling lonely as
a result of the separation from his wife and perhaps also the anniversary of his mother's death. We can assume a feeling of yearning, of longing, to which the spiritual experience responded. The
woman in Report 2 was in search of spiritual experience when she
set out to climb Mount Sinai, praying as she ascended. What she
saw was spiritually exciting, as she expected it to be. The physical
ascent left her affectively elevated too. She set out into an expectant mood, found what she was looking for, and "felt wonderful"
for days thereafter.

The woman described in Report 3 was not alone, but was separated from her family. The scene that stimulated her was joyous
and the people she was with were happy, as was she. The excitement made her affectively sensitive to an appreciation of a transcendent deity.

Report 4 tells of a gentleman who was unexpectedly overcome
by a mystical experience at a time of despondency in the course of
a manic-depressive career, contemplating his death. He felt that he
was in contact with "some power" that communicated a solution
for his problem. His mood was lifted by the experience.

In the account of Saint Teresa's experience there is nothing of her
mood, but she was known to suffer illness, probably psychiatric,
and, since it was recurrent but not continuously disabling, probably affective. She found the experience extremely gratifying: "and
so excessive was the sweetness caused me by this intense pain that

one can never wish to lose it, nor will one's soul be content with anything less than God."

The instance taken from William James, Report 6, concludes with the following affective statement: "In the years following, such moments continued to come, but I wanted them consistently. I knew so well the satisfaction of losing self in a perception of supreme power and love, that I was unhappy that the perception was not constant."

The woman in the seventh report observed, "When I began the evening, I was feeling discouraged," in contrast to the sense of elevation that the mystical encounter had induced.

Report 8 tells of a young woman who was overwhelmed by spiritual excitement as a member of a large group of people, following the victory of the Israeli army in the war of 1967, moving eastward into the rising sun toward the recaptured sacred site of the ruins of the ancient Temple. She found it an inexpressibly exalting feeling.

This review of the exemplary accounts considered shows that those experiences not elicited by the specific, inspiring circumstances are usually preceded by a feeling of longing, reaching out, hope. The experience seems to be a response to the hope. In each of the instances quoted, the experience was followed by a strong feeling of relief or gratification, even elevation and excitement. It is clear that this spiritual experience performed a specific function of elevating the subject's mood, certainly for the moment, but for some, for day and weeks thereafter.

Yet in Otto's accounts, we see a somewhat more variegated description (1966:12 f.).

If we do so we shall find we are dealing with something for which there is only one appropriate expression, "mysterium tremendum." The feeling of it may at times come sweeping like a gentle tide, pervading the mind with a tranquil mood of deepest worship. It may pass over into a more set and lasting attitude of the soul, continuing, as it were, thrillingly vibrant and resonant, until at last it dies away and the soul resumes its "profane," non-religious mood of everyday experience. It may burst in sudden eruption up from the depths of the soul with spasms and convulsions, or lead to the strangest excitements, to intoxicated frenzy, to transport, and to ecstasy. It has its wild and demonic forms and can sink to an almost grisly horror and shuddering. It has its crude, barbaric antecedents and early manifestations, and again it may be developed into something beautiful and pure and glorious. It may become the hushed, trembling, and speechless humility of the creature in the presence of—whom or what? In the presence of that which is a mystery inexpressible and above all creatures.

Otto describes these feelings specifically as religious rather than more generally spiritual. The term he selects, "mysterium tremendum," suggests something more troubling, even frightening, than the benign accounts presented in this book. And he includes "wild and demonic forms," which "can sink to an almost grisly horror and shuddering." I quoted, after the other examples, a description given by Albert Schweitzer, cited by Phyllis Greenacre. Specifically, he recalls from childhood the image of the face of the devil, "terrifying and awful," yet "with some pleasure in it too."

I have not encountered among my patients or in other accounts many instances of anxiety promoting spiritual experience, nor are there many in James's examples. Apparently Otto was dealing with a different population and probably he reported some of his own experiences.

In the classical literature of religious spirituality and mysticism, such frightening scenarios do occur. For example, in the literature of Hekhaloth mysticism (Chamber mysticism; see Isaiah 6), the ascent to heaven is blocked by horses that serve as gatekeepers. According to the description, they are "angry and warlike, strong, harsh, fearsome, terrific, taller than mountains and sharper than peaks. Their bows are strung and stand before them; their swords are sharpened and in their hands. Lightening flows and issues forth from the balls of their eyes, and balls of fire from their nostrils, and tortures of fiery coals from their mouths. They are equipped with coats of mail, and javelins and spears are hung upon their thews."

Why are some spiritual experiences gratifying and others frightening? In the literature of Merkavah mysticism (Chariot mysticism; see Ezekiel 1), the outcome of the descent to the chariot depends upon the state of mind of the aspirant. When he is properly prepared, that is, when he is in a state of ritual and spiritual purity, possesses the requisite seals, and recites the appropriate hymns and incantations, his quest will be rewarded. But if he attempts the approach to the merkavah without proper preparation, the fierce angels guarding it will attack and destroy him.

Translated into contemporary psychological language, the statement seems correct. The outcome of the spiritual quest depends upon the preparation of the questing individual, that is, his psychological preparation in terms of mood. When the subject is yearning for uplift and in the state of mind in which he can properly respond to a spiritual experience, he will find the experience gratifying. Any illusions or hallucinations that accompany it will conform to the mood. When, however, the depressive pull is excessively strong, it will oppose the redemptive tendency of the spiritual endeavor; the latter will fail and will be experienced as a terrifying threat of destruction, or even eventuate in a period of frank depression of short or long duration.

Such dynamics can be seen in the dreams of manic-depressives or borderline patients, that is, when a depressive pull creates a feeling of crisis, the dream may portray some mood-elevating endeavor, a desired recognition, a claim for a reciprocation of love, or vocational success, so that the subject will awaken with a feeling of relief or even elevation. However, when the depressive tendency is too strong, the dream will take a nasty turn, and the hoped-for pleasurable gratification will give way to defeat or even death and destruction. The dream, like the spiritual experience, will reflect the balance of the forces regulating mood.

Mood is a continuing emotional background of life upon which all of the brief emotional perturbations are superimposed. It influences which opportunities we embrace, how strongly we react to frustrations and threats, and what distortions are imposed upon the perceptible stimuli presented to us. When we are in a good mood, we embrace life enthusiastically, think creatively and hopefully, and present a joyous appearance to others. When we are in a bad mood, we fail to appreciate opportunities, lack imagination, and are overcome by pessimism, if not despair. But a bad mood might sometimes generate hope. Under certain circumstances we can hope for improvement and respond to opportunities that might permit it. And there are occasions when, in a good mood, we nevertheless become apprehensive that things might deteriorate.

Obviously mood is influenced by the external forces that impinge upon us. Pleasant experiences, gratifications, the achievement of goals, reciprocation of affection, can all evoke pleasant feelings, which, for a longer or shorter period, will overcome a prevailing bad mood. Other events can cause distress and unhappiness that may briefly overcome a good mood or reinforce a bad one. All of this is self-evident.

What is not generally appreciated, however, is the fact that even in the absence of relevant external influence, mood fluctuates, solely as result of inner psychic or neurophysiologic changes. These fluctuations are usually rhythmic. Ordinarily they are so subtle as to escape observation. However, if one records an analytic session, that is, a subject's spontaneous, unrestrained, continual account of what goes through his mind, one will often find fairly clear-cut, unstimulated alterations of mood, especially in patients with mood volatility. At times, when the mood changes are more pronounced or more abrupt, we become aware of them ourselves. On some occasions, during a dream, we may notice a sudden shift from pleasant to unpleasant or vice versa. So not only prevailing mood but also its fluctuations may determine our perception of how we see the world and how we react to it.

Presumably, as the mood shifts in one direction, for example, upward toward euphoria, a counteractive tendency comes into play, and at a given boundary, reverses the mood downward. Similarly, as the mood declines toward depression, an upward reversal comes into play. So long as the mood remains within the range of normal, we see no more than the common fluctuations of daily life. However, when it transgresses the range of normality, either pathologic depression or mania ensues.

Each affect disease—depression, mania, bipolar disease, borderline personality disorder, the affect component of attention deficit disorder, cyclothymic personality disorder, depressive neurosis—is characterized by excessive mood swings. When the mood deviates in one direction and remains fixed there, we speak of depression or mania. However, the system can fail in permitting excessively frequent, extreme deviations. That is, the pathology consists of volatility, not merely extremeness.

We know something about the basic physiology of this process. From the evidence of psychopharmacology, we know that providing a drug that increases the availability of neurotransmitters called dopamine and/or norepinephrine will usually alleviate depression. Dopamine provides the energy for a neural system described by Jaak Panksepp (1998) that seems to keep in a state of readiness the various instincts that maintain our individual, social, and sexual lives. That neural function seems to correspond closely to Freud's description of what he called libido, that is, a kind of psychic energy.

Depression can also be alleviated by drugs that increase the amount of a neurotransmitter called serotonin. That is an inhibitory substance rather than an activating one. Therefore we must infer that depression involves not only a relative deficiency of an energizing substance like dopamine or norepinephrine but also an excess of a depressing force that can be suppressed by serotonin. We do not know or have any indication of the nature of this depressing force. At the time of this writing, several pharmaceutical companies are reporting promising results with various substances that block the action of a hormone called corticotrophin releasing factor (CRF), which induces the secretion of adrenocorticotrophic hormone (ACTH), which in turn induces the secretion of cortisone and similar steroids in the cortex of the adrenal gland. CRF by itself can induce all these symptoms of stress and depression, but when cortisone is elaborated, the distress is replaced by euphoria. So perhaps the depressing influence, the force that reverses upward fluctuations of mood and in excess, contributes to the genesis of depression, is driven by CRF. But all of this is speculative, and by the time these words reach the reader, the physiology of mood regulation may have been more definitively elucidated.

I have described the function of mood regulation in this much detail because, as we have seen, mood influences spiritual orientation and receptiveness, how ready the individual is for spiritual experience and whether it is gratifying or frightening. In Report 11, a minister felt "screwed to the ground" when he was either low or high, but fully spiritual even when he was sinking into depression or rising out of it. In fact, except when depressed or manic, we do not spend much time at the extremes of the mood swing. Mostly we are either feeling increasingly better or increasingly worse. It is in these states of mood, or tension between euphoric and depressive extremes, within which we live most of the time, that we most welcome spiritual experience. In fact, it is usually in the state of resisting depression rather than rising out of it that the spiritual tendency proper is gratified. Mystical experience may also be facilitated by the experience of rising toward hypomanic or manic euphoria.

This process of mood regulation that I have been describing is not too difficult to visualize, but it becomes much more vivid in the dreams of patients with affect illness, or on the verge of becoming ill. Let me cite here some illustrative material (cited in *Ultimate Intimacy* 1995).

> I got up at 1 a.m. It was very light because of an amusement park nearby that had bluish lights. It was like dawn. I thought I saw lightning, but it was yellowish, like firecrackers. They arched high and came down in a starburst, like a chrysanthemum. Up and down, one after the other. One came near me. It bounced like a tennis ball. We watched a long time. It must [have been] the end of the day, and that's why they had fireworks.

The dream exhibits tension between depression and elevating forces. The patient reports that she saw lightning but then discovered that she had seen nothing dangerous, only firecrackers.

The flaring firecrackers arched high and came down. One bounced like a tennis ball. The rising and falling and rhythmic bouncing reflect the mood fluctuations, which were taking place in the dream. Presumably fluctuations occur at considerably higher frequency in dreams than during waking life.

> I was with mother at our home outdoors, in the evening. Suddenly the northern lights were in the sky, soft and lovely. I said, "How lovely!" They got more and more colorful and violent. They colored the whole sky. Suddenly it was a great bomb attack with missiles. The sky was flooded with falling objects. I hurried her indoors. We were covered with ash and incurably contaminated

by it. It was radioactive fallout. We got into the house. I tried to wash myself off.

This dream starts with a "lovely" reunion with the mother, but the heavenly display quickly becomes a bomb attack with radioactive fallout. The dream reflects an abrupt mood change from happy reunion to poisonous destruction.

> The world was being flooded. The water was reddish and gray-ish. It was turbulent with white crests. I saw rocks and houses. People were drowning. We were on a high level, where there were white houses, I was on a boat—a nice boat, large with blond wood lacquer floors. There was a kitchen on the boat. I became concerned that it would capsize. We landed at a house on some land. We brought things onto the boat, glasses, no, plastic cups for fear that they might break, and food.
>
> What's the point of living if you're going to drown? I thought of suicide and became calmer. No, I said, there is always hope. If you die now, you eliminate hope.
>
> I saw some people drowning, some with hands raised, some protesting, some peacefully.

The dream started on a depressive note: a flood, people drowning in bloody water. The dreamer finds security on a boat, but her depressive tendency threatens her with the possibility of capsizing. She has the boat reach land, where she replenishes the food supply. But the depressive mood reasserts itself in thoughts of suicide. She comforts herself with hope but sees others drowning. The dream reproduces an ancient myth, one version of which is expressed in the Noah's ark story. Unlike the dream, the latter ends with signs of rebirth, the dove's finding food and refuge, the actual landing of the ark, and God's promise that He will never again attempt to destroy the world by floodwater, and His instructions to man to produce progeny. He designates the rainbow as the eternal promise of rebirth.

I add, parenthetically, that the aspect of the dream that most faithfully reflects the subject's waking life is the affect. For this reason dreams are very helpful for the psychopharmacological monitoring of affect and for regulation of medication.

At the beginning of this section I recorded the obvious fact that mood is strongly influenced by the things that influence our lives, gratifications, frustrations, temptations, threats. Then I described a rhythmic oscillation of mood that I presume affects mood regulation. As the subject becomes sober, sad, depressed, a corrective movement sets in and tends to reverse the mood to contentment and happiness. And similarly, as the subject becomes too ebullient, his mood is automatically corrected downward.

These two sources of influence on mood may run parallel or may collide. For example, if a depressing threat appears, the patient may at first resist it with some antidepression maneuver, a subjective change in mood or an action that may offset the threat and change the mood to one of greater optimism. In other words, the response to threat or actual stress occurs in two phases, first resistance, and if that is not successful, then defeat.

I am reminded of the dream reported to me by a manic-depressive patient as he was slipping into a depressive state. He saw himself standing against an attacking army, prepared to fight. He quickly abandoned his weapons and walked away. Here we see an abrupt change in mood in the dream from readiness to resist the adversarial forces of depression to resignation.

My argument is confirmed by the response to a chemical depressing agent. The antipsychosis drugs, which are also antimanic, are basically dopamine blockers. When administered in relatively small doses, especially in resilient patients, they result in improvement in mood, sometimes complete relief from depression. The patient successfully resists the small increment in depression, and reverses it.

However, when the dose is increased to that recommended for the treatment of psychosis or mania, the patient's resistance is overcome and he becomes fully depressed. In fact, at a dose slightly greater than the initial small dose that activates antidepression rebound, the drug often subdues the active depressing agency, whatever that may be, so that the symptoms of depression are alleviated, though in some cases the inertia and anhedonia may remain. Only at the usual antimanic dose is depression definitively reinforced.

Let me restate the argument somewhat differently. Mood is ordinarily permitted to oscillate within a fairly narrow range. However, during the course of the day, we each encounter opportunities and frustrations, gratifications and threats that affect our mood. We tend to resist depressing influences by both trying to do whatever will overcome the threats and by reorienting ourselves so as to regain equanimity. To some extent we do these things deliberately and to some extent automatically, even unconsciously. We tend to reinforce and extend the opportunity for gratification, but unconsciously, the regulating forces may temper the gratification and limit efforts to augment it, and even contrive behavior and mood changes that function to reverse the pleasure. Most of these mental operations are unconscious. Not everything that seems to befall us is accidental. To a greater extent than we realize, we make our own fate. These operations are much more visible in patients who are abnormally volatile than in the rest of the population. The unwitting self-defeating or self-destructive activities of presumably successful individuals are the essence of drama.

Spiritual experience influences mood. The following account given by Saint Bernard of Clairvaux illustrates my claim.

> You will ask then how, since His track is thus traceless, I could know that He is present? Because He is living and full of energy, and as soon as He has entered me, has quickened my sleeping soul, and aroused, softened and goaded my heart, which was torpid and hard as a stone. He has begun to pluck up and destroy, plant and build, to water the dry places, light up the dark places, throw open what was shut, inflame with warmth what was cold, straighten the crooked path and make rough places smooth. . . . In the reformation and renewal of the spirit of my mind, that is my inward man, I have seen something of the loveliness of His Beauty, and meditation on these things have been filled with wonder at the multitude of His greatness. But when the Word withdrew, all these spiritual powers and faculties began to droop and languish, as if the fire were taken from beneath a bubbling pot; and this is to me the sign of His departure. Then my soul must needs be sad and sorry, till He comes back and my heart again

warms within me as it is wont; for this is to me the sign that He has returned. (Cant., 74, condensed) (Underhill 1964:86 f.)

Although Saint Bernard attributes his depression to the withdrawal of spirituality, it is not really clear which is primary, the withdrawal of his spirituality or the onset of depression. But this relation between losing spiritual enthusiasm and clinical depression is what we saw at the beginning of this chapter in Report 11.

The combination relates to what has been called "the dark night of the soul." Although that concept is associated with the name of Saint John of the Cross, it is actually traced back to Pseudo-Dionysius, a sixth-century Syrian scholar. Sidney Spencer, the author of the article on Christian Doctrine in the *Encyclopedia Britannica* (16:376), writes, "A phase of the dying to self that this implies is the 'dark night of the soul,' experienced by many Christian mystics. The primary fact in that experience is the temporary cessation of the divine union, which gives rise to emotional lethargy, followed by a state of desolation and despair sometimes lasting for months or years. The soul that accepts its trials with patience attains to the utmost transcendence of self, through its willingness to be deprived of the greatest of all blessings." Spiritual despair is a depressive state, probably of pathologic intensity. Spirituality returns when enough psychic energy is generated to reach out toward the spirit and thereby to lift the mood.

If, as I argue, we try to control our moods, to regulate them, we do so by employing various techniques and instruments. These include most actions in and on the world around us, and in our own minds. Actions on the environment may include, for example, cultivating family and friends, becoming more active in community affairs, engaging more actively in social enterprises, in business or investment, or in political work. We may attempt to obtain more physical pleasure by pursuing sexual gratification, for example, or pleasure in food, exercise, or the sensual pleasures of a spa. We may attempt to influence our moods by influencing our mental processes and experiences: listening to music; watching theatrical performances; reading for pleasure, inspiration, or learning; mastering an intellectual discipline; learning a new language.

As my exploration of spirituality draws to a close, I am proposing that spirituality too functions as a mood regulator, specifically to lift mood. Unlike the other activities mentioned, it is not under direct, voluntary control. Yet as noted, one can invite it by preparing oneself. It is interesting that the usual techniques for encouraging spiritual experience involve deprivation, separation, frustration. The preparation, that is, consists of removing the usual sources of gratification, of mood-lifting experiences, so a corrective need is established that seems automatically to inspire the spiritual experience in those who are sensitive to it.

In the several exemplary reports that I have presented, in most cases, the event responded to a need. In the initial report, the letter from a friend, the feeling that "the heavens declare the glory of God" responded to his profound loneliness

The woman in the second report, who ascended the mountain hoping for the spiritual experience she ultimately attained, was professionally successful and recognized, but her personal life left her desolate and miserable. The reporter of the third example was away from home but not especially unhappy. She was a religious person but on that occasion was not aware of any specific unhappiness. Apparently she was overcome by the awesome beauty of what she saw. The frankly mystical experience of the fourth patient clearly responded to his unhappiness and frustration and provided him surcease. In Reports 3, 5, 6, and 8, although nothing is said of need and quest, there is pleasure, exaltation, and awe that persisted for some time. In Report 7 we hear about a mystical experience of a woman who had started the evening "discouraged" and unable, she thought, to participate in the celebration. To revert to the example of Hamlet, it is clear that his mystical vision of his father expresses misery and yearning to be reunited with him.

In most antidepression maneuvers such as those listed above, the subject does not realize what he intends to accomplish, though he thinks of the activity as something that gives him pleasure. In the case of the spiritual experience, there is usually no indication of conscious intention. The struggle against distress is evident as we examine the precipitating situation and its consequence, but to the subject the experience seems to arrive unsought, except for cases such as that of the woman in the second report, in which it was deliberately induced.

We have already discussed the spiritual experience as a repetition of the infant's early experience with his mother, an illusion facilitated by the suspension of reality testing. The looseness of ego function is favored by the affective struggle against depression and therefore is probably encountered more often among patients with affect disease.

In conclusion, the Spiritual experience proper and its mystical form may each be understood as an instrument of mood regulation, an effort to overcome a depressive tendency before it eventuates in definitive depression, by reaching out for the comfort experienced in the mother's close presence and finding relief in the illusory feeling, or sometimes a hallucination, of having attained that contact.

By the same token, religious worship, which is essentially a kind of applied spirituality, seeks to achieve a mood of composure and tranquility by reinforcing and maintaining the impression of attachment to the deity.

The Psalms clearly exemplify the religious effort to achieve mood regulation. They are a collection of extraordinarily beautiful poems, most of them originally created as part of the Temple worship of ancient pre-exilic or postexilic Israel, engaging God emotionally on the several significant occasions of the life of the individual or the community: the enthronement of the new king, the annual festival of renewal, praise, lamentation, thanksgiving, petition, propitiation. Psalms and individual verses constitute a large part of the Jewish liturgy, though a much smaller portion of the Christian liturgy. (For a full discussion of the origin and content of the psalms, see Mowinckel 1962.)

This is the answer to the question I posed at the end of the previous chapter. Yes, spiritual and religious experience does have biological value. It plays a part, sometimes an important part, in mood regulation, and therefore in current mental activity and the avoidance of mental illness.

CHAPTER 7

Apocalypse

A discussion of apocalypse seems essential in a study of the psychology of spirituality. I consider the apocalyptic revelation the ultimate spiritual experience and aimed at mood regulation. Apocalypse is a statement that takes the form of a mystical experience and its message is clearly intended to influence mood. While scholars date the earliest classical apocalypses to the second century before the Common Era, elements of the same structure are found much earlier, in the books of the Jewish prophets, in the accounts of the flood in Genesis, and in Mesopotamian myths.

In his book *Maps of Meaning* (1999), Peterson, in the Jungian tradition, tries to establish the relation between unconscious processes and early myths. Although he does not deal with apocalypse by name, he does develop the universal concepts of chaos and cosmos. The image of chaos, as he observes, clearly relates to the state of mind that characterizes melancholic depression, while cosmos is represented in unconscious thought by birth and rebirth, reorganization, and reconstruction. The antinomy between chaos and cosmos designates the two opposite poles of apocalypse.

> The domain of chaos—which is where what to do has not yet been specified—is a "place" characterized by the presence of potent emotions, discouragement, depression, fear, rootlessness, loss and disorientation. It is the affective aspect of chaos that constitutes what is most clearly known about chaos. It is "darkness, drought, the suspension of norms, and death." It is the terror of the dark of the night, which fills itself with demons of the imagination, yet exerts an uncanny fascination; it is the fire that magically reduces one determinate thing to another; it is the horror and curiosity engendered by the stranger and foreigner. (143)

Apocalyptic literature has continued to be produced through medieval and even into modern times. A serious, scholarly review of this history is provided in the recent (1999) *Encyclopedia of Apocalypticism*, edited by McGinn, Collins, and Stein.

How many of these are veridical mystical experiences and how many are contrived to resemble them? I suspect that most were composed for the purpose of influencing groups of people and few were genuine revelations.

Most people think of the word "apocalypse" in association with the last book of the Christian Bible, known as the Apocalypse or the Revelation. It is indeed a classical apocalypse, but it includes many details, images, and symbols that are obscure and require exegetic elucidation. The book opens with a descriptive statement: it is the revelation God gave to Jesus to transmit to his followers. Reading the prophecy confers blessedness, and his promise that the prophecy will be fulfilled soon. Dating the time of fulfillment, usually symbolically, is common in many apocalypses.

The statement takes the form of a classical letter from John of Patmos, with a salutation and a closing. Each of the seven churches that are the named recipients is addressed in turn, with observations about its religious behavior. Chapter 4 describes the actual mystical vision. The speaker finds himself in the heavenly court, which he describes in dramatic and vivid detail. The characteristics owe much to Isaiah 6 and Ezekiel 1, which we have already considered, as well as Daniel 7. There, in the court, John has the opportunity to learn about the prophecies, all of which deal symbolically with the persecution of the Christians by the Romans. There ensues a series of vivid images of world destruction, from which only the faithful will be saved. Characteristic of the apocalypse genre is the symbolic representation of nations, kings, and military forces as animals. The duration of the apocalyptic trial, the time to the End, is given in obscure numerical allusions. The destruction is amplified many times over, as is a struggle between the divine forces and their diabolical antagonist; for example, the angel Michael overcomes the "great dragon who is called the devil and Satan."

Chapter 12 tells of a woman in childbirth, whose infant is threatened by a "red dragon." This image could probably be understood as a reference to the birth of the Church in the face of Roman persecution. I mention this detail because rebirth is an essential component of apocalypse. Here, the rebirth, which is actually a metaphorical recovery, is represented as a literal event.

The definitive rebirth starts with chapter 21:

Then I saw a new heaven and a new earth; for the first heaven and the first earth had passed away, and the sea was no more. I saw the holy city, new Jerusalem, coming down out of heaven from God, prepared as a bride adorned for her husband; and I heard a great voice from the throne saying "Behold, the dwelling of God is with men. He will dwell with them, and they shall be His people, and God himself will be with them; He will wipe away every tear from their eyes, and death shall be no more. Neither shall there be mourning nor crying nor pain any more, for the former things have passed away!" And He who sat upon the throne said "Behold I make old things new."

The book closes as though it were the end of the letter.

My interest relates to the use of the death and rebirth scheme to engage the mood of the audience, to encourage the persecuted, and to instill hope and courage. Death and rebirth fantasies characterize the mood swings discussed in the previous chapter. The swing down to depression is accompanied by fantasies, worries, images, thoughts about death and destruction. The reversal back to normal mood and elevation is accompanied by images associated with re-birth. The alternating moods are accompanied by alternating images. We see these clearly in the apocalyptic-type dream, such as those cited in the previous chapter, which occurs commonly in the presence of mood volatility.

The dreams, symptoms, and fantasies appear concurrently with the mood swings. The spiritual and mystical experiences are unconsciously intended, I argue, to correct a downward mood that threatens to become too extreme. The contact with the transcendent object lifts the mood. When the subject is too high, whatever spiritual experience he may encounter will seem directed toward reversing the mood, that is, threatening him.

Here is a record of a dream apocalypse whose imagery is based upon the Book of Revelation. I quote from *Ultimate Intimacy* (54). The disclosure of the apocalyptic secret saves the dreamer. This material is kindly provided by Dr. Jacob A. Arlow.

> The patient has put his apartment up for sale. He is hoping to get enough money to enable him to leave his law practice and go to Hollywood to pursue a career in film. He intends either to write about film, to write scenarios, or perhaps even to produce. The patient has no experience or training in this field. To him, however, going to Hollywood means throwing off the shackles of inhibition and especially the proscriptions of the church regarding sexuality. In previous months, the patient has produced a great deal of psychoanalytic material of a frankly incestuous nature, coupled with thoughts of castration and damnation for sexual wishes, together with fear of authority figures. This material, however, has come out in an extremely isolated form. The patient repeats what he has learned as if it were a catechism. His insight is reduced to a formula, which is repeated as such. The patient is most isolated in his productions. He gives hardly any details of day-to-day activities, conversations with other individuals, or fleeting fantasies, unless a specific inquiry is made about such items.
>
> Over the past weekend, preceding the Independence Day (July 4) holiday, the patient had as a weekend guest his only close friend. This is a man whom he has known from college days.

Both are Catholics and lawyers with serious sexual problems. Both are dissatisfied with the practice of law and would like to leave it. The friend, Adolph, however, has two children and a wife and feels trapped. During their earlier years, the two would share sexual fantasies and giggle about "exploits" they had with girls. Although this is the patient's closest friend, he sees him perhaps once or twice a year. Adolph's wife is extremely withdrawn, as is their older child. It is clear from the description that the patient and Adolph, who shared sexual fantasies and thoughts, both suffer the same kinds of inhibitions. Over the weekend, they went for a walk together and discussed their sexual inhibitions and the role of the Catholic Church in frightening them with eternal damnation for sexual transgression.

After his friend, Adolph, Adolph's wife Sylvia, and the two children had left, the patient spent a quiet Fourth of July holiday reading a book that was essentially an interview with the Italian movie director, Fellini. On the night of 5–6 July, the patient had the following dream:

"My wife and I were somewhere up in the mountains in some small village. There were four people coming on horseback. They were knights like the Four Horsemen of the Apocalypse. They had stopped to tell us that there was going to be an earthquake and some of the area would be flooded. We were on a small island. They told us to move to a larger island, which we did. While we were there, the earth began to quake, fire began to flow and the small island where we had been was inundated with water. We were clinging close to the ground while the earth was shaking."

The patient stated that the dream must be traced to what he was reading in the Fellini interviews. Fellini spoke about the pervasive influence of the Catholic Church in Italian life. Its two-thousand-year-old influence pervades every aspect of Italian thought. Most particularly, however, Fellini emphasized the role of the Apocalypse. The ultimate vision of the Apocalypse is in the background of every Italian person's thinking, and, as such, it gives vibrancy to the lives of the Italians. Everything is lived against the background of the ultimate great struggle of the Judgment Day, when people will either be damned to eternal perdition or go to heaven with the angels, etc. Fellini felt, and the patient agreed, that it was the Church, not God, that introduced the idea of sexual pleasure as sin, making the apocalyptic vision one fraught with fear and trepidation.

Later in the session the patient quoted a further element from the Fellini interview. Fellini was questioned about the picture *8 1/2* and Anita Ekberg. Fellini said he had not known Anita Ekberg, but when he saw a picture of her in the American film magazine, in which she was dressed in a skimpy leopard-skin, he exclaimed, "I hope to God I never run into her. I could never resist the temptation." In discussing this aspect of the material, the patient said, "There again is a woman as the devil, woman as the temptress and seductress."

To which I added that Anita Ekberg was noted for her large sensuous breasts. The patient agreed, and I then reminded him of the sex play with his mother's "apples."

The patient had been in Italy ten years previously, he recalled, after the earthquake in southern Italy. He was at the Amalfi Drive and saw how the earth had just been torn apart by the quaking, how fragments of roads were separated from each other by dozens of yards as a result of the earthquake. He had also seen a mild eruption of a volcano in Sicily. The flowing lava connected with volcanic eruptions reminded him of visions of fire and brimstone in apocalyptic visions in the Bible in the Apocalypse of St. John.

The four knights in the dream were identified by the patient with the Four Horsemen of the Apocalypse. He could not, however, remember their names nor exactly what they stood for, but he knew that they represented portents of great danger and ultimate destruction. In the dream, however, he was struck by the fact that the Four Horsemen were actually saviors and helpers. While discussing the Four Horsemen, the patient kept fondling his tie reassuringly.

I called the patient's attention to the fact that the Four Horsemen represented tremendous threats—conquest, war, famine, and death. It was when I mentioned Death and the Pale Rider on the white horse that the patient recalled the aspect of the Fellini interview that dealt with Anita Ekberg.

This material was used to demonstrate to the patient how, in spite of his advanced thinking, he still clings to the fear instilled in him by that part of the Catholic teaching about sex (incest) being a mortal sin, punishable by eternal damnation. This is in spite of the fact that earlier in the session he supported Fellini's view that God really takes the total balance of man's deeds, good and evil, over the course of the seventy-or-so-year span and weighs man in the balance, but he would not condemn an individual just for one act of mortal sin, that it was the Church that introduced the idea of eternal perdition. In spite of all this, however, the patient, out of his own castration anxiety and guilt, still has to grapple with fear of damnation (castration).

This case illustrates the prospect of destruction as punishment for sin. In the dream, however, the patient is not punished with the wicked but escapes with the aid of the Four Horsemen, who abandon their classic role of portents of death and destruction and become helpers and rescuers. The reason the threat fails is that, in view of his lifelong masochism and depressive character, at Dr. Arlow's suggestion, the patient had begun a program of antidepression drug therapy with me a year earlier. His response to all medication had been positive, but only temporary. On June 22, 20 milligrams of fluoxetine (Prozac) had been prescribed, in addition to the 60 milligrams of methylphenidate (Ritalin) per day and the 0.5 milligrams of lorazepam (Ativan) three times a day that he had been taking. He had responded nicely to the fluoxetine. The dream, which occurred on July 6, reflects the remedial effects of that drug in the patient's seeing himself as one of the saved rather than one of the doomed, and the Horsemen as friends rather than demons. This case illustrates the influence of mood on the outcome of the mythic drama.

The apocalyptic type of mood swing encountered clinically records the automatic, unconscious regulatory efforts. More enduring elaborate clinical apocalypses occur during episodes of psychosis. An example to which Freud drew attention and that has become classical is the instance of Daniel Paul Schreber. I give here Freud's description (1911c).

At the climax of his illness, under the influence of visions which were "partly of a terrifying character, but partly, too, of an indescribable grandeur," Schreber became convinced of the imminence of a great catastrophe, of the end of the world. Voices told him that the work of the past 14,000 years had now come to nothing, and that the earth's allotted span was only 212 years more; and during the last part of his stay in Flechsig's clinic he believed that the period had already elapsed. He himself was "the only real man left alive" and the few human shapes that he still saw—the doctor, the attendants, the other patients—he explained as being "miracled up, cursorily improvised men." Occasionally the converse current of feeling also made itself apparent: a newspaper was put into his hands in which there was a report of his own death; he himself existed in a second, inferior shape, and in this second shape he one day quietly passed away. But the form of his delusion in which his ego was retained and the world sacrificed proved itself by far the more powerful. He had various theories of the cause of the catastrophe. At one time he had in mind a process of glaciation owing to the withdrawal of the sun; at another it was to be destruction by an earthquake, in the occurrence of which he, in his capacity of "seer of spirits," was to act a leading part, just as another seer was alleged to have done in the Lisbon earthquake of 1755. Or again, Flechsig (his psychiatrist) was the culprit, since through his magic arts he had sown fear and terror among men, had wrecked the foundations of religion, and spread abroad general nervous disorders and immorality, so that devastating pestilences had descended upon mankind. In any case the end of the world was the consequence of the conflict which had broken out between him and Flechsig, or, according to the aetiology adopted in the second phase of his delusion, of the indissoluble bond which had been formed between him and God; it was, in fact, the inevitable result of his illness.

The text makes clear that Schreber's delusional fantasies dealt with the conflict between his wish to be dead and his wish to be reborn. The death of the world replaced his own death. Despite Schreber's attempt to displace his death wish onto the world, derivatives of the wish nevertheless appear in his delusional ideas that he had, in fact died. Yet the new world represents an attempt at rebirth, though it is not successful.

In addition to the conflict between destructive and reconstructive forces found here and in profusion in the rest of the Schreber memoir and clinical record, other features of apocalypse are clearly represented: striking and terrifying visions and auditory experiences; the concept of the seer; numbers denominating the passage of time until "the end"; a villain; direct communication and an emotional bond between the individual and his God: a vision of God in His heavenly court; and a messianic mission by the patient.

The classical apocalypses, on the other hand, whether veridical or fictitious, seem designed to influence the mood of the audience to whom they are addressed. The mystical vision that is said to have declared the apocalyptic prophecy is claimed as authority for the message. "This is not my idea. I heard it directly from God or some semidivine intermediary." It is aimed simultaneously at the despairing, hoping to give them courage, and at the villains, threatening them. While such apocalypses seem benign and even constructive, sometimes the population that considers itself victimized and without hope retrieves hope by viciously attacking a designated enemy.

Apocalypses, as I have described them, are literary pieces with a social message. But they achieve a certain amount of credibility because apocalyptic destruction does occur, whether natural, as for example earthquakes or floods, or executed by human hands, as for example the Nazi apocalypse of our times.

In the clinical apocalypses, the subject who is too high is warned of retribution; the subject who is too low is encouraged to hope, though sometimes his expectation of recovery takes the form of fury. The public apocalypse warns the perpetrator and encourages the victim at the same time.

This is a time of apocalyptic events and expectations. It might be helpful, even if not especially comforting, to keep in mind the historical and psychological regularity and cogency of this phenomenon.

CHAPTER 8

Demonic Spirituality

Infanticide, Self-Sacrifice,
and Fundamentalism

Aggression in Mood Regulation

In this chapter I shall consider more systematically what I have
called negative spirituality, that is, spiritual experience that is associated with anxiety, depression, despair, anger, or aggressive attack.

My description of the process of mood regulation in chapter
6 was incomplete in that it did not fully describe the role of aggression. I argued that mood fluctuates continually in everyone,
whether in response to external events, gratification, frustration,
threats, and so on, or spontaneously as result of internal regulatory
processes.

Specifically, as mood declines toward depression, mood-elevating forces come into play so as to reverse the decline and initiate
ascent toward euphoria, a process that in turn, at the top of the
excursion, is reversed. When the mood swings are restricted within boundaries compatible with normal function, we either do not

notice them or consider them unremarkable. When, on the other hand, they transgress the boundary that delineates normal mental functioning for each of us, we recognize pathology.

As mood departs from euthymia, corrective forces come into play that facilitate the reversal. The descent toward depression may not be noticed consciously, or it may become evident only in feelings of discontent, unhappiness, or malaise. In response, one may attempt to repair or correct whatever has gone wrong: to reinforce important attachments (see friends, spend time with spouse or other family members, repair a rift); seek some gratifying activities (exercise, vacation, entertainment, a sexual encounter); retreat from the world briefly to encourage restitution to a more felicitous mood in solitude. Or one may take refuge in a chemical substance that alleviates the stress or elicits a dissociative state or both.

On the other hand, when mood begins to ascend toward the limit tolerated by the individual, a sense of discomfort may or may not set in. Some activity may be initiated to deter an untempered euphoria and thereby prevent a reactive decline toward depression. One may feel that success or gratification cannot continue unchecked and automatically invoke small superstitious gestures, such as crossing fingers (to drive the devil away) or knocking on wood (of the true cross). One may feel moved to give someone a gift, to make a philanthropic contribution, or help someone, do a favor.

I have argued in chapter 6 that, for want of a better term, what might be called the spiritual "instinct" can also contribute importantly to mood regulation. As we have seen, in the effort to repair depressive decline, the successful pursuit of spiritual fulfillment by attachment to a transcendent other, can create a feeling of gratification and elevation of mood. On the other hand, for spiritual individuals, as mood improves beyond a tolerable degree, the spiritual appetite subsides and then disappears, so that ultimately, if the quest is not renewed, the individual may become dispirited (see Report 11).

However, my description is incomplete. Mood regulation may, and often does, involve aggression. In chapter 6, I described some of the expressions of aggression found in spiritual experience. I quoted Otto's description of the spiritual experience as a "mysterium tremendum," the mystery that makes one tremble. "It has its wild and demonic forces and can sink to almost grisly horror and shuddering. It has its crude and barbaric antecedents." I described two examples of frightening scenarios in the classical literature of religious spirituality and mysticism. And I explained these distressing variants of spirituality as the consequence of an excessively strong depressive tendency that appears during the spiritual quest and either frustrates it or perverts it into the demonic.

Aggression is a necessary and powerful component of human behavior, frequent and recurrent, and of serious consequence. It finds expression in many ways and defies definition. Jaak Panksepp starts his chapter on aggression in *Affective Neuroscience* (1998) as follows:

> At times animals threaten, bite and kill each other. Such behavior is known as aggression. Its manifestations range from a threatening baring of teeth to the tearing of flesh, from the graceful dive of a hunting hawk to the spitting spectacle of a cornered cat, from the display of pompous sexual plumage to the catastrophes of well-oiled guns and hidden bombs. Aggression is neither a universal nor a unidimensional phenomenon. Many invertebrates, like mollusks, exhibit no apparent aggression during their life cycles. However, nearly all vertebrates exhibit aggression from time to time, and such behavior can have several distinct environmental and brain causes. (188)

Panksepp's further description of aggression includes angry attack aggression as well as the aggression of sexual rivalry and predation, that is, interspecies aggression. These three forms are biologically distinct, but at times they cross over and reinforce one another.

Angry attack aggression may be regarded as instrumental in the sense that it is available to be deployed when needed, in response to a threat or an attack by another person. The implications of this proposition include psychopharmacological considerations and also the question whether aggression is always something that is elicited *de novo* by threat or attack, or whether its potential for discharge stands ready to be released by an adequate stimulus. In any case, for our present purposes, I argue that aggression can also be elicited by threatening shifts of mood away from the normal range for that individual. Of course a threat or attack may bring about such a mood deviation or directly release an aggressive response, or both.

As mood descends toward depression, a person tends to become irritable and cranky as well as sad. The greater the shift and the more rapid, the stronger the display of aggression. The mildly or moderately depressed individual often burdens his family and friends with anger and distemper. Borderline personality disorder is characterized by frequent, abrupt mood changes. When a depressive segment begins, the patient exhibits sharp, angry explosions. The mood changes are often or usually generated internally rather than precipitated by an external event, so that no truly culpable object can be recognized. Therefore the resultant attack is usually directed against whoever might be in the immediate neighborhood at the time, a parent, a spouse, a friend, or a co-worker.

In chapter 6, I briefly described the dream of a manic-depressive patient who was slipping into depression. He saw himself armed to fight an enemy, but at a certain point, he laid down his arms and walked away. The dream shows that early in the depressive process the patient may be impelled to fight an identified enemy, but as the depression deepens, he becomes resigned and loses his belligerence.

Usually, the phase of anger follows the initial antidepression attempts to reinforce attachments, to cling to loved individuals. In this initial phase, as I demonstrated, spiritual tendencies are initiated or strengthened. However, I have not seen accounts of any gratifying spiritual quest or fulfillment occurring during an angry, depressive mood. Apparently, with the onset of anger, benign spirituality disappears. In religious literature, we read that hope rather than anger and despair facilitates the helpful spiritual revelation.

The aggression that is occasioned by an identifiable external individual antagonist differs from the aggression that is precipitated by an impersonal event, such as a natural catastrophe or prevailing economic or political circumstance, or that occurs in the course of internal mood regulation. In the former case, the aggression is directed outward at the adversary, the source of the distress; it is appropriate. In the latter case, it may be directed at an inappropriate individual toward whom the subject entertains preexisting hostile or ambivalent feelings, or at a mythical enemy. In the case of children and adolescents, the parents, and especially the mother, receive the force of the anger; for adults, the spouse, or partner or close friend or associate or fellow worker, is targeted. Alternatively, the anger may be directed at a mythical enemy.

Such mythical animosity creates prejudice and persecution. In my 1996 book, *Myth and Madness,* I demonstrated that the classical anti-Semite has two enemies, a real one, that is a real person or circumstance, and a mythical one, the stereotypic Jew.

REPORT 12

After a weekend during which a man described himself as having been "peevish" because, as result of his wife's indisposition, he had been obligated to look after their small children whom he loved very much, he dreamed: "Walking through a park, I noticed a pile of stones, and further on another and then another. There were more, maybe thirty of them. As I walked further I noticed that under each pile, a cat was buried, but enough of the cat protruded so that it was visible, but just visible. There was a rumor that a satanic cult was killing cats. I looked for my cat, but could not find it. However I felt reassured."

I commented that this scene suggested animal sacrifice. He replied, "There is a lot of that in the Old Testament." I agreed and asked what the number thirty suggested to him. "Thirty pieces of silver" he replied.

The man had exhibited no trace of antisemitism before or since, and I believe that he was not knowingly antisemitic. But faced with his ambivalence to his children, unconsciously classical antisemitic myths of the murder of Christian children by Jews came to mind. He had had a favorite cat for many years and its recent death had thrown him into an episode of depression, from which he was emerging only with difficulty. Some weeks later, and in an entirely different context, he observed that it seemed to him that in his industry, Jews received more favored treatment than other ethnic groups.

Hsia (1988) records instances from the sixteenth and seventeenth centuries when men murdered their own sons and accused the Jews. Not only are Jews labeled the mythic enemy but also they are often considered an obstacle between the antisemite and his god.

The minister who had spoken of being screwed into the ground when he was depressed, had been paying me only one half my usual fee because he had been in a poor financial position and so I had extended courtesy to him out of respect for his position. At one point in the course of a successful treatment, he unexpectedly inherited a small sum with which he planned to purchase a country place for his family. On that occasion, I asked whether he might consider increasing the fee slightly, still considerably below the usual fee. He seemed dismayed and said that he would discuss it with his wife. I replied that I would be satisfied with whatever decision they reached.

At the next session he reported a dream. His pen had fallen into a privy on my property. The property reminded us both of the property that he intended to purchase. I asked about the pen and he showed me his favorite pen, a Cross pen, and it was gold. I told him that it seemed that my request for a fee increase suggested that I was desecrating his gold Cross. He was astonished and disavowed such a sentiment. I believe that he was innocent of conscious antisemitic sentiments, but the dream revealed his mythic ideas of Jewish lust for gold, and the wish to desecrate the cross. In this case one may argue that I was a real "enemy" in that I had requested an increase in fee, but more important, I was also a mythic enemy.

Aggression is oppositely directed but not quite symmetrical when the mood is ascending too high. Clinically, the manic patient becomes more and more self-satisfied and arrogant. Though he exhibits little anger, he does attack when frustrated. However, as mood ascends to extremes, the subject begins to expect punitive reversal; he becomes sensitive to criticism and ultimately paranoid, that is, persuaded that he is being persecuted.

In 2003, an actor called Gibson created, filmed, and produced a motion picture called *The Passion of the Christ*. It depicted the story of the crucifixion, not quite as given in the Gospels, and with some contribution from the published anti-Semitic hallucinations of Catherine Emmerich, a nineteenth-century German stigmatic nun. An article by Peter J. Boyer in *The New Yorker* of September 15, 2003, included an account of an episode of severe depression that Gibson described, during which he had seriously contemplated suicide. He recovered fairly abruptly after an unspecified time, we are told, and as he did so, he felt inspired by the Holy Spirit to make this motion picture to tell the story not only of the crucifixion but of the resurrection as well. The author of the essay reports that in the depiction of Christ's resurrection, he recognized a symbol of Gibson's vigorous recovery from his depression. "Gibson's resurrected Christ rises in the tomb with a steely glare, and then strides purposefully into the light, to the insistent beat of martial drums." Gibson, we learned, had not been consistently religious previously, and had recovered from a period of dissoluteness and substance abuse, presumably as he became depressed, and subsequently with his emergence from depression.

So Gibson's recovery can be construed as a conversion experience or what Boyer saw as an altered personality, specifically, preoccupation with violence and conspiracy theories. Jewish organizations were reminded of the medieval passion plays that had inspired pogroms, and especially the continuing production of the passion play at Oberammergau, Germany. They protested the viciousness attributed to the Jews and the repetition of the quotation from Matthew (27:25) (alone of the four Gospels), "May his blood be upon us and upon our children." They requested an attenuating statement in the movie or at its end, explaining that this was a literal rendition of a religious document that had been written tendentiously by unknown authors or editors decades after the event; that the context of the document was seriously anti-Jewish; that the Vatican statement, Nostra Aetate, had declared that the Jews as a community then and now are not culpable. Gibson complained that the Jews were persecuting him and expressed in vivid language, his wish to dismember one of his Jewish newspaper critics. The motion picture was released to the public on Ash Wednesday 2004, making it virtually a religious event.

My point here is that Gibson made a movie of his recovery from depression using the passion of Christ as a metaphor. The physical abuse that was visited upon Christ by the Romans—represented as instigated by the Jews—demonstrated the suffering that Gibson described having experienced in his depressive state. By telling the story as he did, he was encouraging outrage against the Romans, who have disappeared into history, but also against the Jews, who are his neighbors today. We are told that a preoccupation with violence and conspiracy accompanied Gibson's recovery from depression and his return to religion. If, as Boyer suggests, he saw himself as the Christ, then he saw the Jews as his enemies.

In contrast to the man in Report 12, where there was perhaps a mild feeling of injustice, and the man in Report 11, who felt threatened by raising the issue of a professional fee, in the Gibson case, there was no evident provocation. The invocation and attack upon the mythic enemy expressed his attempt to defend against and overcome his depression.

Let me cite a more commonplace example of a mythic persecutor invoked by a depressing experience. A man learned one day, quite unexpectedly, that it was likely he had a very serious illness. That night he dreamed that he was being persecuted by several acquaintances who, he suspected, had ambivalent feelings toward him. In other words, the depressing news, attributable to no human agency, nevertheless invoked feelings of being persecuted by individuals whose adversarial attitudes were entirely mythic.

But aggressive tendencies can be elicited not only by depressive tendencies and moods but also by success and the elevated mood that accompanies it. The aggression released by the ascending mood is directed at oneself; it is self-defeating. I recognize three mechanisms. The ebullient individual will often provoke antagonism by arrogance, overreaching, for example as a business executive or political figure. He may be encouraged to do so by his energy and enthusiasm and so unintentionally or even deliberately provoke resentment.

Second, he may expect an antagonistic response even if he does not see himself as deliberately provocative, perhaps as a result of envy. A paranoid attitude may follow, which, if the patient becomes psychotic, might eventuate in a psychotic paranoia. Gibson's response to the concern about the consequences of the release of

The Passion created in him a feeling of being persecuted, which he disclosed to the *New Yorker* journalist.

Third, this paranoid expectation of retribution for unacceptable success may result in a corrective depressive tendency, an expression of mood regulation. Freud (1916) described a personality disorder that he called "Those Wrecked by Success." He speaks of illness following "close upon the fulfillment of a wish" that "puts an end to all enjoyment of it," referring to a specific gratification rather than to the situation of unacceptable mood elevation. The principle, I believe, is the same. The danger incurred by success exemplifies the irrational forces that appear in daily life. Martin Bergmann (1992), as a preface to his discussion of infanticide (which I shall consider below), cites the myth of Polykrates as given in a poem by Schiller. I quote his description.

> As the eighteenth century was turning into the nineteenth, the German poet Friedrich Schiller wrote a ballad entitled "The Ring of Polykrates." Polykrates, king of the island of Samos, is visited by the king of Egypt. When Polykrates boasts of his good fortune to his visitor, the more cautious Egyptian declares that one should not regard oneself as happy as long as one's enemy is alive and one's fleet exposed to danger on the high seas. As he speaks a messenger arrives with the head of Polykrates' enemy, and soon the fleet returns victorious. The guest suggests that there is only one remedy to appease the jealousy of the gods: Polykrates should throw a ring, his dearest possession, into the ocean. Polykrates follows the Egyptian's advice, but the next morning, when a fisherman brings a large fish as a gift to the king, it is found to contain the ring. With a shudder the guest flees his lucky host.
>
> "The poem evokes," Bergmann says, "the feeling of dread that many men and women, burdened with a sense of guilt, experience when they are particularly successful or when good fortune beyond their expectations befalls them." (7 f.)

Since Polykrates is a historic character, I went to the *Encyclopedia Britannica* (1985) to ascertain how accurate the Egyptian king's prediction had been. Here is the account in *Britannica* 9:578.

Polycrates (fl. 6th century B.C.) tyrant (c. 535–522 B.C.) of the island of Samos, in the Aegean Sea, who established Samian naval
supremacy in the eastern Aegean and strove for control of the
archipelago and mainland towns of Ionia.

Polycrates seized control of the city of Samos during a celebration of a festival of Hera outside city walls. After eliminating his
two brothers, who had at first shared his power, he established
a despotism, and ships from his 100-vessel fleet committed acts
of piracy that made him notorious throughout Greece. He made
an alliance with Egypt, but when the Persians advanced against
Egypt in 525 B.C. he abandoned his ally and sent a squadron of
40 ships to join the Persian fleet. He took the opportunity to send
his main political opponents with this squadron and they deserted, however, and supported by Spartans they attempted un-
successfully to dislodge the tyrant. He maintained his ascendance
until c. 522 when Oroetes, Persian governor of Sardis, lured him
to the mainland and had him crucified.

Evidently Polykrates' unrestrained arrogance led to his comeup-
pance, as Sehiller had predicted.

I am proposing that, confronted with a degree of success that
he is apparently unable to tolerate, the subject experiences fear of
punishment in the form of expectations of misfortune, illness, fail-
ure, loss, or even death. Sometimes these expectations are conscious
as fears and worries; sometimes we see only the termination of the
drive for success and its replacement by a depressive decline. Clinically the subject may become paranoid, even to the point of psychosis, or simply anxious or even depressed. The internal struggle
might be projected out onto a mythical adversary; may be accompanied by a feeling of guilt, a feeling that punishment is inevitable
because it is deserved; it may present simply as a depressive mood.
It may present as some obviously self-destructive behavior, poor
judgment in a person who would otherwise achieve success by hard
work. One encounters businessmen and businesswomen who, over
several cycles, have won and lost fortunes.

This phenomenon resembles the psychodynamics of depressive
illness. One can usually detect two separate component processes.
The first is inertia, a loss of energy, an inability to enjoy life, a

classical feeling of helplessness and hopelessness. The second is the expectation of destruction of one form or another, defeat, rejection, illness, or death. This component leaves a feeling of being persecuted by an enemy or being punished for some real or imagined misbehavior. It is an actual aggressive tendency directed against the self. In cases of an arrested or reversed hypomanic or manic tendency, the aggression can be seen as an obvious correction of the Promethean aspiration. However, in quality, the attack against the self is no different from what we see in ordinary depression. It seems that the first component, the inertia, is the result of an inadequate supply of the neurotransmitter dopamine, whereas the second, the self-destructive component, is not attributable to any single mechanism that we know at the time I am writing this. Some clues suggest that it might be related to a hormone called corticotrophin releasing hormone, or at least that that hormone may play some intermediate role in the pathogenesis of this second component of depression. Since serotonin, another neurotransmitter, is provided by various antidepression drugs called serotonin reuptake inhibitors and is generally an inhibitory rather than a stimulating drug, it may achieve its antidepression effect by inhibiting the second depressogenic mechanism, namely, the self-directed aggression. Interestingly, antipsychosis and antimania substances, which in adequate doses act to suppress what may be relatively excessive amounts of dopamine, in smaller doses often alleviate depression, perhaps by inhibiting this aggression.

I have tried in this section to emphasize the role of aggression in mood regulation—both externally directed aggression to combat a depressive tendency and internally directed aggression to combat an inappropriate elevation of mood.

Spirituality and Aggression

In this discussion of the various forms of spirituality, I have mentioned variants I called negative, referring to experiences that were disagreeable and discomfiting rather than reassuring and gratifying. In the discussion of awe in chapter 2, as an example of awful versus awesome, I drew attention to the well-known Munch painting *The*

Scream, which portrays what seemed to the artist to be a scene of awful horror. According to newspaper accounts, the blood-red sky he painted had been created by clouds emanating from the eruption of the Krakatoa volcano, half a world away. But it also expressed the state of mind of a painter who had been hospitalized for what was probably called, in retrospect, depressive illness. The combination gave rise to an experience of awe that was powerful and horrid rather than a gratifying experience. I also referred to the barracks and death chambers and ovens of Auschwitz. These too evoked feelings of awe, but the awe created shuddering and horror rather than a sense of comfort and yearning. Similarly, in the discussion of spirituality proper, I called attention to Greenacre's report of Albert Schweitzer's memory from childhood of encountering the devil in his father's church.

Spirituality expressed as enjoying the reassurance and comfort of God's smiling personality is complemented by its negative, God's withdrawal of his smile and his face. I count approximately 28 times that the biblical text mentions God's hiding his face from Israel.

Look at Isaiah 1:14–15.

And when you spread your hands (to pray) I will turn my eyes away from you. And when you extend prayer, I will not listen.

Again 2:10–11:

Enter into the rock and hide yourself in the ground for fear of the terror of the Lord and his awesome pride.

Such examples can be multiplied many times over. They threaten that the spiritual gratification that flows from God's favor can be reversed to punitive horror in the presence of disobedience.

Similarly, mystical experiences in which the presence of God is sought can easily be transformed into experiences of horrible persecution. In the classic texts of Chariot and Temple mysticism, the ascent to the divine throne, unless meticulously prepared for with prayer and ritual, elicits only death and destruction. I described also the story of the four scholars who presumed to peer into the forbidden garden; three of them suffered devastating blows.

The following is the report of a man who was impressed by the coincidence of the death of a goldfish and of his infant son.

"We bought our two-year-old son some goldfish not only to teach him about pets and responsibility, but also about death at an early age. Our goldfish had its ups and downs but there came a time when it wasn't too well. Then suddenly, it got better without any interventions. Around this time frame we had a new baby who was born oxygen deprived at birth and suffered from seizures in his first few days of life. The baby was hospitalized for about three weeks and then, just like the goldfish, made a remarkable recovery. I always liked to compare the two lives.

Then in June the goldfish just suddenly died with no signs of sickness. I remember very clearly being out in the driveway with my two sons and thinking that if the fish died, that means our infant will die. I also remember exactly what I said to myself upon thinking that thought: 'The analogy ends here.'

On July 7, just three weeks later, our three-month-old baby died of sudden infant death syndrome. The scary thought is that perhaps God was talking to me and giving me a message. I felt disappointed when I was told there is no special prayer in Judaism to say when you sense the presence of God in this way."

It seemed to him that "perhaps God was talking to me and giving me a message." The father's "scary thought" was that in a mystical experience he had come to feel that all events in the universe are interrelated. In his mind, what he encountered was not simply a coincidence but a demonstration of the essential connectedness of everything in the universe, a common mystical concept. There are no boundaries. Having experienced the union in this tragic way was uncanny.

So the loving God, when ignored or disobeyed—or even unaccountably—can become furious and murderous. This transformation from the gratifying aspects of spirituality to its horrifying aspects I call negative spirituality. Perhaps it would be fair to say that when mood regulation fails or threatens to fail, other regulatory strategies, aggressive maneuvers, may be mobilized.

The Demonic God

The demonic God or rather, the demonic face of God reacts against overreaching, presumptuousness, disobedience, and immorality. An individual who suffers misfortune, of whatever origin, may see himself as having been abandoned, if not actually persecuted, by God. The two faces, the benign and the malign, are given nowhere more vividly than in chapter 28 of Deuteronomy, where rewards for obedience and punishment for disobedience are specified in powerful detail. Such a God needs to be obeyed, but also propitiated and appeased.

Among students of the subject, it seems to be generally believed that animal sacrifice was preceded by human sacrifice, and specifically infanticide. Bergmann, in his book *The Shadow of Moloch*, lists the examples given in the Bible as well as what is known of human sacrifice elsewhere in the Middle East. The Bible stories include the story of the aborted sacrifice of Isaac, the sacrifice of Jephthah's daughter, and the sacrifice of his son by the king of Moab. We read in the Joshua and in I Kings 16 that when the walls of Jericho were rebuilt, the builder's sons were immured in them.

Here we are dealing with a more complex situation than merely propitiating a ferocious God. The murder of another individual is also involved. The prospect of infanticide elicits horror because it violates not only our ideas of the repugnance of murder but also our actual genuine and intense love for our children.

To understand infanticide, we must understand that many normal human behaviors that we take for granted as natural are actually complex in construction. That is, they are created as the resolution of conflicting instinctual tendencies. For example, males and females have an instinctual aversion to each other's bodies (Freud 1927). This is clear in the case of prepubertal children, who aggregate in same-sex groups. Although some older people who are widowed sometimes remarry soon afterward, others refuse, feeling that no matter how well the spouse was loved, his or her death creates a sense of relief that the survivor is reluctant to complicate by entering into another committed relationship. During adolescence and the early years of adult life, sexual aversion is overcome by sexual attraction that appears with puberty, but as is well known, that desire subsides later in life. After the subsidence of sexual needs, husband and wife stay together because they have developed a close social bond, a vital attachment. But when the attachment is severed by the death of one spouse, unless a strong attachment need persists, the survivor may have little interest in a new partner. Over the years, the nature of marital attachment changes as the component instinctual tendencies each rise and subside independently. Similarly, competition for the love of parents and for goods and resources among siblings conflicts with the tendency toward family solidarity and so produces the famous ambivalence of sibling rivalry.

To come back to infanticide, Panksepp (1998) reports that lower mammals display aversion to newborn infants and will kill or eat them when anything goes wrong with the normal process of parturition. He exhibits a graph demonstrating that infanticidal behavior in male rats diminishes to a minimum 21 to 30 days after a sexual encounter when the pup is born of that encounter, and then infanticidal behavior gradually rises once more thereafter (201). So we infer that infanticidal behavior is normally overcome by what might be the parental instinct, but gradually resumes when parental instinctual behavior diminishes. The point of this digression is to argue that counterintuitive as it may seem, humans too would not tolerate small children if their infanticidal tendency were not overcome by loving parental instinctual needs. This argument may be supported by citing the pathologic escape of infanticidal wishes from this normal inhibition.

On April 3 and 4, 2004, the Associated Press reported that a woman killed two of her three very young sons by crushing their heads with rocks, and severely injured the third, in response to hallucinated orders from God. Her three children all had biblical names. After she killed the first two and started to attack the third, she found that she couldn't complete the murder and told God, "You are just going to have to do the rest." She asserted that she believed that she was divinely chosen by God to kill her children on Mother's Day weekend. The woman was plainly psychotic and was acquitted of murder on that basis, but the case demonstrates a latent infanticidal tendency that can be liberated by psychosis. The account of this story appeared on AOL News and the following day, April 5, in *The New York Times*. I quoted above the dream of the dead cats, which I surmise represented an infanticidal wish that would be completely unrecognizable and horribly repugnant to the dreamer.

I infer that sacrificial infanticide represents the activation of an unconscious, infanticidal, instinctual tendency under the influence of the need to propitiate the gods.

When animal sacrifice replaced human sacrifice, the animal was not regarded as an enemy but rather as food. The interspecies predatory instinct reinforces the instinctual tendency to propitiate the god. Bergmann calls attention to the varieties of sacrifice described in the Bible: the Olah that is the holocaust, the sacrifice that is completely consumed by fire, at one extreme; and at the other, the Zevah, most of the variants of which are consumed as food meant to be shared by the sacrificer and by the priest and Levites, symbolically a way of sharing food with God. Bergmann points to similar distinctions among the sacrifices of other peoples.

Bergmann describes further the difference between what Burkert calls "the Olympian feast sacrifice" and "chthonic holocaust." The latter corresponds to the Olah. The animal is completely burned. The Chthonioi were the Greek gods of the underworld and the chthonic holocaust was an attempt to appease them. The Olympian feast sacrifice, on the other hand, consisted in sharing a communal meal with a beneficent god. That corresponds to the Jewish Zevah. These two forms of sacrifice then correspond, respectively, to the demonic god who must be appeased and to the loving god with whom one shares a sacred meal. The demonic god expresses negative spirituality; the loving god is associated with benevolent spirituality. Infanticide is a holocaust, obviously intended to placate a demonic God. In Greek mythology, as elsewhere in the polytheistic world, the multiplicity of gods permitted a designation of some as friendly and benevolent, in contradistinction to others who were demonic. In Judaism, however, monotheism made it necessary to look upon these two qualities as aspects of a single God. The advantage of this arrangement is that it brings morality into the realm of religious behavior.

I contend that we see God in our monotheistic world the way the infant sees his mother: at times smiling lovingly and at other times scowling threateningly. In Scripture and in liturgy, the hostile image seldom appears alone. It usually alternates closely with the smiling one, or the two overlap. In each of the theophanies of Isaiah 6 and Ezekiel 1 we see mixtures of God's fierceness and his comforting love.

In the few instances of infanticide in the Bible, the behavior is cultic and moral issues do not seem to enter. However, by the period of Prophets, issues of morality are emphasized over cultic concerns. The Prophet Micah deals with this issue (6:6–8).

6. With what should I approach the Lord, bow before God on high?
Shall I approach him with *oloth* (holocausts), with year-old calves?
7. Will the Lord be pleased with thousands of rams, with myriads of streams of oil?
Shall I give my first born for my transgression, the fruit of my womb as penance for my sins?
8. Man, He has told you what is good, and what the Lord requires of you, but to do justice, to love kindness, and to walk humbly with your God.

The God of the Prophets supersedes the God of Exodus 4:24–26, who sought to kill Moses in the desert but was appeased by his son's foreskin; and the God of the desert who accepted the ritual scapegoat. Interestingly, the God who exiled Ishmael to the desert and demanded the sacrifice of Isaac is transformed in those very tales, when these sacrifices are aborted. Rabbinic Judaism speaks of God's two attitudes toward man: his *middath harahamim*, his quality of love and compassion; and his *middath hadin*, his quality of stern justice. The God of the prophets as well as of the rabbis is not to be appeased by cultic practice, but by moral behavior.

10. Hear the word of YHVH, you chieftains of Sodom; give ear to our God's instruction, you folk of Gomorrah.

11. "What need have I of all your sacrifices (*zivhekhem*)?" Says YHVH, "I am sated with *oloth* (burnt offerings) of rams, and suet of fatted cattle, and blood of bulls; and I have no desire for lambs and he-goats.

12. That you come to appear before Me, who requested that of you, to trample My courts?

13. Do not continue to bring worthless gifts. Incense is offensive to Me. New moon and Sabbath, convoked assemblies, iniquitous meetings, I cannot abide.

14. Your new moons and fixed seasons are hateful; they have become a burden to Me, I cannot endure them.

15. And when you raise your hands, I will turn My eyes away from you; though you pray at length, I will not listen.

16. Your hands are full of blood. Wash yourselves clean; remove your evil doings from My sight, cease to do evil.

17. Learn to do good, seek to do justice; aid the wronged; treat the orphan justly; defend the widow.

18. Come, let us discuss this, says YHVH. If your sins are like crimson, they can become white as snow; if they are red as scarlet, they can become like wool.

19. If you agree and obey, you will feed on the best produce of the land.

20. But if you refuse and rebel, you will be consumed by the sword."

The word of YHVH.

Isaiah 1:10–19

The prophet demands moral behavior; cultic practice alone is repugnant. The loving God will reward the former and the demonic God will punish the latter.

I suggest that the concept of the negative, demonic God prevails when one's mood is despondent, demoralized, defeated, and hopeless. The demonic images that ensue are not sought, as the beneficent images are; they intrude and frighten us, as does the persecutory force of depression. They create the need to appease the demon in whatever way might be efficacious. In the ancient world, sacrifices, both human and animal, were considered appropriate. But they no longer are—or are they?

What remains with us from the days of human and animal sacrifice is the idea of murder as a form of worship, the idea that religion sanctions murder. And that is a reminder of all the religious wars of history, "holy wars" in whatever language designated.

"When Pope Urban II summoned the chivalry of Christendom to the Crusade, He released in the masses, hopes and hatreds which were to express themselves in ways quite alien to the aims of papal policy. [That was in 1095.—MO]. . . . And nevertheless it is clear that already amongst the prelates and priests and nobles who heard Urban's appeal at Clermont, something was at work which was not simply an expectation of individual gain, whether material or spiritual. As the assembly listened it was swept by emotions of overwhelming power. Thousands cried with one voice; 'Deus le volt!'—'It is God's will!' Crowding around the Pope, and kneeling before him they begged leave to take part in the holy war. A cardinal fell on his knees and recited the Confiteor in the name of the whole multitude and as they echoed it after him, many burst into tears and many were seized with convulsive trembling. For a brief moment there reigned in that predominantly aristocratic assembly an atmosphere of collective enthusiasm such as was to become normal in the contingents of common folk which were formed later." (Cohn 1970:61 f.)

At the prospect of communal murder in the name of God, the crusader knights together with masses of impoverished peasants joined in the march across Europe, in the course of which perhaps 80 percent perished.

The compulsion to fight to defend and to submit to a godlike leader, ignoring other humane obligations, is captured by Heinrich Heine in his well-known poem, "Two Grenadiers."

Two of Napoleon's soldiers who had been captured in Russia, bedraggled, make their way back to France. When they reached Germany they heard the news that France had been defeated and that their emperor had been captured. They wept over the sad news and considered death an option. But one objected, fearing that his wife and child would perish without him. The second dismisses concern for wife and child. He is preoccupied with the capture of his emperor. He asks his companion to promise him that he will, after his death, carry him to France and bury him there. In the grave, fully armed, he will wait until he once more hears the sounds of war. When his emperor arrives over his grave, he will emerge to fight and protect his emperor.

Religious worship involves not only a transaction between man and his gods, but also a murderous transaction between men, sanctioned by a warlike god.

Mine eyes have seen the Glory of the coming of the Lord.
He is trampling out the vintage where the grapes of wrath
are stored.

(from the "Battle Hymn of the Republic";
cf. Revelation 14:18–20 and Isaiah 3:3)

Religion and murder, even fratricide, become mutually reinforcing and encouraging.

Self-Sacrifice

The subject of human sacrifice compels us to discuss the phenomenon of suicide, self-immolation, and other forms of self-destruction. I would assume that self-sacrifice like infanticide has a biological root. Specifically, one may speculate that humans and perhaps other mammals possess an instinctual mechanism for self-destruction, which most of the time is overridden and inhibited by an instinct for self-preservation, a need to maintain one's physical and mental integrity, ultimate narcissism. This self-destructive tendency becomes manifest when the self-preservative instinct is weakened or the self-destructive tendency is strengthened, or both. The most common occasion for suicide is depressive illness. The self-critical and self-destructive force that becomes activated in depression is powerful enough to overcome the self-preservative restraint and liberate the potential for self-destruction. The suicidal act is rationalized as escape from pain; or as death deserved because of guilt; or as beneficence to the survivor, for example, by leaving money or an insurance policy. Any of these rationalizations may be activated by the depression-driven suicidal need. The immediate cause might be either the intolerable depressive pain or the irresistibility of the depressive force. It is not clear whether the depression strengthens the self-destructive urge so that it overcomes the self-preservative inhibition, or whether the instinct for self-preservation becomes weakened by the depression so that the self-destructive urge can escape from inhibition, or both.

Depressed individuals seldom refer to God, and they usually reject religious objection to suicide. Observers may speak of "possession" by a devil or a *dibbuk*. Such a statement reifies the self-destructive urge of depression. The survivors will profit, the suicide declares, and they will be freed from a burden.

One may commit suicide to thwart an enemy, to prevent torture, or to frustrate the executioner. In other words, such suicide may be used to protect the individual against pain and mental catastrophe.

Suicide can also serve as a mode of attack. For example, a suicide bomber may kill the enemy. The story of Samson, who pulled down the pillars of the Philistine temple, is an early instance of suicide as a means of attack. As he did so, he is reported to have said, "Let my soul perish together with the Philistines" (Judges 16:30).

Suicide sometimes serves the altruistic motive of protecting others; for example, on the battlefield, one soldier may take a blow to save comrades who are in danger. In civil life, when a family or a group is in danger, an individual may heroically attempt to rescue them, knowing he is risking his life. Many such instances are recorded to have occurred in the aftermath of the destructive terrorist attack on the World Trade Center of September 11, 2001. The individual who courageously participates in battle, whether as a volunteer or drafted by his government, is exposing himself to mortal danger. He may be motivated by an idealistic fidelity to his country and flag, knowing that the odds are good that he may be seriously wounded or killed. Here devotion to the community supersedes self-preservation.

In the heat of battle, the soldier often feels invulnerable and exposes himself unwisely to excessive danger. Motivation here is based upon commitment to community, that is, an altruistic attitude rather than personal gratification. If the war is designated a "holy war" or the equivalent by the community, then the motivation is reinforced by the wish to serve God as well as the community in the hope of being rewarded appropriately.

Martyrdom is undertaken to remain faithful to religious belief or to political commitment or community solidarity. Usually the subject hopes to be rewarded in the world after death for making the "supreme sacrifice." By killing himself, he defies the enemy's demands; the martyr fights him. He protects the belief commitment of his religion, which might otherwise be undermined.

Bergmann's discussion of Schiller's poem "The Ring of Polykrates" illuminates our subject further.

> The poem was written over a thousand years after sacrifices were no longer practiced in the Western world. Yet it is not possible to read Schiller's poem without getting in contact with some of the feelings that underlie the need for sacrifice. The poem evokes the feeling of dread that many men and women, burdened with a sense of guilt, experience when they are particularly successful or when good fortune beyond their expectations befalls them. According to some investigators these feelings of guilt are the source of sacrifice (Henninger 1987). If Schiller's intuition was correct, then envy or jealousy projected on the deity is the basic emotion that gave rise to sacrifices. From very early times people must have felt that they must give up something dear to them in order to prevent destruction by an envious or jealous god. Both sacrifice and circumcision can be seen as religious defenses against the projected image of a jealous and murderous god.

I am not persuaded that it is necessarily "envy or jealousy projected onto the deity is the basic emotion that gave rise to sacrifices." I suspect that an angry god is sufficient justification for the need to propitiate.

The form of the sacrifice varies with the culture. In medieval Europe monks took vows of poverty, chastity, and obedience. The sect calling themselves Flagellants submitted one another to painful flagellations, but as comrades, and also flagellated their tormentors in turn, exercises in religious sado-masochism.

Although the context of this discussion is religion as the principal locus of negative spirituality, the urge to sacrifice may be determined by the need to overcome and forestall depression. In religious rationalization, depression or the misfortune that elicits it is attributed to an angry god or to a diabolical agent that precludes divine providence, as, for example, in the incidents of anti-Semitism that I quoted above.

Self-sacrifice, an exercise in moral masochism, need not be based upon overt religious consideration or dedication. The *New Yorker* magazine of August 2, 2004 contains a story written by Ian Parker, "The Gift," under the heading of "Annals of Philanthropy." It tells of a man in his thirties and forties who rapidly made millions of dollars by sagacious real estate investments and soon gave all of it away to eleemosynary institutions, mostly in the field of public health. He did it, over the objections of wife and friends, out of the sense of moral obligation. He did not understand why he should possess things while others might be dying for lack of money. But what made the story even more striking was that having given away most of his money, he then searched for something else to donate, and donated one of his kidneys to a young woman whom he had not known. And having done that, much to the dismay of his family, he considered donating the other kidney, proposing to survive on dialysis, and other organs as well. He did not speak of religion, merely of moral obligation. Of course, motivating this behavior was a need to contend with recurrent depression. The author gives enough detail to make clear that the subject of the story exhibited both highs and lows, that is, a bipolar course. Before going into business, he had earned two Ph.D.s with a brilliant thesis about writing. He taught both grammar school and university classes. He undertook business enterprises, invariably brilliantly successful, only to drop each in turn and give away what he had earned. He defended his strange behavior to family and friends as moral necessity, but not once did he invoke religious considerations. One might argue that the religious thoughts were repressed, not conscious, but we have no evidence for that view.

If we try to ascertain the biological source of the self-destructive instinct, we do not find it in the child's relation to his parent. We find it in the dynamics of depressive illness in which a self-destructive force appears and in some instances succeeds in destroying the individual. It seems to be an outgrowth and exaggeration of the tendency toward self-criticism, feelings of guilt and shame, lowered self-esteem, all of which are mobilized to prevent an excessive mood swing toward the upside, toward hypomania and mania, and to reverse it toward a more neutral position. However in the presence of a tendency toward excessive mood volatility, the downward swing continues beyond equanimity and toward depression itself and the self-defeating and self-destructive tendency continues beyond correction of the mania or hypomania and toward frank depression. I don't know how to decide whether the self-destructive tendency is something disclosed by the depressive pull or is created *de novo* in the pathogenesis of the illness. By an act of self-sacrifice, such as those that I have adduced, the subject hopes to prevent or reverse the threatening depression.

As I suggested above, spiritual experience, positive or negative, helps with mood regulation, and sometimes the process of mood regulation creates a spiritual experience.

Fundamentalism

We consider a religious community fundamentalist if it displays several of the following qualities: unusual zeal, separatism, authoritarianism, religious stringency, intolerance of the deviations of others, aggressiveness or defensiveness or both, an apocalyptic frame of mind, a belief in the inerrancy of the scripture that they value, intolerance of alternative translations and of modern commentaries, intolerance of all sexual language and activity except for marital sex. Theweleit (1987) described a secular proto-Nazi fundamentalist group, the Freikorps. They distinguished among three kinds of women: those who are absent, such as the wives and fiancées left behind, generally unnamed and unnoted in the Freikorp men's most intimate diaries; the women who appear in the imagination and on the literal battle front as "white nurses," chaste, upper-class German women; and who are class enemies—the "red women" whom men face in angry mobs and sometimes in single combat. These women are actively sexual, whores, aggressive, and possibly armed. While the fundamentalist can tolerate women who are absent or sterile and Madonna-like, he cannot tolerate a woman who is attractive and sexually active.

How can we understand the fundamentalist syndrome? Let us assume that fundamentalists are trying to appease a fearsome god, though he is not recognized as such. Their attitude, in each of the several defining characteristics, is consistent with an attempt to appear stringent and zealous in obedience to the rules of the cult and its narrow ideas and practice of morality. Contact with any who might introduce more liberal ideas might possibly dilute theirs and therefore must be phobically avoided. So must the temptations of sexuality, lest temptation lead to violation. Fundamentalists can tolerate no version of Scripture that might cast doubt on the inerrancy and absolute authority of their own. In short, they are trying to appease a demonic and hostile god by extraordinarily stringent—if not masochistic—self-denial and self-control.

This understanding of the nature of fundamentalism can be illustrated, I believe, by the story of the apostasy of Israel with the Midianite worshippers of Baal Peor. The account is given in chapters 25 and 31 of the Book of Numbers. In the manifest account in the text, the Israelite men engaged in sexual relations with the Midianite women and participated in the sexual worship of Baal Peor. A plague broke out in punishment, and YHVH told Moses to execute the leaders of the apostasy. Just as Moses gave the order to execute all those who had attached themselves to Midian, a young man of the civil elite of Israel led a Midianite princess into the Israelite camp and, in brazen defiance of Moses and the religious establishment, performed an act of sexual intercourse in a *kubbah*, that is, a small marriage tent. Pinehas, the son of Eleazar, the High Priest, pursued them into the enclosure and impaled them both on his spear while they were coupled together. The plague was arrested immediately, after 24,000 had died. YHVH praised Pinehas for his devotion and for having acted to requite his passionate fury. Had Pinehas not done so, YHVH declared, he would have wiped out the entire people of Israel. Subsequently YHVH instructed Moses to attack the Midianites so as to avenge their having led Israel into apostasy. The Israelites slew every male but spared the women and children. Moses protested sparing the women because it was they who had seduced the Israelite men. The virgins who did not participate in the sexual seduction were to be spared, but not the seductresses.

I repeat the story in some detail because it illustrates my thesis. Although in the text, the story starts with the apostasy and the plague is seen as punishment, one commonly finds in Scripture that misfortune is attributed to prior misbehavior. Here the plague is attributed to sexual apostasy, which was dramatized by the public defiance of Israel's religious authorities. Pinehas, I contend, acted as a fundamentalist, publicly murdering descendants of civil authority who violated religious proscription and thereby, he assumed, had provoked YHVH to initiate the punitive plague. Israel was to be protected by murdering the enemies of YHVH. Here, as in most other fundamentalist scenarios, sexuality elicits the greatest fury of the religious authorities, so that ultimately all the sexual women of Midian were executed. In summary, a murderous fury against non-observant men and against sexually active women was considered justified by fear of divine punishment. The fundamentalists attack and murder to propitiate their god, to prevent him from becoming angry and destroying them. In fundamentalism, the murderous anger is often preceded by depression. Chapter 25, verse 6 says, "and then one of the Israelite men appeared and brought this Midianite woman to his companions in the presence of Moses and the entire congregation of Israel who were standing and weeping at the entrance to the Tent of Meeting."

It is interesting that while Pinehas's fundamentalist murder is praised in the Bible, the rabbis of the Talmud registered a different view. Some of them treated him as though he were a vigilante. In Sanhedrin 82a, the rabbis stated explicitly that anyone consulting them about how to act in a similar situation would not have been instructed to follow Pinehas's example.

If we subscribe to the reasoning that I have proposed, the fear of a punitive, hostile god would be attributed to a depressive threat, in this instance an expression of a communitywide sense of defeat, desolation, and despair. This fear is complemented by a belligerent response to an enemy who is held responsible for that state of mind. If the sense of victimization is attributable to no real enemy, it's attributed to a mythic enemy. In the case of the current militant factions of Islam, the mythic enemy is the West, especially the United States and Israel and world Jewry. In other words, the fundamentalist's resistance to depression consists of appeasing God or fate or his own superego, any of which might persecute him, and also fighting a mythic enemy. As mentioned above, when Pope Urban II preached the crusade, at Clermont in 1095, his listeners are reported to have replied with almost one voice, "Deus le volt!" that is, "God wishes it!" Perhaps unconsciously the fury at the mythic enemy is displaced from anger at the demonic god.

Not all fundamentalist communities are identical. The mechanisms to which I have drawn attention are probably similar among the various groups, but the actual manifestations may vary. For example, in current militant Islamic fundamentalism, infanticide returns in the form of suicide bombing, attacking an enemy who has in fact no hostile designs on the Islamic community but whose status as an enemy is determined by history based either purely on myth or on events that occurred several centuries in the past. Infanticide in the interest of destroying an enemy is not promoted by Christian or Jewish fundamentalism, to my knowledge. Among these, we have seen occasional bombings, sometimes with serious loss of life, but young people were not sent out to blow themselves up. Suicide bombing represents infanticide and attack on the mythic enemy in the same act.

Fundamentalist communities tend to split into warring segments, sometimes allied by sharing the same enemies, but otherwise seeing one another as infidels.

Apocalypse

In chapter 7, I described apocalypse, its manifestations and psychodynamic background, but here I shall try to put it into the context of negative spirituality. I have tried to demonstrate that the phenomenon of spontaneous mood regulation plays an obvious role in all of the various spiritual phenomena discussed, aggression as well as pacific, serene spirituality. I have tried to demonstrate too that aggression internally directed by a depressive tendency can reinforce the depressive syndrome, and when it is directed outward in the presence of rebirth tendencies, aggression can accompany and reinforce antidepression efforts. The hope and wish of the discontented individual or community to achieve recovery can invoke great anger and murderous belligerence. I have suggested that that mechanism conforms to the need of the fundamentalist to destroy others, complementing his stringent self-restraint.

The apocalyptic mechanism focuses not on the principle of individual, self-denying righteousness so much as upon the belief that one's rebirth or triumph rides upon the defeat of the other, the wicked. The polarization of the world into the righteous and the wicked resembles the polarization assumed by the fundamentalist. But whereas the fundamentalist sees his rebirth as depending primarily upon his extraordinary restraint, his masochistic submissiveness, and his war against infidels, the apocalyptic focuses primarily on the expectation of the physical destruction of the enemy, either miraculous or natural.

The essence of apocalyptic expectation is annunciated by a prophet, who reports a mystical contact with the deity exemplified classically by the accounts given in Isaiah 6 and Ezekiel 1 and 2, quoted above. Most mystical experiences yield revelation, and the apocalyptic revelation is paradigmatic; in essence, the prophet claims divine inspiration. The prophecy is intended to warn the wicked of ultimate, if not imminent catastrophic destruction, and to encourage the suffering righteous to anticipate their subsequent rebirth. All of this is to occur at the "end of days," the eschaton. Primarily, apocalypticism is expectant.

As noted in the previous chapter, sometimes it is anticipated that destruction and rebirth will recur cyclically for a while before the ultimate and definitive consummation at the end of days, for example, the various millennial and dispensational beliefs.

What is spiritual about apocalypse is the individual subjective experience of comfort derived from a divinely given revelation and promise. It is the parental promise and reassurance of protection against the attacks of the stranger, the enemy. But it also invokes the principles of morality, and perhaps to a lesser extent, cultic righteousness, in distinguishing between the wicked who will be destroyed and the righteous who will be "saved," vindicated, and reborn.

The fundamentalist polarizes the world into his own holy group that epitomizes religious and moral virtue and everyone else as infidel, wicked, and deserving of condemnation and death. The apocalyptic prophet addresses himself primarily to the destruction of the world except that the righteous will be saved. The difference is subtle but clear. The fundamentalist claim is: it's we against them. The apocalyptic prophet speaks in terms of categories. The wicked know who they are and the righteous know who they are. This distinction may not be self-evident to the population to which the prophecy is addressed. In Ezekiel 9:3,

> The Presence of the God of Israel ascended from the cherub upon which He rested, to the platform of the Temple and He called to the man clothed in linen who carried the writing instrument at his waist. And the Lord said to him, "Pass through the city, Jerusalem, and place a mark upon the foreheads of the men who are suffering and distraught because of all the abominations that are committed in it." And to the others, he said in my hearing, "Pass through the city after him and smite, let not your eyes spare any, nor show pity. Old and young, maidens and little children, as well as women, utterly destroy, but do not touch any person who bears the mark."

In Revelation 3 and 14, some had the "mark of the beast," on their right hands and foreheads, and in contradistinction, the 144,000 who stood on Mount Zion with the Lamb had the Father's name written on their foreheads.

My point is that the fundamentalists constitute a coherent, recognizable community, whereas in apocalypticism, the righteous and the wicked may mingle in the same community and therefore may require some external mark to distinguish them. However, in other apocalyptic scenarios, righteous and wicked are each distinct and recognizable.

Yet the differences between fundamentalists and apocalyptics are sometimes obscured. Some apocalytics, impatient for the "end time," abandon the expectant attitude and act to effect the prophecy themselves. They become a violent band of religious zealots determined to bring the apocalyptic prophecy to fruition, as described, for example, in the texts of Ezekiel and Revelation that I have quoted. Sometimes they complement their externally directed aggression with attacks on themselves and one another, attacks that seem to make them even more vicious. The Flagellants of the Middle Ages exemplify this variant. This category of activist apocalyptic is described in Norman Cohn's *Pursuit of the Millennium* (1970).

Messianism

With messianism we return to the redemptive aspect of spirituality. The notion of a redeemer associates naturally with the rebirth component of the apocalyptic oscillation, as suggested above. Redemption is psychodynamically equivalent to being retrieved by the mother, so that messianic redemption, being "saved," is being rescued by a mother substitute. Commonly, the advent of the messiah is preceded by a period of tribulation, "the birth pangs of the Messiah" (Sanh 98b). While messianism is not confined to apocalyptic speculation, it is associated with it. The messiah is the rescuing parent whom we hope to reach in our spiritual aspiration. Fundamentalism claims that God sanctions self-denial and the demonization of others. Apocalypticism claims that God threatens the wicked and promises redemption to the righteous. Messianism claims that a divine redeemer will arrive to save his faithful from the apocalyptic destroyer or the ravages of reality.

While messianism is a mythic concept, realistic movements of self-assertion and political independence often receive a mythic, messianic coloring that not only gives them romance but also encourages zealous, conscious hopes for magical rescue, communal and individual, hopes that we all entertain.

Terrorism

In the *New York Times* of September 22, 2002, Elaine Sciolino published excerpts from three autobiographical essays written by a twenty-eight-year-old prisoner in France who was suspected of participating in an Al Qaeda plot to blow up the American embassy in Paris and of directing communications between a cell in France and Al Qaeda. In France he was charged with associating with criminals connected with a terrorist plot and carrying false identification papers. From prison, the man composed three essays about his childhood, his turn to Islam, and his political radicalization, and he sent them to a French television network. "The result," wrote Sciolino, "is an unusually personal—if one sided—glimpse into the mind set of a young, educated Arab who calls himself a terrorist, even as he denies involvement in any terrorist plot" ("Roots: Portrait of the Arab as Young Radical" 9). The apologia that he offered relates to the concerns of this chapter, although he did not voice fundamentalist or apocalyptic doctrine openly but rather the more general category of "terrorism." Obviously the story is a presentation of the world as he sees it and need not, except for certain circumstantial facts, be considered to represent the literal truth.

Sciolino's report starts: "Allah the Great says in the Koran that neither Jews nor Christians will ever be satisfied with you until you follow their religion. But Allah's way is the true way . . . this is without a doubt the verse of the Koran that sums up . . . the twenty-eight years of my life." The author begins with a statement that the Jews and Christians are his enemies, a mythic belief that he attributes to the Qur'an. This is the mythic enemy, already considered in several contexts, that usually arises as a projection of the internal self-punitive force that appears in the process of enveloping depression and then becomes the target of the belligerent struggle to resist depression.

Until he was five, he lived with his mother and younger brother and was spoiled by uncles and aunts who tried to compensate for the absence of his father, who was working in France to support his family. When the boy turned five, his father brought the family to France, and the writer had lived in Paris ever since. "I was condemned to be my father's foot soldier while he was working. I was ultimately an interpreter, guide, an accountant for my poor mother, who had a great deal of trouble getting used to this barbarian language. . . . Very early on I had adult responsibilities which literally ate into my childhood, which I wanted to live in the same way as other children."

Note that the subject sees himself as exploited by his father and already he uses a military metaphor, "I was condemned to be my father's foot soldier," to describe his family responsibilities. Clearly he is antagonistic to his father because his early "adult responsibilities" literally "ate into my childhood." He felt persecuted by his father as early as age five. Remember that during the first five years the patient lived with his mother, without the father whose occasional visits seem to have represented intrusions. He writes later that his father beat him with a wooden paddle when he failed to excel in school.

"People were jealous of me because of my good grades but they made fun of me for the way I acted and for my excessive modesty in the eyes of the French children. They made jokes about my first name." He felt persecuted and abused not only by his father but also by his classmates. In his early years his ambition was "to be a pilot on a fighter plane. But I knew that my poor eyesight would never allow this . . . so I decided to become an aeronautical engineer." The military fantasies continue.

Just as I came close to achieving my dream, I started to worry about religious and political questions. The context of the time was the war in Algeria, where they were about to set up a regime based on Islamic law.

The West hated us because we were Arabs and Muslims. . . . The massacres committed by the Algerian army was the last straw for me. I could no longer study serenely.

All of the pressure that had been put on me during my school years so that I would succeed at any price suddenly transformed itself into energy to challenge radically my environment and my father. . . . From that moment on I did not want anything to do with the West.

The political and military events of those years, that is, when he was eighteen, precipitated a crystallization of an oppositional personality leaning toward hatred of both his father and the West, identifying with militant Islam. As he puts it, the energy hitherto employed in the effort to please his father by excelling at his studies was now redirected to oppose his father. That opposition and the loyalty to his mother adds an oedipal motivation to what he saw as political and personal.

Somewhat later, the family fell on hard times again, and he saw himself exploited by the French for political purposes. Then came the signal event. "There were only two choices left for me, either to sink into a deep depression, and I did for more than six months at the end of my second year at the university, or to react by taking part in the universal struggle against this overwhelming unjust cynicism.

So I reviewed everything that I had learned and put all of my knowledge into a new perspective. I then understood that the only person worth devoting my life to was Allah . . . everything suddenly became clear to me and I understood why Abraham went into exile, why Moses rebelled against Pharaoh, why Jesus was spat upon and why Muhammad said, "I come with the sword on judgment day." My battle was and will be to eradicate all powers that are opposed to the law of Allah, the most high, whatever the price may be because only our Creator has the power to make laws and any system based on the laws of men is artifice and lies. The glorious battle will not stop until the law of Allah has been reestablished and applied by a just and honest caliph.

"Everything suddenly became clear to me" is a statement commonly heard from patients during the course of mental illness. It generally marks the point at which an individual is becoming psychotic and begins to see the world in a different light, as a delusional fantasy replacing the grim reality or painful affect he prefers not to face. At that point in this biographical account, it becomes clear to the writer that his destiny is to become a rebel in the name of his God. Note the aspiration for rebirth of the community, that is, the expectation that as a result of his military action, "this glorious battle," religious law will be established and the world will be ruled by an Islamic monarch.

Thereafter he immersed himself in religious and political literature and justified his new identification because "I knew that a victory of Islam over the West was possible." He went to Algiers in the middle of the war and observed the struggle between the Algerian military security forces and the Islamists. "The Algerian war, the Bosnian, the Gulf War, Kosovo, Afghanistan, Palestine, Lebanon—all of these events strengthen my conviction that the Judeo-Christian community influenced by atheism has a visceral hatred of the community of Muhammad. . . . For all these reasons and because of all these events which have left indelible wounds, I went over to the forces of the 'dark side.'" The conversion is completed together with a reinforcement of his paranoid belief in the mythical enemy.

> My ideological commitment is total and the reward of glory for this relentless battle is to be called a terrorist. I accept the name of terrorist if it is used to mean that I terrorize a one-sided system of iniquitous power and a perversity that comes in many forms. I have never terrorized innocent individuals and I will never do so. But I will fight any form of injustice and those who support it. My fight will only end in my death or in my madness.

Note that he emerges from his depressive illness into political and religious conversion, much as Mr. Gibson did in accounting for his sudden decision to return to religious life and to present a picture of his depression, using the Passion of Christ as a metaphor. The Algerian terrorist came out of his experience fighting, and so did Gibson. The need to battle a mythic enemy, the expectation of communal as well as individual rebirth, the preoccupation with apocalyptic destruction, the expectation of the attack and, in this case, the expectation of either relapsing into depression or provoking his own death—all of these are themes we have encountered in this chapter. The zeal of fundamentalism is easily recognizable here.

What is missing from this account is the influence of his fellow Arabs and Muslims in the community where he grew up and his suicidal need to put his life in jeopardy.

One question that can be asked of this material is whether the pathology of depression influences so very many youths so as to force them into membership in militant Islamic movements. Most religious conversions occur during the later teen years, a period of emotional turmoil and a struggle to position oneself in the adult community. Much of that turmoil takes a depressive form, though perhaps not intense enough to warrant a diagnosis of clinical depression. It is generally believed in the psychiatric community in the United States that one or another form of mood pathology affects between 10 and 20 percent of the population at some point during their lives. Perhaps that figure is too low and mood disturbances that are not labeled with a diagnosis or do not even warrant one are even more common. Perhaps a demoralized community may create a depressive orientation to life in many of its members. The translation from individual experience to community experience and back requires further study.

CHAPTER 9

Analyzing an Account
of a Spiritual Experience

After I had completed the first draft of this manuscript, I read an account of a "vision quest." It was presented as an autobiographical description of an adventure entered into by Dr. Donald M. Marcus, a respected and experienced psychoanalyst, who hoped to find a week's diversion in natural surroundings. Paula Hamm, a close colleague and mutual friend, had been chairing discussion groups at meetings of the American Psychoanalytic Association on the subject of the psychodynamics of spirituality for several years. A close friend of Dr. Marcus, she knew of his manuscript and suggested that he present it to the group; he gladly did so.

With his permission, I reproduce it here to illustrate an extended spiritual experience and to demonstrate how the type of analysis that I have been describing applies.

A PSYCHOANALYST GOES ON A VISION QUEST

The Vision Quest is an important part of the Native American culture. Young men use it to discover what their life path should be while tribal elders may use it as a way to find out the best course of action for the tribe in times of danger. While the actual procedure varies from tribe to tribe, in general it consists of a man's going out alone into the wilderness with only the clothes he is wearing. He does not eat and in some cases does not drink water for about a week. He has little or no protection from the elements. He is given a ceremonial blessing when he leaves and when he returns the whole tribe is waiting for him. As might be expected, the altered state of consciousness that it produces almost always results in a vision. For a number of years wilderness guides have made this experience available in a modified form to anyone who was interested. I will describe such an experience from which I have recently returned.

The adventure actually began several months prior to the quest when the list of needed items arrived. Unlike the Native Americans, we would require a tent, sleeping bag and pad, warm clothing and rain gear. In addition, our guide, Michael Eller, requested that we bring along something precious to give away to make room to take in something new. This was no easy task, and made me think through what I found to be precious and what I could easily give away. I first chose a medal for Excellence in Classics that I had received when I was graduated from high school. It was precious at the time I got it but it did not cause me any great pain to think of giving it away, so I knew it was no longer precious. Next I chose a pin I received at MIT when I was made a member of Sigma Xi, the honorary research society. Again, it did not cause me any great pain to think of giving it away so I knew it was no longer precious to me. My wife suggested that I give away the trophy I got for making a hole-in-one in golf. That would hurt. The only problem was that it weighed five pounds and was really too heavy to carry up the mountain. I decided to take the medal and the pin and leave the trophy behind.

The trip started auspiciously at 6 a.m. on a Saturday in August when, on the way to the airport, I saw a deer in Encino, a rare occurrence these days. Michael, with two assistants, met our group of two men and five women questors at the Reno airport and drove us to the Hunewill ranch in Bridgeport, California where we met our sixth woman questor and where we were going to camp the first night. As we were touring the ranch a woman's voice called out, "I know you." It was Beth Trawick, an old friend and colleague whose office is only a block from mine. She was spending a week as a guest at the ranch. It seemed like another good omen.

It was almost dark as we were pitching our tents and I was unable to figure out how to set mine up. Even Michael had some difficulty in the gathering darkness because my rental tent had been packed inside out. Eventually I got into my sleeping bag close to Buckeye Creek, where I could hear the sound of the rushing water. As is usual for me the first night camping out, I got very little sleep, but the air was clear and the stars were spectacular. We arose early the next morning, ate a breakfast of oatmeal, packed a lunch for the climb in and segregated our gear. In our day packs we had water, lunch, rain gear and sundries we would need for the hike. Everything else was packed in a duffel bag to be carried in by horse. We stopped in Bridgeport to buy a few last minute items like fresh bread, and then headed by car to the trailhead, stopping on the way to get a permit at the Ranger Station.

At the trailhead Michael told us about the climb to our base camp and how it was important that we each walk at a pace that was right for us. We formed a circle around a sage bush and pledged to take good care of each other as well as the sacred land into which we were going. In addition he insisted on what he called his 'no discount' policy in which we were not to discount any pain or symptom of illness of any kind. After agreeing to meet again at that sage bush in a week's time, we put our packs on our backs and headed up the mountain. We began our climb at an altitude of 7000 feet and our base camp was at 9600 feet. About a half hour into our walk we saw a hawk suddenly rise out of the bush near our path. When we got to that spot we could see a small dead and bloody rodent which the hawk had killed and abandoned when we approached. Ever since I had an encounter with a hawk two years ago I have thoughts of hawks as "my animal." On that occasion, I was sitting on a bench in the Santa Monica Mountains, and a hawk kept flying back and forth in front of me, often no more than thirty feet away. It continued this for about five minutes before it flew away. I had the feeling that it was being friendly and eager to communicate.

Because of the altitude, the heat and the steady uphill climb, it was slow going, but the views were spectacular: the valley below and the lakes, trees, mountains and glaciers above. At first we saw two off-road vehicles, but soon the trail narrowed and was passable only on foot. We stopped often for the group to rest and to allow the slow walkers to catch up; when we came to a rushing stream we stopped for lunch. I was actually too tired to eat but forced down one of my peanut butter and jelly sandwiches. It was a beautiful spot, but we could not tarry because we needed to get to our base camp to set it up before dark. Shortly after lunch, Noah, Michael's godson and our assistant guide, noticing my increasing fatigue, asked me whether I would like him to carry my pack. I said no at first, but as we began to ascend another steep hill, I thought better of it. I was beginning to wonder whether I would make it to the base camp. Even with Noah carrying my pack I found the last half hour very tiring. We finally arrived at the campsite after a five hour walk and our gear was waiting for us, neatly stacked by the cowboys who had brought it in by horse. Because of my great fatigue, I decided that it would be too much for me to set up my campsite, pack it to take to my solo spot, set it up again and then take it down and repack it again after three days only to set it up once more before having to take it down and repack it for the trip out. Instead, I found a spot about a hundred yards from the base camp, far enough away so that I could not see it or be seen, where I could pitch my tent once and still have solo time.

I lay exhausted in my tent until dinner time, arising only because I knew it was important to drink as much as possible of the mineral soup that Michael had prepared with a thick broth, tofu and snow peas. I told the group that although I was not certain why I had come on the vision quest, I had already learned something very important: I really was 76 and not as young as I liked to think. As I said this I began to cry and I became aware of a deep sadness which enveloped my heart. While some of it had to do with my awareness of my aging and approaching death, I knew that it was too deep and overwhelming to be only that. It felt more like a sadness that was always with me, but was kept out of consciousness by the pressure of everyday living. The altitude and my physical weakness had broken down my defenses and the sadness had emerged. I was at first embarrassed by my crying that broke through almost every time I spoke, but Michael and the group were appreciative of my honesty, welcoming it as an important part of me. Perhaps what characterized this whole experience for me is how welcome I felt without my usual defenses. Instead of being shamed, I was admired for my openness. It was the kind of environment we try to create when we do psychoanalysis. Despite my pain, I knew that something good would come from this opportunity to contact my deeper truth.

That night we put on warm clothes and gathered around as Noah built and tended a wilderness campfire, which differs from the usual campfire in that it is small and has to be tended constantly because just enough wood is used to keep it going. Meanwhile, Michael gave us information and told us stories to prepare us for our solo time. We all asked questions about the things that worried us. What about bears? Michael said he had never seen evidence of a bear near or around our campsite, but we were near Yosemite where there were lots of bears so we should not keep any food in our tents at night. One of our questors told us of her fear of fire ever since she was burned as a child. Almost everyone was able to divulge something about themselves which they would never have been able to do if not for the unusual circumstances of being in this mountain wilderness.

It was another perfect night with millions of stars shining through the clear thin air. An almost full moon appeared over the East canyon wall casting enough light to make a flashlight unnecessary. I slept better and had a dream which was comforting in that I awoke thinking that I would certainly get acclimated to the altitude in a few days. We awoke to the noise of Michael and Noah fixing breakfast and heating water for a hot drink. It was another perfect morning and I took time to go down to Lake Tamarack, some 50 yards from our base camp, from which I could get a good view of the whole area. Directly South of us lay a ridge of mountain peaks which formed the Northeast border of Yosemite National Park. Descending from these peaks were about 10 small glaciers. We were in a canyon which extended North from the ridge which was about 2–3 miles distant. The canyon was about a half mile wide with walls consisting mainly of scree, although there were some trees on the West wall. We were camped in a forest on a plateau with the lake in the shape of a crescent nestled against the East wall of the canyon.

Before breakfast, Michael had us all congregate by the lake to observe the sun rising over the East canyon wall. He stood on a rock and sang a Navajo song of greeting, the same song he had recently sung to his son as he was being born. As I felt the warmth of the sun and heard the beauty of the song I began to cry uncontrollably. As nearly as I could make out it seemed to have to do with the beauty of the experience and the fact that I felt so welcome. After breakfast we gathered around a medicine circle which Michael had laid out with different colored stones marking the four points of the compass. While the color of the stones varies from tribe to tribe, the directions always have the same meaning: North is winter, dormancy, the beginning; East is spring, youth and first bloom; South is summer, adulthood, and full bloom; West is fall, old-age and wisdom. It describes our planet, our lives, and different aspects of our lives, so that our lives spiral many times around the circle. In addition to learning something of native American psychology, we all got to know each other better.

After the circle, Michael took us on a tour of the area, stopping at different places to give us a feel of this beautiful land. The first place we stopped was next to a strange yet magnificent tree. Actually it was two very large old trees joined at the base up to about 3 feet above the ground, leaving a space in which one could sit comfortably. It was the first of a small stand of trees, so positioned that it would break the wind for the other trees when winter storms hit. It seemed to be very old and very wise. I went up to it and introduced myself, explaining why my group had come. The tree answered that it knew we were coming and it had already noticed that we were a loving group which would take good care of this sacred land. He welcomed us, hoping that we would all find what we were seeking. After I thanked him, he said "You have become a good and wise person and it is time for you to forgive yourself for your past misdeeds and failings. You have suffered enough."

While this male voice seemed to come from the tree, I was aware that it sounded like the voice of my superego, except that my superego is rarely so benign. In retrospect, I think I made contact with an aspect of my superego that is very loving and usually hidden by another more cruel part. I am not likely to forget that benign part of my conscience which will always be associated with that tree. I was so pleased with that tree that I spoke to two other trees. The first was a short tree which had the appearance of being old despite its height and I asked it why it was so short. It replied, "As you can see I am growing in this area where it is almost all scree and no soil. Just as with you humans, our growth depends on the environment." It made good sense to me. Later, I spoke to another tree which intrigued me because its narrow trunk was bent first one way and then the opposite way over its whole length of some five feet. When I asked why its trunk was so crooked, it replied that it had responded to the elements, having been bent by the winter storms and then in the summer growing straight again. That way it had bent but not broken, and it was the same for humans. Again a tree made sense to me.

When night fell, Michael showed us another campfire style and told us more of what we would need to know to survive on our own for the three days of our solo. Among other things, we were each to have a "buddy." The buddies would decide on a place where they could leave a message for each other once a day to let the other know that they were well. If a message was not present, the buddy would then check to see what happened. One would go to the message circle in the morning and the other in the afternoon. My buddy was Sandy, who at 49 was the youngest of our group. Interestingly, she and I each seemed to know what the other needed, which I will take up later.

The next morning we gathered around our medicine circle where Michael fanned us with the smoke of burning sage to purify us, then blessed us and sent us on our way, one at a time. Because I was not yet acclimated to the altitude I had decided that I would not fast, but would limit my food intake to about 500 calories a day. We had all the water we required since we each had a filter to purify the lake water.

I spent my time attempting to understand why I felt so sad. I suspected that it was something that had escaped notice during my years of analysis, and was breaking through because my defenses were down. My dreams suggested that it was something that I was afraid to look at. Still I felt that this was a good time to face my fear. That afternoon when I went to our message circle, I found a note from Sandy which touched me deeply. She called me "grandfather" because I reminded her of the grandfather she loved. She also told me how much she respected me for my wisdom and how good it was to have me as an elder. It made me think that perhaps I could accept myself as an elder.

Toward mid-afternoon the clouds began to gather and soon there were rain drops. While in my tent, waiting for the rain to stop, I thought about my situation. I was alone in the rain, feeling weak, my back was hurting, my nose was running and the lightning and thunder seemed close. I hoped that the trees nearby were not the tallest around. What, I wondered, had ever possessed me to go on this trip? With whom could I discuss it? I feared my wife would tell me "I told you so!" I decided to check with my massage therapist. She was quick to reply "Stick it out, and when you get back I'll massage your back." I felt much better after she spoke to me. Soon the rain stopped, the sky cleared and it was another magnificent night.

The next day I felt stronger and went exploring. I could understand why the Indians believed that this was sacred land. When I got back to my tent, there was a note from Michael telling me that I was welcome to use the medicine circle. I broke out sobbing feeling so welcome. As I thought about this odd occurrence, I realized that I had rarely ever felt welcome just for myself; I had been a problem for my depressed mother because I was such an active boy. She loved me very much but worried about me and that added to her anxiety. While I loved her dearly, the only way I could separate from her was to harden my heart and deny my love. This hurt her deeply. We were not a good match and failed each other. I also believed I failed her in that I could not help relieve her depression. This was heartbreaking for me. As I thought about this, my sadness intensified and I knew I was on to something. Neither of us was to blame; it was just sad. Now, however, I could know the full extent of my love for her and remain separate. It was relieving, but I suspect that my sadness is going to be with me for the rest of my life. That is the price I have to pay for loving my beautiful mother; the reward is that I can love others more deeply.

I slept very well that night and had a dream which suggested to me that I was on the right track to understanding my sadness. I had not built a fire thus far and I decided that since this was to be our last night of solo time I would build a fire and have a ceremony to use the new knowledge I had gained about my relationship with my mother. What was especially curious to me is that Sandy seemed to intuit what I wished to do, although I made no mention of it to her. She left me a package of dried sage, a shell in which to burn it and some bound straw to waft the smoke over my body; I had all the ingredients necessary for a ritual ceremony. At the same time I found a feather and I seemed to know intuitively that is was meant for Sandy so I left it for her. Later, I learned that feathers always appeared when important things occurred in her life.

As darkness closed in, I built my ceremonial fire, lit the sage, and purified myself with its smoke. I imagined taking my mother (and my father) into my heart where I could show them how much I had always loved them. I told them that I knew that they had loved me, too, and had done their best to be good parents. I told them that I forgave them for all the ways in which they failed me, and I hoped that they forgave me for all the ways that I failed them. At that point they slowly disappeared. It was as though I had let go of them and they were free to leave. It was beautiful but sad.

The next morning we all came back to the base camp and Michael welcomed us in another ceremony around our medicine circle. We shared our experiences, many of which were quite extraordinary. The other male questor, Bob, had found the mandible of a bear which still had some flesh on it indicating that it had not been dead for long. We had no way of knowing what had happened to it, but we knew with certainty that bears were in the vicinity. One of the women, Joyce, who had confessed to a life-long fear of fire, dared to build a fire of her own. We had all survived and grown from our experience.

In the afternoon, after showers with water heated by the sun in solar bags, we again gathered around the medicine circle. This was the time to show our precious things and to tell why they were precious to us. As we did so, we placed them in the circle. We were then told that it was now time to line up around the circle and on Michael's signal, fight for the object we wanted most. Because Sandy had given gifts to me on our solo time, I had given my precious things to her, not realizing that we were going to play this game. Since they were very meaningful to her I requested that she be allowed to keep them and Michael agreed to it. There were many interesting items, but the one I wanted most was a tiny paper accordion given away by Catherine, another psychoanalyst. (What are the odds that I would find another analyst on this trip?) Catherine had said that it was given to her by a man she had loved who had died. The analyst in me was very intrigued. After we had procured our items, it was time for those who had not gotten what they wanted to try to bargain for it. There were a couple of successful transactions. Suzanne wanted to give me a valuable book for the accordion, saying that it was a token of the kind of love she had never had and believed she would never have. I told her that I was deeply touched by her request, but that I was more interested in emotional value and it was important for me to see what I could intuit about Catherine's love. I was pleased with myself for standing my emotional ground even though a voice in me told me that Suzanne needed it more than I. Perhaps I *had* let my needy mother go.

Before going to sleep that night. I played with the paper accordion and tried without success to get a sense of the kind of energy that it contained. However, I proceeded to have a wildly sexual dream which was quite different from any of the other dreams I had had on the mountain. I was not conscious of having any great sexual feelings toward her.

The next day as we hiked out of the mountains, I began to feel much stronger, and soon found that Catherine and I were alone, ahead of most of the others. I asked her if she would like to hear my dream and what I had intuited from her accordion. When she said yes, I told her that I thought her love had been very passionate and wildly sexual. She did not seem terribly surprised and readily acknowledged that what I told her was true. I wondered if giving away the accordion was part of an attempt to free herself of this old love. When we got back to the ranch, I knew that I no longer needed the accordion and that it properly belonged with Suzanne. In exchange for the accordion she gave me the book completing the deal that she had wanted to make so passionately.

Unfortunately Noah had to drive two of our questors to Reno to catch an early flight and Suzanne left early to drive back to her home near San Francisco, so there were only seven of us at our makeshift farewell dinner. It was a great pleasure to remind each other of the special time we had spent in our special place, but it was also sad that it was time to go back to our regular life. Michael warned us that not everyone would understand what we had to tell and that it was best to be careful about whom we told.

It is exactly a month since I walked down from the mountain. What can I say about the experience which would sum it up? It broke down my defenses and allowed me to make contact with aspects of myself I usually keep hidden. In a subtle way I have changed. I am less afraid and this allows me to be more open. My family, friends and patients have all noticed it. Several patients claim my work has improved markedly. Would I recommend this vision quest to others? Yes, if you love the outdoors and getting close to mother nature. It was an experience I will never forget.

Dr. Marcus describes the Native American "vision quest" as a search for revelation intended to provide guidance for Indian tribes at critical times. It reminds me of the practice of incubation. A troubled individual in search of guidance would go to the temple of the god whose advice he sought, and sleep there in the hope of recalling a dream whose interpretation would provide him with the counsel he needed. As Dr. Marcus notes, the altitude, the deprivation of food and water and the exposure to the elements results in an altered state of consciousness that favors the appearance of the desired vision. Dr. Marcus's experience was a modified one, the privation considerably less extreme.

Note that the vision quest is not described as a religious experience, although some of the ideas suggest religion. It seems to be closer to pure spirituality. It does not deal with morality as religion does, but it does involve a social group as religion does.

At the meeting, Dr. Marcus told us that he signed up for the vision quest when it was offered as a week's vacation adventure opportunity. However, from the text of the essay it seems evident that he was attracted also by the opportunity to profit from whatever comfort and wisdom he could acquire from this traditional Native American method of obtaining guidance in crisis. He had been trying courageously to deal with his aging. We see that initially he hoped to be able to contend with the physical rigors of the program and only when he realized that he could not, he accepted some help, and limited food restriction. He expected that the various privations as well as the altitude might result in an altered state of consciousness and thereby a vision.

In preparation, the guide suggested that each of the participants bring "something precious" to give away, "to make room to take in something new." In my discussion of religious spirituality, I described transactional worship, a modality in which God is induced to favor the worshipper in response to the latter's offering.

At the outset, Dr. Marcus seems to be seeking out good omens, a kind of magical guarantee of the success of the quest and perhaps alleviation of anxiety.

Throughout the experience he was sensitive to and recorded natural phenomena that inspired him, the sound of rushing water, spectacular stars, a bright moon, clear air, magnificent trees. Throughout the essay he records his impressions of nature. Usually he found positive elements that encouraged him, delighted him, and caused him to enjoy the adventure. His description suggests a sense of awe as he looked down at the landscape from the heights.

I am reminded here once more of Report 1. The subject in the presence of the pool and the bay is reminded of the beginning of

Psalm 19, "The heavens tell of the glory of God and the sky declares of the work of his hands." Natural phenomena, in this spiritual frame of mind, convey a heartening message—a revelation.

Actually, at some points Marcus animistically attributed cognition and intention to lower animals or inanimate objects, the hawk, the trees. He perceived that they were communicating with him. He actually heard the trees talking to him, he told us at the meeting, but at the same time as a psychoanalyst, he knew that his experience was a hallucination. His description reminds me of Shakespeare's metaphor in *As You Like It*, quoted above: "Tongues in trees, books in running brooks, sermons in stones and good in everything."

Nature not only inspires the psalmist but participates in the revelation that he is seeking, Psalm 19 tells us. "Day to day gives voice to speech and night to night communicates knowledge. There is no speech and there are no words whose sound is unheard."

Alone, Dr. Marcus's mind drifted to thoughts of his mother and of their uncomfortable relationship during his childhood. We find numerous symbolic and indirect allusions to his mother throughout the essay: the sacred land, seeking comfort from the massage therapist, the comforting trees (though he thinks of them as male, perhaps an allusion to his father), the beauty of nature, his response to the song sung as a child was being born.

He found himself weeping on two types of occasion: as he was forced to acknowledge his age and his weakness, and when he recognized that he was accepted and welcomed by his new companions. Tears of separation and tears of reunion.

The "revelation" then consisted of his coming to terms with the ambivalence of his relation to his mother. The trees and his quest companions assured him that he is a good and wise person, and that assurance brought him comfort; it undoes his depressive self-recrimination.

Note that here again, as observed above in the discussion of religious congregational life, the spiritual quest took two directions, upward to the memory of his mother, and laterally to his new companions, who provided him with the emotional support that he needed. Although it is clear that his interest in his companions as fraternal rather than sexual, it is equally clear that a sexual element broke through. My formulation is that the spiritual need recruits the sexual instinct to its service, as in the case of the mystical vision of Saint Teresa, described above.

At one point, while alone, that is, in the absence of the support of his companions, there was a brief episode of despair when he felt sick and weak and threatened by thunder and lightning. At that point he had to make contact with another person and called his massage therapist, someone who was not there but who had taken care of him physically in the past.

As distinct from the individual exemplary reports with which I introduced the discussions, this was an extended experience, lasting a week, in which Marcus reported a number of spiritual experiences. He described the awe he felt in response to the beautiful surroundings, mountains, valleys, water. The experience of hearing the guide sing the song, which greeted the rising sun and which he had also sung upon the recent birth of his son, left Marcus in tears. He did not know how to explain his emotional response, other than feeling welcome since the song was a song of welcome. But reading it, I have the impression that he experienced contact with a spiritual essence that seems to have been invoked for him by the scene he saw and heard. His conversation with the trees was clearly a mystical experience, as was his report of "taking my parents into my heart," after which "they slowly disappeared." That the members of what I have called the spiritual triad all occurred during the same vision quest confirms their intimate relationship. Evidently, awe, Spirituality, and mysticism are three facets that engage the same emotional disposition.

On the surface, there is no indication here of intended religious observance. However, certain elements suggest rudimentary religious attitudes. Welcoming the sun with a song reminds one of sun worship of premonotheistic Mediterranean religions. Spiritual experiences as we ordinarily hear of them are individual, whereas religious experiences are usually social or congregational. On this vision quest, the mutual support of the group was important to all, as if it were a religious group. In pure, nonreligious spirituality, morality seldom plays a significant role. Here there is a suggestion of morality in the commitment of the members of the group to take care of one another and also in the procedure for dividing up the gifts, the "precious things." I don't know how much of this represents

Native American religion that has colored the vision quest. At any rate, the experience was clearly primarily spiritual, with only a secondary hint of a religious component.

Throughout this book, I have repeatedly adverted to Psalm 19, to which my attention was drawn initially by Report 1. The psalm is an interesting one, including many elements of religious import and in a way comparable to the vision quest that we have been studying.

PSALM 19

1. For the leader, a psalm of David.
2. The heavens declare the glory of God, and the sky recites the work of His hands.
3. Day to day gives voice to speech and night to night communicates knowledge.
4. Their is no speech and there are no words whose sound is unheard (or, but their sound is unheard).
5. Their voice issues from the entire earth and their words throughout the universe. He created a tent (in the heavens) for the sun.
6. And the sun emerges from his canopy, eager as a hero to run his course.
7. He starts from one end of the heavens and his destination is at the other, no one can escape the sun.
8. The teaching of YHVH is perfect, restoring the soul; the testimonies of YHVH are reliable, making the simple wise.
9. The precepts of YHVH are just, causing the heart to rejoice; the commandments of YHVH are wholesome, lighting up the eyes.
10. The fear of YHVH is pure, abiding forever; the judgments of YHVH are true, altogether righteous.
11. More desirable than gold, and much pure gold, sweeter than honey and the drippings of the honey comb.
12. Your servant is instructed by them, observing them is rewarding.
13. Who can be aware of errors? Clear me of unperceived guilt.

14. And protect your servant from the arrogant, let them not control me, so I may remain innocent and I shall be clear of serious violation.

15. May the words of my mouth and the murmurs of my heart be acceptable to you, YHVH, my rock and my redeemer.

The first verse, "a psalm of David," merely means that this is a song intended to be sung to the accompaniment of a musical instrument, attributed to King David and intended for use in the course of Temple worship.

In verse 2 the heavens declare the glory of God and the sky recites the work of his hands. This is a verse to which I have repeatedly referred. In Report 1, it occured to the writer when his attention was drawn to the strangely beautiful and arresting view of the heavens. The verse means that he interpreted what he saw as a communication from God, a demonstration of what God had created. This, despite his disavowal of religious belief. In the vision quest there are many references to the beauty of the natural surround, with special reference to the stars and the moon and the "spectacular" views.

Verses 3, 4, and 5 of the psalm describe continual communication day and night as distinct, as if it were verbal. In the vision quest, Marcus responded to the many natural phenomena that moved him as though there were some direct communication. He made that explicit in the case of the hawk and later in the case of the talking trees.

Verses 6 and 7 almost seem out of place in a biblical song, for they refer to sun worship much as it was practiced by the pagans of the eastern Mediterranean before the advent of monotheism. Here the power of the sun has been placed under the rule of YHVH. In the vision quest, the Indian song to the rising sun, a celebration of rebirth, was also sung upon the birth of the singer's child. To this point, the correspondence between the vision quest and Psalm 19 is amazingly close.

With verses 8 through 11, there is a sudden change of subject. The singer praises the "teaching of YHVH," namely the Pentateuch. There is nothing like that in the vision quest. However, if we consider that the teachings, the decrees, the precepts, and the instructions of YHVH are all revelations from him, then we may ask what are the revelations in the vision quest. As I noted above, they are clear: the hallucinated voices of the trees, assuring him, among other things, that he is a good and wise man, and the realization that a major unresolved unconscious issue in Marcus's childhood was his conflict with his mother. These are both vision revelations that Marcus discovered on his quest. So both the vision quest and Psalm 19 start with inspiration by the beauties of nature and proceed to appreciation of revelation.

Verses 12 and 13 deal with morality, commitment to conform to the law of the revelation that the singer has just acknowledged. As observed above, there is not much explicit morality in the vision quest and only a suggestion of it in the agreement of the group to take care of one another and in their orderly dividing up of the gifts. However, verse 13 of the psalm talks about misbehavior, error, and guilt. We do find guilt in the vision quest, in Marcus's thoughts that his misbehavior had caused his parents grief, and his regret. He included first his mother and then both parents in the responsibility for the disaffection between him and them, and his personal feeling of guilt. He concluded that his ruminations had an expiating effect.

In verse 14, the singer prays that he will not succumb to inappropriate inclinations so that he will be innocent of misbehavior. The Hebrew word should properly be translated as "I shall become pure." In other words, purity is achieved by moral conduct. Note that purity is also mentioned in the vision quest on two occasions: first when the questors are each sent out on their solitary missions, and once on the last night of the missions when Marcus purified himself, in each case with the smoke of burning sage. Both the psalmist and the questor hope to achieve the feeling of purity, probably associated with holiness, but in different ways, the psalm by moral behavior and the questor by ritual.

Finally verse 15 is addressed directly to YHVH, asking that the song and the prayer be found acceptable, and YHVH is identified at "my rock and my redeemer." This statement seems to have no parallel in the vision quest unless we associate the word "redeemer" with mother, as discussed above. On the last night of the solitary portion of Marcus's adventure, while he was purifying himself with sage smoke, "I imagined taking my mother (and my father) into my heart so I could show them how much I had always loved them. I told them that I knew that they had loved me too, and had done their best to be good parents. I told them that I forgave them for all the ways in which they failed me, and I hoped that they forgave me for all the ways that I failed them." I see this as a statement comparable to verse 15, "May the words of my mouth and the murmurs of my heart be acceptable to you, YHVH, my rock and my redeemer." In the same category I would include also the final statement, "Would I recommend this vision quest to others? Yes, if you love the outdoors and getting close to mother nature."

Considering the disparate sources of these two accounts, the one a description of a contemporary week's adventure and the other a song composed 3,000 years ago for religious worship in the Temple, the similarity is striking.

The differences are also significant. In the first place, in the vision quest, there is a sexual element, confined to fantasy and never acted out but nevertheless experienced as an emotion. The psalm contains no such element. Sexual behavior was characteristic of pagan worship in the ancient Near East and strictly prohibited by the monotheistic religions. The vision quest is a more or less purely spiritual experience, with only a few hints of rudimentary religious components. The primary difference is that religion incorporates morality as an essential component and is almost always observed in a social context. In the vision quest, while the social component is important, the element of morality, if there is one, is subordinate and limited.

I present this material in this concluding chapter because I believe that it summarizes much of the book's discussion. It is also a reminder of the difference between pure spirituality and pure religion. Spirituality recapitulates and retrieves the baby's feeling of attachment to his mother; religion recapitulates and retrieves the older child's feelings and modes of relating to his family.

References

Ainsworth, M. D. S. 1973. "The Development of Infant-Mother Attachment." In *Review of Child Development Research*, ed. B. M. Caldwell and H. N. Ricciuti, 3:1–94. Chicago: University of Chicago Press.

Austin, J. 1998. *Zen and the Brain*. Boston: MIT Press.

Bear, D. M. and P. Fedio. 1977. "Quantitative Analysis of Interictal Behavior in Temporal Lobe Epilepsy." *Archives of Neurology* 34 (Aug.): 454–467.

Bergmann, M. 1992. *In the Shadow of Moloch: The Sacrifice of Children and Its Impact on Western Religions*. New York: Columbia University Press, 17.

Bilu, Y. 2000. "Oneirobiography and Oneirocommunity in Saint Worship in Israel: A Two-Tier Model for Dream-Inspired Religious Revivals." *Dreaming* 10 (2): 85.

Borg, J., B. Andree, H. Soderstrom, and L. Farde. 2003. "The Serotonin System and Spiritual Experiences." *American Journal of Psychiatry* 160 (11): 1965–1969.

Bouchard, T. J., Jr., D. Lykken, M. McGue, N. L. Segal, and A. Tellegen. 1990. "Sources of Human Psychological Differences: The Minnesota Study of Twins Reared Apart." *Science* 250:223–228.

Bouchard, T. J., Jr., M. McGue, D. Lykken, and A. Tellegen. 1999. *Intrinsic and Extrinsic Religiousness: Genetic and Environmental Influences and Personality Correlate.*, *Twin Research* 2 (2) (June 1, 1999): 88–98.

Bowlby, J. 1969. *Attachment and Loss*. Vol. 1: *Attachment*. New York: Basic Books.

——. 1973. *Attachment and Loss*. Vol. 2: *Separation, Anxiety and Anger*. New York: Basic Books.

Burkert, W. 1996. *Creation of the Sacred*. Cambridge, MA: Harvard University Press.

Churchland, P. S. and P. M. Churchland. 2002. "Neural Worlds and Real Worlds." *Nature Reviews/Neuroscience* 3 (Nov.): 903–907.

Cohn, N. 1970. *The Pursuit of the Millennium*. New York: Oxford University Press.

D'Aquili, E. G. and A. B. Newberg. 1999. *The Mystical Mind*. Minneapolis: Fortress.

Eichenbaum, H. 2002. *The Cognitive Neuroscience of Memory*. New York: Oxford University Press.

Einstein, A. 1956. *Out of My Later Years*. New York: Random House.

Filoramo, G. 1990. *A History of Gnosticism*. Trans. A. Alcock. Oxford, UK and Cambridge, MA: Basil Blackwell.

Fowler, J. W. 1981. *Stages of Faith*. San Francisco: HarperSanFrancisco.

Freud, S. 1911b. *Formulations on Two Principles of Mental Functioning*. In *The Complete Psychological Works of Sigmund Freud*, 13:218–226. London: The Hogarth Press and the Institute of Psychoanalysis.

——. 1911c. *Psycho-Analytic Notes on an Autobiographical Account of a Case of Paranoia (Dementia Paranoides)*. In *The Complete Psychological Works of Sigmund Freud*, 12. London: The Hogarth Press and the Institute of Psychoanalysis.

——. 1916. *Some Character Types Met with in Psychoanalytic Work: Those Wrecked by Success*. In *The Complete Psychological Works of Sigmund Freud*, 14:316. London: The Hogarth Press and the Institute of Psychoanalysis.

——. 1926. *Inhibition Symptoms and Anxiety*. In *The Complete Psychological Works of Sigmund Freud*, 20. London: The Hogarth Press and the Institute of Psychoanalysis.

——. 1927. *Fetishism*. In *The Complete Psychological Works of Sigmund Freud*, 21:154. London: The Hogarth Press and the Institute of Psychoanalysis.

——. 1930. *Civilization and Its Discontents*. In *The Complete Psychological Works of Sigmund Freud*, 21. London: The Hogarth Press and the Institute of Psychoanalysis.

Halevi, Jehudah. 1974 (1924). "Your Glory Fills the Universe." In *Selected Poems of Jehudah Halevi*, ed. H. Brody. Philadelphia: Jewish Publication Society.

——. "Lord Where Shall I Find You." In *The Penguin Book of Hebrew Verse*, ed. J. Carmi, 338. New York: Penguin.

Halperin, D. 1995. "UFO Abduction Narratives and the Religious Tradition of Heavenly Ascent: A Comparative Study." Unpublished manuscript.

Holmes, O. W. 1877. *Mechanism and Thought and Morals*. Boston: Osgood.

Hsai, R. P. 1988. *The Myth of Ritual Murder, Jews and Magic.* New Haven: Yale University Press.

Idel, M. 1998. *Kabbalah: New Perspectives.* New Haven: Yale University Press.

Idel, M. and M. Ostow. 1998. *Jewish Mystical Leaders and Leadership in the Thirteenth Century.* Northvale, NJ: Jason Aronson.

James, W. 1902. *The Varieties of Religious Experience.* New York: Random House.

Jellinek, A., ed. 1960. *Hekhaloth Rabbati in Bet ha-Midrasch.* Vol. 1 (part 3). Jerusalem: Wahrman.

Joseph, R. 2001. *The Transmitter to God.* San Jose: University of California Press.

Kadushin, M. 1952. *The Rabbinic Mind.* New York: Jewish Theological Seminary, 222.

Koenig, H. G. 1994. *Aging and God: Spiritual Pathways to Mental Health in Midlife and Later Years.* New York: Haworth.

Libet, B. 1992. "The Neural Time-Factor in Perception, Volition and Free Will." *Revue de Métaphysique et de Morale* 97:255–272.

Lorenz, K. 1974. *On Aggression.* New York: Harcourt Brace Jovanovich.

McGinn, B., J. Collins, and S. J. Stein. 1999. *Encyclopedia of Apocalypticism.* 3 vols. New York: Continuum.

Meissner, W. M. 1984. *Psychoanalysis and Religious Experience.* New Haven: Yale University Press.

Mowinckel, S. 1967. *The Psalms in Israel's Worship.* Trans. D. R. Ap-Thomas. Nashville: Abingdon.

Muffs, Y. 1992. *Love and Joy: Law, Language and Religion in Ancient Israel.* New York: Jewish Theological Seminary.

Ostow, M. 1955. "Linkage Fantasies and Representations." *International Journal of Psychoanalysis* 36 (6): 1–6.

——. 1995. *Ultimate Intimacy: The Psychodynamics of Jewish Mysticism.* London: Karnac.

——. 1996. *Myth and Madness: The Psychodynamics of Antisemitism.* New Brunswick, NJ: Transaction.

Otto, R. 1966 (1923). *The Idea of the Holy.* Oxford: Oxford University Press.

Panksepp, J. 1995. "The Emotional Sources of 'Chills' Induced by Music." *Music Perception* 13:171–207.

——. 1998. *Affective Neuroscience.* Oxford: Oxford University Press.

Panksepp, J. and G. Bernatzky. 2002. "Emotional Sounds and the Brain: The Neuro-Affective Foundations of Musical Appreciation." *Behavioral Processes* 60:133–155.

Pargament, K. I. 1997. *The Psychology of Religion and Coping: Theory, Research, Practice.* New York: Guilford.

Parker, I. 2004. "Annals of Philanthropy: The Gift." *The New Yorker* (August 2, 2004):54.

Peers, E. A., trans. and ed. 1960. *The Life of Teresa of Jesus: The Autobiography of St. Teresa of Avila.* Garden City, NY: Image Books.

Penfield, W. and H. Jasper. 1954. *Epilepsy and the Functional Anatomy of the Human Brain.* Boston: Little, Brown.

Persinger, M. A. 1987. *Neuropsychological Bases of God Beliefs.* New York: Praeger.

Peterson, J. B. 1999. *Maps of Meaning: The Architecture of Belief.* New York: Routledge.

Proust, M. 1981. *In Search of Lost Time.* New York: Modern Library.

Rizzuto, A. 1979. *The Birth of the Living God.* Chicago: University of Chicago Press.

Sarna, N. M. 1993. *Songs of the Heart.* New York: Schocken.

Scheidlinger, S. 1974. "On the Concept of the Mother-Group." *International Journal of Group Psychotherapy* 19:417–428.

Scholem, G. 1954 (1941). *Major Trends in Jewish Mysticism.* 3rd ed. New York: Schocken.

——. 1960. *Jewish Gnosticism: Merkabah Mysticism and Talmudic Tradition.* New York: Jewish Theological Seminary.

Schomer, D. L., M. O'Connor, P. Spiers, M. Seeck, M. Mesulam, and D. Bear. 2000. "Temporolimbic Epilepsy and Behavior." In *Principles of Behavioral and Cognitive Neurology*, ed. M. Mesulam, 373–405. Oxford: Oxford University Press.

Seeger, T. F., G. A. Sforzo, C. V. Pert, and A. Pert. 1984. "In Vivo Autoradiography: Visualization of Stress-Induced Changes in Opiate Receptor Occupancy in the Rat Brain." *Brain Research* 305:301–311.

Spencer, S. 1985. "The Dark Night of the Soul." In *Encyclopedia Britannica,* 15th ed., 16:376. Chicago: Encyclopedia Britannica.

Theweleit, K. 1987. *Male Fantasies.* Vol. 1. Minneapolis: University of Minnesota Press.

Underhill, E. 1964. *The Mystics of the Church.* New York: Schocken.

Wegner, D. M. 2003. *The Illusion of Conscious Will.* Cambridge, MA: Radford Books.

Weinfeld, M. 1991. Deuteronomy 1–11. *Anchor Bible.* Vol. 5. New York: Doubleday.

——. 1992. *Deuteronomy and the Deuteronomic School.* Winoma Lake, IN: Eisenbrauns.

Winnicott, D. W. 1953. "Transitional Objects and Transitional Phenomena." *International Journal of Psychoanalysis* 34:2.

Index

apocalypse, 2, 142; components of, 143–44, 150; demonic spirituality and, 177–80; designed to influence mood of audience, 150; in dream imagery, 145–48; as genre, 143–44; historical instances of, 150; opposite poles of, 142–43; during psychotic episodes, 148–50; rebirth and, 142–44, 178–79

Apocalypse, book of. *See* Revelation, book of

appetitive behavior, 123

Arab terrorist, account of, 181–85

Arlow, Jacob A., 145–48

As You Like It (Shakespeare), 32, 198

attachment instinct, 33, 42, 44–45; brain function and, 114, 117–18, 120–23; lateral and vertical, 83–84, 101–2, 198–99; religion and, 61–62, 65; sexual awareness and, 82; transference of to contemporaries, 83–86; variety of forms and intensities, 86; *see also* yearning

Augustine, St., 92

Austin, J., 112

authority, hierarchy of, 126

autonomy, 86–87

awe, 1, 10–16, 56–57; brain function and, 42–43; dependent upon external impression, 15–16, 19–20; dictionary definitions, 16, 27, 43; fearsome aspects of, 16, 27–28, 43, 161–62; group experience of, 88; infant-mother bond and, 36–37, 42–43, 107–8; inviting forms of, 16, 27; natural background and, 34–35; nostalgia and, 42–43; overwhelming of perceptual apparatus, 35–36; reality of, 6; revelation and, 197–98; size of parent as perceived by child, 107–8, 126; sound and, 35, 71–72; as spectacle/sound alone, 15–16; visual percepts and,

34–35; water imagery, 10–11, 14–15, 34–35

Baal Peor, 175–76

Bar Kokhba, 98

Bear, D. M., 115

belief, as irrelevant to spiritual experience, 12–14, 21, 31

berakha (blessing), 68

Bergmann, Martin, 159, 164, 166, 172

Bernard of Clairvaux, 138–39

Bible/Scripture: Deuteronomy, 55, 95, 164; as encoded, 23; Exodus, 57, 71, 74, 89, 96, 98–99, 126, 167; I Chronicles, 89; I Kings, 164; I Samuel, chapter 29, 28; Joshua, 164; Judges, 171; Kings I, 71; Micah, 167; Numbers, 175–76; Psalm 24, 106–7, 109; Psalm 29, 56–57, 71; Psalm 145, 77; Psalms, 73, 141; Revelation, 179, 180; Song of Songs, 70; *see also* Ezekiel; Genesis; Isaiah; Psalm 19

Bilu, Y., 48

Blake, William, 47

blessing, source in smiling response, 67–69, 75

Borg, J., 118–20

Bouchard, T. J., Jr., 121

Bowlby, J., 123

Boyer, Peter J., 157, 158

brain function, 2, 8; accompanied by affective state, 41–42; archaic structures, role in, 114; attachment instinct and, 114, 117–18, 120–23; awe and, 42–43; dissociation of affective and iconic memory, 37–42; hardwired responses, 36–37; intrinsic meaning and, 116–17; localization of, 112–13; mental illness/damage and, 115–16; mysticism and, 45–47; opioids, 123–24; process of spiritual experience, 117–18; seeking system, 114; serotonin

Deuteronomy, 55, 79, 95, 164
dibbuk, 28, 171
dopamine, 134, 137, 161
dreams, 6, 46; affect and, 135–37;
    aggression in, 154; apocalyptic
    imagery in, 145–48; hypnagogic
    hallucinations, 48–49; incubation,
    48, 196–97; moods and, 132, 133,
    135–37, 145–48; of patriarchs
    in Genesis, 48, 49; regulation of
    medication and, 136–37
drug addiction, 88–89
drugs, for mood regulation, 134,
    136–37, 148, 161
drugs, hallucinogenic, 119

ego function, 44–45, 50–51; dissolu-
    tion of boundaries, 19, 22–23
Eichenbaum, Howard, 37–38, 42
Einstein, Albert, 4
Eller, Michael, 187–91
Emmerich, Catherine, 157
Encyclopedia Britannica, 139, 159–60
Encyclopedia Judaica, 93, 105
Encyclopedia of Apocalypticism (ed.
    McGinn, Collins, and Stein), 143
enemy: mythical, 154–59, 177, 181;
    psychologic concept of, 73–74
entreating, 77
epigenetic scheme of religion: behav-
    ioral codes and, 81–82; enemy,
    psychologic concept of, 73–74;
    food and ritual meals, 74–76;
    God as illusory transitional ob-
    ject, 63–65; lateral attachment of
    child, 83–84; marriage outside
    of community, 86–87; modes of
    religious experience, 65–67; odors,
    70–71; prayer/propitiation, 76–78;
    redemption, 72–73; sexual devel-
    opment, 81–82; smiling response,
    67–69, 75, 76; socialization phase,
    83–86; sound and, 71–72; stages of
    faith, 62–63; touching and, 69–70;

transactional worship, 80–82, 89;
    transition from mother to father,
    90–93; *see also* religion
epilepsy, 114–16
*Epilepsy and the Functional Anatomy
    of the Human Brain* (Penfield and
    Jasper), 114–15
eschaton, 178
eternity, 100
existence, as essential attribute of
    God, 94
Exodus, 57, 71, 74, 126; image of
    God and, 89, 96, 98–99
"Experiences of Awe in Childhood"
    (Greenacre), 27–28
extraterrestrials, 73
extraterrestrial travel, 48
Ezekiel, 22, 91; apocalypse in, 178,
    179, 180; dream mysticism in, 48,
    49; moral messages in, 104; stranger
    concept in, 73; vehicular travel in,
    58–59; visibility of God in, 96, 99

faith: Conjunctive, 62–63; Individual-
    Reflective, 62, 63; Intuitive-Pro-
    jective, 62; Mythic-Literal, 62;
    Synthetic-Conventional, 62; Uni-
    versalistic, 63
familiarity, sense of, 16
family loyalties, 101–2
fantasies, 47
fasting, 117
Fedio, P., 115
fellowship, 62, 100–103
fire, symbolism of, 75
Flagellants, 172–73
flood, accounts of in Genesis, 142
food and ritual meals, 74–76
founders of the United States, 2
Fowler, James W., 62–63
Frankist movement, 102
Freikorps, 174–75
Freud, Sigmund, 3, 67; God, view of,
    64; infant hallucinates gratifica-

tion, 45; instance of Daniel Paul Schreber, 148–50; oceanic feeling, concept of, 3, 11, 19, 56; Oedipus complex, 85; preconscious, concept of, 40; "Those Wrecked by Success," 159

garden imagery, 97
Genesis, 48–49, 75, 126, 127, 142; recapitulation of mental development of infant, 54–55
gesture, 82
Gibson, Mel, 156–59, 184
"Gift, The" (Parker), 173
glory, 109
Gnostics, 92
God: communication with, 13, 16–17, 23, 30, 201; demonic face of, 164–70; developmental sources of images of, 63–65; existence as essential attribute of, 94; as illusory transitional object, 63–65; as indescribable, 18–19; as invisible, 95–96; location of, 95, 99–100; natural phenomena and, 56–57; as purely spiritual, 30, 108, 110; *see also* image of God; name of God; qualities of God
gods, pagan: female, 90; multiplicity of, 166; sexual behavior of, 83; sibling, 90; sun and moon gods, 99
grace and comfort, affect of, 32–33
gratification, sense of, 17
Greenacre, Phyllis, 27–28, 131, 162
group, as symbolic of mother, 102
group behavior, 81–82, 87–89

Hagigah, 110–11
Halevi, Judah (Yehudah), 57, 99, 105–6, 108
hallucinations, 6; attachment needs and, 120–23; hypnagogic, 48–49; image of God and, 90; infant-mother bond and, 45–46

Ham, 71
Hamlet (Shakespeare), 28, 47, 140
Hamm, Paula, 186
Hartman, L. F., 93
Hasidim, 102–3
Havdalah service, 71
heaven, 99
heights, 79, 107–9, 126; Mount Sinai, 13, 23, 26, 27, 57, 71; as sites of religious worship, 99–100
Heine, Heinrich, 169–70
Hekhaloth mysticism, 23, 48, 131
hestaer panim (hiding one's face), 68
hierarchy of authority, 126
holiness, 104–11; eligibility for, 109–10; infant-mother bond as origin of, 106–7; mysterium tremendum and, 105, 109; sexuality as incompatible with, 83; terms for, 105; as transcendence, 106
Holmes, Oliver Wendell, 41
Holocaust, 79, 102
Holy Spirit, as term, 55
holy wars, 169–70, 172, 177
hormones, 83
Hsia, R. P., 155
hypnagogic hallucinations, 48–49

iconic memories, 36, 94
Idea of the Holy, The (Otto), 105
Idel, Moshe, 19, 23, 103
illusion, 5–6; transitional objects and, 63–65
Illusion of Conscious Will, The (Wegner), 40–41
image of God, 3, 89–93; androgynous qualities, 92; as on or in container, 91; transition from female to male deity, 90–92
immanent presence of God, 91
incest taboo, 86–87
incubation, 48, 196–97
individual, 103; group behavior and, 81–82, 87–89

ineffability of spiritual experience,
24–26
inertia, 160–61
infant, 3; Genesis as recapitulation of
development of, 54–55; sense of
power over parent, 81–82; stranger
anxiety, 72–74
infanticide, 159, 164–66
infant-mother bond: awe and, 36–37,
42–43, 107–8; breath of mother,
55; faith and, 66; feeding, 74–76;
height concept and, 79, 99–100,
107–9; morality, development of,
103–4; mysticism and, 45–49;
odors and, 70–71; as origin of
holiness, 106–7; as origin of
spiritual experience, 1–2; posture
of prayer and, 79–80; propitiation and, 76–78; redemption and,
72–73; regression and, 45–46, 51;
rewards and punishment, 77–78,
81–82; smiling response, 67–69,
75, 76; Spiritual experience and,
43–45; toilet hygiene, 110; touching, 69–70; undifferentiated phase,
3, 66, 67; voice of mother, 71–72;
yearning for attachment, 42, 56,
107–8; see also child
Inhibitions, Symptoms and Anxiety
(Freud), 123
In Search of Lost Time (Proust),
38–39, 42
instincts, 5, 40; activation of, 121–22;
conflicting, 164–65; marriage and,
121, 164–65; sexual, 18, 70, 82,
121, 122, 198–99; social, development of, 83–86; see also attachment instinct
Isaac, 84
Isaiah, 57, 60, 73, 82, 91; apocalypse
in, 178; holiness in, 108, 109;
moral messages in, 104; sacrifice
in, 167–68; visibility of God in, 96,
99; withdrawal of God's smile, 162

Islamic fundamentalism, 177, 181–85
isolation, 117, 122–23

Jacob, 84
James, William, 1, 3, 23, 46, 61, 130;
on consciousness, 40; defining cri-
teria of spiritual experience, 24–26;
mystical experience of, 18–19
Jasper, Herbert, 114–15
Jerusalem, as mystical mother, 47
Jewish folklore, 28
*Jewish Mystical Leaders and Leader-
ship in the Thirteenth Century*
(Idel and Ostow), 103
Jews: Moroccan immigrants, 48;
revolt against Rome, 98; see also
Judaism
John of Patmos, 143–44
John of the Cross, 139
Joseph, R., 112, 113
Judaism: monotheism, 166–67; move-
ments within, 102–3; transactional
worship, 80–81; see also Hekha-
loth mysticism; Kabbalistic mysti-
cism; Merkavah mysticism
Jungian tradition, 142–43

Kabbalistic mysticism, 19, 23, 91–92,
94
Kaddish, 95, 108
kadosh (holiness), 105
Kadushin, Max, 32, 106
Keats, John, 11, 13
kedushah (holiness), 105–6
King James Bible, 54, 72
knowledge, states of, 25, 46
korban (sacrifice), 75
Krakatoa, 16, 162
"Kubla Khan" (Coleridge), 47–48

Libet, Benjamin, 40–41
libido, 134
life expectancy, 124–25
lifestyle changes, 117

visibility of God (*continued*)
    and punishment for looking, 96–99
vision quest, 2, 186–200; Psalm 19
    correlated with, 201–3; as search
    for revelation, 196–97; superego
    and, 191–92; transactional wor-
    ship, 197
visions, mystical, 17–18

water imagery, 10–11, 14–15, 34–35;
    see also oceanic feeling
Wegner, Daniel L., 40–41
Weinfeld, Moshe, 95
wind, 54
Winnicott, D. W., 63, 64–65
wish fulfillment, 47–49
Wordsworth, William, 11, 13, 32, 47,
    52–53
"World Is Too Much with Us, The"

(Wordsworth), 52–53
worship, 61; mood regulation and,
    141; sun worship, 99, 199, 201;
    transactional, 80–82, 89, 197

Yahweh, 93–94
yearning: for contact with the unat-
    tainable, 12–13, 23; dreams and,
    48; infant-mother bond and, 42,
    56, 107–8; literary expression
    of, 47–48; mood regulation and,
    129–30; name of God and, 94–95;
    perverse fulfillments, 47; Psalm 19
    and, 44; for reunion, 12–13, 31–
    32; *see also* attachment instinct
YHVH, 93–95, 96
YHVH Zevaoth, 109

Zevah sacrifice, 166